Making Media Content

The Influence
of Constituency Groups
on Mass Media

LEA's COMMUNICATION SERIES
Jennings Bryant and Dolf Zillmann, General Editors

Selected titles include:

Berger • *Planning Strategic Interaction: Attaining Goals Through Communicative Action*

Bryant/Zillmann • *Media Effects: Advances and Theory in Research, Second Edition*

Ellis • *Crafting Society: Ethnicity, Class, and Communication Theory*

Greene • *Message Production: Advances in Communication Theory*

Reichert/Lambiase • *Sex in Advertising: Perspectives on the Erotic Appeal*

Shepherd/Rothenbuhler • *Communication and Community*

Singhal/Rogers • *Entertainment Education: A Communication Strategy for Social Change*

Zillmann/Vorderer • *Media Entertainment: The Psychology of Its Appeal*

Making Media Content

The Influence
of Constituency Groups
on Mass Media

John A. Fortunato
University of Texas

 LAWRENCE ERLBAUM ASSOCIATES, PUBLISHERS
2005   Mahwah, New Jersey   London

Lawrence Erlbaum Associates, Inc., Publishers
10 Industrial Avenue
Mahwah, New Jersey 07430
www.erlbaum.com

Cover design by Sean Sciarrone

Library of Congress Cataloging-in-Publication Data

Fortunato, John A.
Making media content : the influence of constituency groups on
    mass media / John A. Fortunato
        p. cm.
Includes bibliographical references and index.
ISBN 0-8058-4748-0 (cloth : alk. paper)
1. Mass media. 2. Content analysis (Communication) I. Title.

P91.F673 2005
302.23—dc22   2004056416
                                                        CIP

Books published by Lawrence Erlbaum Associates are printed
on acid-free paper, and their bindings are chosen for strength
and durability.

Printed in the United States of America
10   9   8   7   6   5   4   3   2   1

To My Mother and Father:

The most fortunate thing is something I had
nothing to do with. It occurred the moment
I was born to great parents.

Thank You for Everything.

Contents

III: The External Mass Media Organization: Constituency Groups

Tables

Figures

Preface

The idea for *Making Media Content* was conceived when I was asked to teach a media business course. Upon organizing the class, I first attempted to finish the statement, "The media business is ..." This statement led to a few central questions necessary to study the mass media business: What are the goods or services that the organizations of the mass media produce? How do these mass media organizations develop and distribute their products? How do the aspirations of the business aspects of the mass media coexist with any societal responsibilities? And, how do the people who work in the mass media deal with all of the pressures that are incorporated into decision making involved in their job?

In responding to the initial question of what is it that mass media organizations produce (i.e., the media business is ...), I arrived at the general conclusion that the primary business of the mass media is to produce content—fill the broadcast hours, the print pages, the Internet site. Before forming any ideas of how the mass media function to inform or to entertain, or before responding to why people use the media, it must be recognized that all decision making emanates from the mass media responsibility to produce content.

The questions of the standards and practices of how these mass media organizations arrive at producing their content are more complicated than responding to what is the media business. *Media* can be a very ambiguous term, with each mass media organization having a different audience reach, different resources to gather and distribute content, and different types of content they desire. This ambiguity makes producing a volume that encompasses any singular explanation of the mass media industry virtually impossible. To try to limit this immense field, this book focuses on national news, as this content has the important function of helping move the democracy forward.

Determining what becomes content is a powerful position for a mass media organization. The people employed by these organizations have the ability to select and frame the content that will potentially be seen, heard, or read by the audience. In thinking of the business of media as the production of content, however, the mass media organizations are not acting unilaterally. For example, mass media organizations need advertisers to buy time and space on their broadcast or in their publication. Advertisers are, however, most interested in reaching an audience to promote their products. Mass media organizations thus need to obtain quality content so as to attract an audience. Finally, people with content are using the mass media to reach the audience. All of these constituency groups are constantly, simultaneously trying to influence the content decision-making process, with all of these efforts converging at the mass media organizations' decision-making efforts.

The purpose of the media business course I was asked to teach, and eventually the purpose of this book, became to examine the mass media industry and provide insight into the complex relationships between the mass media organization and the various constituency groups that try to, and in some instances do, influence the media business. The rationale for achieving this purpose is that the mass media are such an important component of society, with a tremendous impact on the daily functions of so many people as well as on the daily functions of the government, other industries, and the economy as a whole. Because of the mass media's profound impact on society, it is important for people to have some understanding about their business practices and how they gather, organize, and distribute their content. My simple goal is for people to learn something about how the mass media operate and to provide some insight into the complex processes of an important industry so that they can better evaluate what they are seeing, hearing, or reading.

To achieve this goal I implement two tactics. The first tactic is to examine some of the essential communication literature that has already provided tremendous insight into the media industry. The second tactic is to provide some commentary from people in the mass media and the various constituency groups with which a mass media organization must interact. This combination of a theoretical overview and practitioner perspective will hopefully create a more complete explanation of the decision-making process.

From the project's inception until its publication, many people are deserving of credit. At the earliest stages, the members of the St. Peter's

College communication and English departments were very helpful. The advertising department at the University of Texas at Austin has been extremely supportive of my efforts. Conversations with Dr. Max McCombs from the University of Texas were always insightful. I also need to recognize the communication Ph.D. program at Rutgers University for the incredible training I received—I am always thankful. The careful review and suggestions from Dr. Robert Wicks were invaluable in the evolution of the project. Finally, Linda Bathgate was very patient and supportive in assisting me in this work. I could not have asked for a better advocate for this project.

I would like to acknowledge the people who helped me coordinate interviews and offered assistance in providing data: Edward Farmer, John Gault, Kelley Gott, Terry Hemeyer, and Peter King. I am greatly appreciative of the people who willingly gave up some of their time and allowed themselves to be interviewed. The hope was their professional perspective would illuminate some of the critical concepts: Mark Beal, Mike Bevans, Karen Blumenthal, Mandy Bogan, Lorraine Branham, Tom Breedlove, Sally Brooks, Mike Emanuel, Kelley Gott, Terry Hemeyer, Peter King, Alain Sanders, Bob Sommer, Rachel Sunbarger, David Wald, Jeff Webber, David Westin, Kinsey Wilson, and Clint Woods.

—John A. Fortunato

About the Author

John A. Fortunato, PhD is an assistant professor at the University of Texas at Austin in the Department of Advertising, College of Communication. He previously was the chair of the communication program at St. Peter's College. Dr. Fortunato wrote *The Ultimate Assist: The Relationship and Broadcast Strategies of the NBA and Television Networks* (Hampton Press). His research articles have appeared in *Public Relations Review, Communications and the Law, New Jersey Journal of Communication, Fordham Intellectual Property, Media & Entertainment Law Journal, Rutgers Law Record*, and *Journal of Sport Management* special issue on sports media. Before earning his PhD from Rutgers University, he gained industry experience as a production assistant for NBC Sports, including NFL Live, NBA, Showtime, and the 1992 and 1996 Summer Olympics, and as a part-time sports producer for WWOR-TV Channel 9 (New York).

Introduction

As an industry with such a profound impact on society, it seems the mass media and their functions would be greatly understood by the general public. The mass media, however, can be one of the more misinterpreted and misunderstood industries. The term *mass media* can be better understood by breaking down the meaning of each of the two words. When used as an adjective, the word *mass* denotatively means large. Because of communication technological advances, *mass* is appropriate in describing the current media environment, as the media are at unprecedented size. The term *mass* indicates size but also conveys a sense of speed with which information can reach the many. It can simply be stated that every time technology changes, the communication and mass media environment changes. Through the technology of cable, satellite, and Internet communication vehicles there are more opportunities for gathering, distributing, and retrieving mass media content and these opportunities are almost certain to grow.

The term *media* is much more difficult to define. The term is ambiguous but often used in a monolithic fashion. For example, hearing statements such as, "The media are to blame" or "The media are blowing this story out of proportion" are not uncommon. By using the term *media* in a general, all-encompassing manner, certain mass media organizations are immediately elevated to a higher status and others disparaged by being lumped together into one entity. Mass media organizations are not homogenous and differ in some fundamental ways: (a) size: the resources (money, equipment, and personnel) that the particular media organization has access to, the amount of time and space they have to fill content, and the audience reach of their output;

(b) delivery mechanism of the message: print, audio, video, and Internet based; and (c) scope: the types of content they provide to the audience. Add in the quality of content produced and the decision-making philosophies of each mass media organization, as well as the skills and philosophy of each individual who is a part of the content decision-making process, and there can be as many definitions of *media* as there are organizations that produce content.

Disparities of how content is gathered, distributed, and retrieved by the audience can exist among mediums or even within one medium. Clear disparities exist among the different mediums by simple transmission capabilities of audio, video, and print; how quickly the mass media organization can distribute that content; and how quickly, when, and where the audience can access that content. Within one medium the disparities exist more on the amount of resources and the types of content that the mass media organizations are trying to gather and distribute to the audience.

To amplify the difficulty of defining media, disparities can exist within one mass media organization, using essentially one medium and producing content of only one genre. For example, look at the components of NBC News, which are made up of:

- *NBC Nightly News*
- *The Today Show*
- *Dateline NBC*
- *Meet the Press*
- MSNBC (*Imus in the Morning, Hardball with Chris Matthews, Countdown with Keith Olberman*, and *Scarborough Country*)
- CNBC
- Local affiliates *NBC News*

Each of these television programs (therefore, a similar delivery mechanism) has a far different mandate in the types of stories they are looking for, the types of content they produce, the amount of time and analysis they provide to each story, and the overall resources devoted to each of these programs despite all being within the single genre of news. In addition to the television programs, NBC News has its own Internet site, msnbc.msn.com, which has links to stories on news, business, sports, entertainment, technology science, and health. On the Internet site there is also a link to *Newsweek* magazine and all of the individual NBC News programs. The larger television networks, such as NBC, are more than just a news organization. The news division is but one area of a larger mass media organization, as NBC has its prime-time division, sports division, daytime division, and late night programming division.

All of these divisions can draw some of the resources away from the news division. NBC is also part of a larger corporation, General Electric, which is involved in numerous other industries that can potentially draw resources away from NBC.

Thus, the difficulty in describing the decision-making process of mass media content is that not all mass media organizations are the same, and in fact, no two are the same. When you factor in the individual aspect of every person that has a role in the decision-making process, the difficulty in offering a description is only exacerbated. Trying to develop any generalities or standard operating procedures for the mass media industry as a whole is next to impossible.

Although mass media organizations are different and using the term *media* in any generic fashion that encompasses all types of mass media organizations is incorrect, there are some critical similarities among all mass media organizations. The initial major similarity is that all mass media organizations need content. No industry exists without a product or service to offer customers, which it hopes customers will desire. A second similarity emerges as every mass media organization, whether entertainment or news oriented, needs content to attract an audience. Within this need, the personnel at all mass media organizations have to obtain quality content and make critical decisions in evaluating their options and determining which content to provide to an audience. With the mass media being limited by time and space available, content is always subject to a complex decision-making process of what will appear on the air, in print, or on the Internet. Once a story or issue has been selected to receive exposure, decisions still need to be made about how that content will be presented or framed to the audience. Framing decisions include the location (the lead story of a news broadcast or somewhere in the middle, the front page above the fold in a newspaper or on the back page, what first appears when visiting an Internet site or a link that needs to be clicked to another site), overall time spent on a particular story, and pictures or language to be used in the story.

Shoemaker and Reese (1996) defined content as "the complete quantitative and qualitative range of verbal and visual information distributed by the mass media" (p. 4). For this book, content is simply defined as the messages that the audience actually has the potential to see, hear, read, or click onto—the messages that are given exposure by a mass media organization that the audience has the opportunity to retrieve. Through this definition there is an indication that some stories never become content and are not exposed to a mass audience.

The decision-making process of what becomes and does not become content is even more critical for the national news media. The importance of understanding the process of content decision making for news is enhanced by a few critical factors: (a) in a democratic society, people need information to make the proper decisions about their governance; (b) with news happening all over the world, people need the mass media and their resources to gather and distribute information; and (c) with the limitations of time and space, the mass media cannot provide all the happenings of the world and therefore must make careful evaluations about the stories they select and the perspectives of the stories that they present.

The purpose of this book is to examine the complex decision-making process of national mass media organizations in determining what news content to put on the air, in print, or on an Internet site. Trying to lend some insight into this complex decision-making process is important because of the profound impact and power that the mass media have in society. Their power originates through the extensive and consistent media use on the part of the audience and the potential for the audience to be influenced by mass media content.

The power also emanates from the mass media organizations' ability to be in locations where the audience is not. The mass media are then entrusted with the responsibility and ability to select and frame content. The process of how that content arrives to the audience is one of complex decision making by the people who work for mass media organizations. Although the responsibility of the mass media is to make content decisions, this book begins with the premise that the mass media organization is not the sole entity involved in the content decision-making process. Mass media employees are not making decisions unilaterally, as there are several people and organizations trying to influence simultaneously the mass media organization decision-making process. In addition to mere exposure and getting stories selected, these constituency groups are equally focused on how that content is framed, that is, the facts and perspectives that will be featured in the story. Because selection and framing are necessary components of the system, there is tremendous competition to be included in the news content, and constituency groups try to influence the mass media organization content decisions through a series of communication initiatives.

Complicating the process is the business side of the news media industry, as the companies that produce news content are part of larger private corporations. Another major premise of this book is that the business of the media is to produce content that will attract an audience. The audience is then offered to advertisers, giving the mass media organization its opportunity for economic profit. The business objective of the decision-making process of a mass media organization can thus be defined as producing content with the objective of getting the audience to use the media in a way that will bring advertiser support, and eventual profit, to the mass media organization.

Therefore, critical to explaining the content decision-making process is examining the strategic relationships that mass media organizations have with the many constituency groups that attempt to influence the process. The phrase "attempt to influence" implies the question: Do, or to what extent do, these constituency groups influence the content decision-making process? All mass media organizations, whether it is NBC, Fox News, *Sports Illustrated, The New York Times*, abc.com, or a local town newspaper, do, however, have to deal with many or all of these constituency groups. The extent of influence from each constituency group might vary based on each mass media organization and on each situation. Any constituency group can have a direct impact only under certain conditions. It is also necessary to note that constituency groups, and the people that represent these constituency groups, are not equal.

Constituency groups for a mass media organization can be separated by internal or external affiliation. The internal groups are employed or financially involved with the mass media organization and include the ownership level (both CEOs and stockholders) and the day-to-day decision-maker level (producers, directors, editors, writers, reporters, camera operators, and announcers). There is much complexity to the decision-making process simply within the mass media organization.

The complexity is only increased as external constituency groups are continuously and simultaneously trying to influence the process. External constituency groups are not directly employed by mass media organizations but attempt to establish relationships with many mass media organizations and influence them in any decision making regarding content. The external constituency groups are: (a) media content providers, (b) advertisers, and (c) the audience.

Mass media content providers are broadly defined as any group or person with a message designed to reach an audience. It is often through the various vehicles of the mass media that they attempt to receive exposure for their messages. Content providers include: politicians, government departments, companies making news, public relations practitioners, publicists, marketing professionals, artists, athletes and professional sports leagues, entertainment production companies, actors and actresses, musical performers, and authors. Media content providers are critical in any description of the content decision-making process in that although they need the mass media to obtain exposure, they, too, can be a powerful entity in the process, as mass media organizations need quality content that will attract an audience. In the news industry, the powerful content providers are the organizations or the prominent people that have desirable content, such as government officials or corporate leaders.

Advertisers are an essential external constituency group in any evaluation of the business aspects of the mass media, as they generate all of the revenue for the broadcast media and most of the revenue for the print and Internet media. Many theorists argue that the economic factions of ownership, stockholders, and advertisers are the most influential constituency group in the content decision-making process. Others contend the desire on the part of advertisers is merely for exposure of their brands and products to the largest possible audience.

The arguments that the mass media organizations are only trying to please the economic constituency groups of owners, stockholders, and advertisers is a little misleading in that the business can only thrive financially if there are customers, an audience. Advertisers most want an audience, particularly a desired target audience, that might buy their product and will invest in commercials and other promotional communication strategies only if that content delivers an audience. Mass media organizations most please advertisers not by allowing them to influence overtly the decision-making process but by producing content that does indeed attract a large audience. The relationship between mass media organizations and advertisers does not necessitate interference in the editorial aspects of content decision making. That level of influence is not a prerequisite for advertisers to achieve their goals of: (a) exposure to the desired target audience, (b) increased product brand recall, and (c) increased sales.

Although all constituency groups have an opportunity to influence decision making, one characteristic of the process that appears throughout this book is that the audience is a constant factor in content decision making. So much of the content decision-making process is dictated by the expectations, desires, dependencies, and behavior of the audience. The behavior of all other constituency groups, especially content providers and advertisers, often follow the behavior of the audience and their mass media use in terms of the medium and the types of content they are participating in.

Audience behavior can influence future content decision making based on their participation in the media through critical behavior feedback measures of television ratings, newspaper or magazine circulation, attendance at or rental of movies, hits on an Internet site, and book or compact disc sales. It is the media use behavior of the audience that is primarily of interest to content providers so they can learn the best location to place their messages. Mass media use on the part of the audience is important in that there are a variety of reasons that people participate in the mass media, notably, for information, entertainment, and social needs. For these reasons there will always be a steady stream of media users. Thus, I argue here that the most critical group in the decision-making process is the audience.

It is a large audience that generates advertising revenue and a profit for the mass media organization. For example, a statement might be made about the television industry that content decisions are made only to get audience ratings. Saying a mass media organization is under ratings pressure is akin to saying that it is under pressure to obtain and maintain an audience. Saying that the goal is to get ratings is the same as saying the goal is to obtain an audience. The mass media organization simply tries to acquire or create content that will generate an audience. The important caveat for content existing in the public dialogue is that there is not a need for all or even a majority of the audience to participate in the content, just enough participants of the audience to attract advertisers and sustain a business. Another important caveat is that the audience can only choose from the content offered.

Because there are so many different mass media organizations and so many constituency groups, with many individuals within these organizations, there are many relationships simultaneously at play, and the process of content decision making is not a standard formula that operates the same way every time. Therefore, trying to explain definitively such a process, even within one genre of national news, is daunting. This book is not designed to present a standard formula of how the process of mass media content decision making should operate but instead to provide perspectives that can illuminate an understanding of how the process does operate in certain circumstances— this or any volume cannot cover every situation encountered in the decision-making process. The similarities of each mass media organization that goes through a process of content decision making, which can be influenced by constituency groups, might lend to some common philosophies and consistent features that can be examined.

In addition to providing insight about how mass media organizations function, I hope this book encourages thought and debate about the mass media decision-making process itself. Jamieson and Campbell (2001) stated, "The mass media are so familiar, so much a part of our everyday lives, that we all feel we know and understand them. But it is precisely because they are so familiar that we need to study them" (p. 4). Shoemaker and Reese (1996) simply posited the question of "what factors inside and outside media organizations affect media content" (p. 1). In explaining the value of studying media content, they argued that this area of study "helps us infer things about phenomena that are less open and visible: the people and organizations that produce the content" (p. 27).

Theory helps illuminate the plausibility of actions in a complex system. Mass communication and mass media theories of uses and gratifications, media dependency, framing, and agenda setting are used in analyzing the content decision-making process. Each of these theoretical frameworks provides explanations at various stages of the process. The uses and gratifications framework focuses on the desires and behavior of the audience, depicting an active audience where individuals make decisions about selecting and interpreting content. Media dependency provides an explanation of the interaction between the mass media organization and its constituency groups and the mass media organization and the audience. This theory depicts a series of interdependent relationships, with the mass media positioned in the middle, and needs are satisfied through the resources possessed by others. Agenda setting speaks to the ability and responsibility of the mass media organization selecting and framing messages, understanding that selecting some issues and emphasizing certain perspectives can increase audience salience regarding these issues and perspectives. Conversely, issues and perspectives that are not selected are relegated to a less important status.

With content as the outcome of the process, the mass media organization, the group that is always in the center of the process, and its relationships are the unit of analysis. The process is interactive among all groups involved. Mass media organizations need advertisers for revenue, and advertisers need mass media organizations for exposure of their products and services to the audience. Mass media organizations need content providers for quality content, and content providers need mass media organizations for exposure of their messages. On certain occasions content providers are also advertisers and use advertising as a communication strategy where they are willing to pay for time and space to ensure the desired media placement and control the message, thus eliminating media gatekeepers.

The audience influences all of the other constituency groups and every aspect of the process through watching, listening, reading, visiting Internet sites, evaluating and reacting to the content, and purchasing sponsor products. The audience behavior influences: (a) the mass media organization that is trying to produce content to attract an audience, (b) content providers who might adjust their message, and (c) content providers and advertisers who need to be where the audience is for exposure of their products and services (see Fig. 1).

The model in Fig. 1 depicts the interactive relationships and shows that all of these constituency groups still have to go through the mass

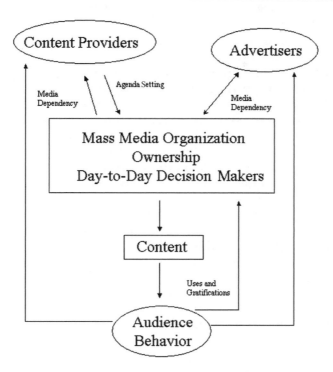

FIG. I.1. The process of mass media content decision making.

media organization, which can fulfill or deny these requests. The model does not depict the nature of these relationships, other than that they are interactive. The nature of these relationships can be as varied as the number of organizations and people involved. The speed of the process is also difficult to capture. The model merely offers a snapshot of a never-ending, continuous process. The model does not show the great competition among content providers to receive coverage and exposure. There is great inequality of constituency groups and audiences. Certain audiences are more valuable than others based on demographic variables of gender, age, income, or geography. Some constituency groups, sources that provide quality content that the audience desires or advertisers who spend more money with that organization, are more valuable to the mass media organization. Mass media organizations therefore vociferously compete for quality content from the many content providers, hoping to obtain the messages from the most prestigious. This process is occurring for every mass media organization through every delivery system. The audience has a multitude of media choices. Among all of these choices, mass media organizations are not equal, as some have established a brand credibility that helps attract an audience.

Although providing a theoretical foundation helps allude to the responsibility of the mass media organization, the model does not depict that selection and framing of content is a necessary condition because of time and space restrictions that are at the core of the decision-making process. Once there is content selection and framing inevitably there will be complaints: Why was this story covered? Why wasn't that story covered? Why were certain facts emphasized or ignored? Why was the story covered from this angle? How should the mass media operate and how do the mass media operate are two entirely different questions. How should they operate invites as many opinions and answers as there are people, with the presumed response being the mass media should operate in a way beneficial to the respondent's views. It becomes virtually impossible to please everyone because essentially everyone has a vested interest in what becomes content. It is this necessary condition of selection and framing that begins to set up a logical conclusion: The mass media system is not, and can never be, perfect.

The mass media system is market driven, similar to other industries. The notion that the audience most dictates the process is not a bad thing; it is not a perfect system, but perhaps it is the best possible. Is it the best system that mass media organizations only provide content they believe will attract an audience? Perhaps not. Are there some stories or issues that people should learn about but are not being covered as extensively because they will not deliver a larger audience? Probably. The criticism about the media system as currently constructed is: What stories are we not learning about?

If the audience is one of the major constituency groups that can influence the process of content decision making in a variety of ways, it is incumbent on them to learn about the process itself and all of its intricacies. The audience must become enlightened about the complex content decision-making process—that is the point of this book.

The book is organized in three sections. The first section explores the power of the mass media and their importance and prominence in the culture. The second section examines the internal environment of a mass media organization. The third section looks at the external constituency groups that try to influence the mass media content decision-making process.

Chapter 1 provides a debate about the mass media responsibility, focusing on their role in a democratic society but also examining that ideal positioned next to the potential contradiction as private corporations designed to make a profit. The mass media technological environment is described in this chapter to explain the possibilities of gathering, distributing, and retrieving messages that must always be factored into the process. Chapter 2 explains how and why the audience uses the mass media. The theoretical frameworks of uses and gratifications, and mass media dependency demonstrate that the power of the mass media is that people use the media to satisfy a variety of needs, notably, information, entertainment, and social inclusion. Dependency, however, demonstrates the interactive characteristic of the process in which mass media organizations also need content providers for obtaining quality content and attracting an audience. With mass media use being an important factor, chapter 3 looks at the mass media organization's responsibility to select and frame messages. Using the agenda-setting theoretical model, the role of the mass media in determining which messages receive exposure emerges, with the stories and perspectives selected having a greater opportunity to be perceived as more important by the audience. The idea that constituency groups try to influence this process and the way agendas are established also begin to develop.

In examining the internal mass media organization, chapter 4 explains that selection and framing is not based on all of the stories possible and that overall philosophies and mass media routines are developed to help a mass media organization limit the scope of its content. The decisions at the routines level help simplify a complex process. Through media routines, a mass media organization can differentiate itself from the competition and establish itself as a brand that relates to audience expectations. Chapter 5 looks at the impact of ownership on mass media content decision making. In addition to establishing any overall standards of practice or allocating resources, the relationship between owner and day-to-day decision makers is discussed. Chapter 6 peers into the working of the day-to-day decision makers at a mass media organization and demonstrates the complexity of the process within the mass media organization. The day-to-day decision makers are at the center of the process, as all of the other constituency groups have to go through this group. The day-to-day decision makers have to select and frame content, but the process is more complex than unilateral decisions being made by this group and ignoring the demands and behavior of all others.

External constituency groups, their pivotal relationships with the mass media organization and their potential influence on content decision making are examined in the third section of this book. Chapter 7 examines content providers, the groups that actually have the quality content that mass media organizations desire. The critical relationship between content providers, particularly the most sought after and used sources, and mass media decision makers is the core of this chapter. Chapter 8 examines the role of advertisers and their potential influence in the content decision-making process. The chapter focuses on the desires of advertisers, which mainly are in obtaining exposure for their brand to an audience, product brand recall, and sales. Chapter 9 looks at the vital role the audience plays in the process, arguing that the behavior of the audience is always a factor in the process, as every other group is reacting to the behavior of the audience. A conclusion is presented to offer a final overview and additional commentary of the entire mass media decision-making process.

Each chapter provides insight into the relationship between a mass media organization and each constituency group, and how it might influence the decision-making process. To support the previous research and the theoretical frameworks presented in section 1, and in comparing theoretical philosophy with practice, several key informant interviews were conducted. The rationale for interviewing professionals intimately involved in the content decision-making process is explained by Ball-Rokeach (1985) who claimed "that the average individual, as opposed to groups and organizations, does not come into direct contact with media information creators, gatherers, or processors" (p. 487).

Interviews were conducted with: Mark Beal, executive vice president, Alan Taylor Communications public relations firm; Mike Bevans, executive editor, *Sports Illustrated*; Karen Blumenthal, Dallas bureau chief, *The Wall Street Journal*; Mandy Bogan, broadcast buying director, GSD&M advertising agency; Lorraine Branham, director of the School of Journalism, University of Texas at Austin; Tom Breedlove, managing director, Ruff, Coffin, and Breedlove advertising agency; Sally Brooks, vice president and group media director, GSD&M advertising agency; Mike Emanuel, correspondent, Fox News Channel; Kelley Gott, sales managing director, *Time*; Terry Hemeyer, former communication executive, Pennzoil; Peter King, senior writer, *Sports Illustrated*; Alain Sanders, former senior reporter, *Time*; Bob Sommer, executive vice president, MWW Group public relations firm; Rachel Sunbarger, spokeswoman, U.S. Department of Homeland Security; David Wald, director of communication; New Jersey Senator Jon Corzine; Jeff Webber, senior vice president and publisher, usatoday.com; David Westin, president, ABC News; Kinsey Wilson, vice president and editor-in-chief, usatoday.com; and Clint Woods, account supervisor, Pierpoint Communications public relations firm.

Media Powers

1

The Mass Media
Responsibility

To explain better the content decision-making process of a mass media organization, some context and understanding of the debate about the perceived role of the mass media in society need to be provided. It is the believed philosophical function of the mass media responsibility that affects the practical content decision-making process. The philosophy can be on an organizational level as a whole and on an individual level, from the people who are employed by the mass media organization, as to the types of content they should provide. There are clearly strong opinions as to what the mass media should be and the types of content they should provide. These philosophies are as varied as the people and organizations, both internal and external to the mass media organization, that have a vested interest in the content provided to an audience. How the mass media should do their job is reflective in what people view as the responsibility of the media. With so many opinions coming from so many groups the mass media cannot please everyone with their decisions.

Mass media organizations receive pressure and criticism about their content decisions in the context of a responsibility to the larger societal ideals and needs. A central conflict for mass media organizations in the United States is their service to democracy, as they are by law supposed to serve the public interest, convenience, and necessity (e.g., Communications Act of 1934, Telecommunications Reform Act of 1996) while operating as profit-oriented companies. The vital role of the mass media in a democracy might be the most important rationale for studying their content decision making. Rachlin (1988) commented on the value of studying the mass media and their processes, stating, "If indeed a free press is necessary to provide the communication that is indispensable to the survival of democracy, we need examine our own press, the forces that guide it, and evaluate its contribution to democracy" (p. 3).

Trying to serve both the public interests and economic interests can be problematic (e.g., Compaine, 2000; Ehrlich, 1995; Jamieson & Campbell, 2001; Lee & Solomon, 1990). For many scholars there should not be a conflict, as an informed citizenry, and not economic profit, is the only laudable goal of any mass media organization (e.g., Alger, 1998; Bagdikian, 2000; Ehrlich, 1995; Gans, 1979; Gitlin, 1972, 1980, 1982; Husselbee, 1994; Mazzocco, 1994; McManus, 1994, 1995; Mosco, 1996; Rachlin, 1988; Rideout, 1993; Siebert, Peterson, & Schramm, 1974; Slattery, Doremus, & Marcus, 2001). Siebert et al. (1974) described a social responsibility of the press that contends the news media are obligated to present information that will enlighten citizens of democracy and support their efforts of self-governance through rational decision making. Croteau and Hoynes (2001) argued "The media also have the special task of providing independent information to citizens. Ideally, they are watchdogs of our freedoms, informing citizens about current events and debates, and alerting us to potential abuses of power. In this context, a free press is a means by which the public is served" (p. 6).

Although serving the democratic citizenry is a noble objective, the reality is that the economics of any industry have to be a part of any evaluation of the goods or services being produced. The mass media are no different in evaluating the economic impact of their output, their content. The production of news can be a very expensive endeavor. The business of the media is to produce content within certain economic parameters but with the desire of attracting the largest possible audience that can be offered to advertisers, thereby attaining the greatest revenues for the mass media organization. Kellner (1990) pointed out that television corporations are no different from other corporations that are organized to extract maximum profit from the production process. Jamieson and Campbell (2001) simply commented "One important distinction between mass communication and other forms of communication in the United States is their commercial basis: *the primary function of the mass media is to attract and hold large audiences for advertisers*" (p. 4).

It is determining the content and the investment made in obtaining content that will attract an audience that is being played against the information that the mass media should be gathering and providing to an audience but is not because it is to costly to produce. Gathering and distributing information take enormous amounts of money in terms of technology needed and payment required for the people who perform these tasks for a mass media organization. The media business is the business of planning, gathering, evaluating, processing, organizing, and distributing content (information and entertainment messages) to an audience. In this simple business objective of producing goods or services available for consumption by an audience, mass media organizations are no different from other companies and the mass media business is no different from other industries.

The content of a mass media organization is the product it offers to an audience and that audience is sold to advertisers to make a profit for the mass media organization. Coca-Cola produces soft drinks; General Motors produces automobiles; Continental Airlines offers airline service; and the Walt Disney Company produces mass media content such as films, books, music, and television programs. All of these companies have the simple objective of producing products or services that will attract customers to sustain their business. Baron (2003) commented, "It is a strange but powerful testament to the American democratic and market system to have one of its most important democratic institutions to be a resounding market success" (p. 67).

To some authors, comparing the mass media with other industries is a false analogy because of the central democratic information function the mass media provide. To some, earning a profit should not be a factor in the business of providing information to the public. Baker (1992) contended, "Anything preventing the press from effectively providing information and commentary that the public would want or that an 'independent' press would conclude the public needs, is a serious threat to sound social policy and a properly functioning democracy" (p. 2153). Croteau and Hoynes (2001) argued that the media are unique for three reasons: (a) the central function of advertising in creating relationships with the media and therefore the media is not responsive to the audience; (b) the fact that the media are not merely a product used by consumers but rather are resources for citizens with important information, education, and integrative functions; and (c) the role the media play in a democracy (pp. 25–26).

Many of these theorists suggest that there is not a conflict, as democratic ideals of an informed citizenry are secondary to the profit earnings. This position is articulated by the political economy approach to mass communication, which focuses on the economic relationships among powerful industries and how these relationships affect government policy, limit diversity of media content, and exert some form of control on the flow of information (e.g., Mazzocco, 1994; Mosco, 1996; a more detailed explanation of the political economy approach is provided in chap. 5). The idea often argued is that the mass media organization simply cannot be both a profit-oriented business and a true disseminator of information. Gitlin (1972) argued that "the mass media in capitalism are private properties before all else. Their prime self-conscious function is profit-making" (p. 338). Schudson (1978, 1995) described the situation of a mass media organization as a fair dispenser of news and a company that is a profit industry as an inherent contradiction. The two positions are mutually exclusive.

The difficulty is: How does a mass media organization exist in a system dependent on money but operate with the belief that it does not have a justifiable right to factor economics into the decision-making process and produce content that might earn a profit? In terms of attempting to earn a profit, it is important to point out the fallacy that the mass media are the sole entity in which the democracy rests. Some authors have blamed the mass media for contributing to political discontent (e.g., Fallows, 1996; Lichter & Noyes, 1996). Although unquestionably vital, the mass media relationships with important constituency groups begin to emerge, and other factors involved in their perceived responsibility as to the content they should provide can be addressed.

Any group that provides information to the public is a major stakeholder in the democratic process and has the responsibility to provide the mass media with accurate, factual content. It is the relationships that the mass media have with the people who control power, most notably government officials, that become a central criticism. Black, Steele, and Barney (1993) argued, "Society is committed to the free flow of information as a means of educating the population, so that its members may make informed decisions. Information control is related to power. Distribution of information is a redistribution of power. Thus, the journalist is often at odds with individuals and entities wishing to retain power by controlling the free flow of information or withholding information altogether" (pp. 25–26). In having relationships with those who control power, and by association having power through having access to information and the ability to evaluate and disseminate information, questions of the nature of these relationships need to be raised.

The determination of what is the proper and valuable information that best serves the public is subjective and open for debate. The processes of how these mass media organizations obtain their information and the relationships between the mass media organization and content providers who have the actual information all become critical. Mass media organizations simply do not have information. It has to be gathered, evaluated, organized, and distributed. All of the activities involved in these relationships have crucial decisions that are made at every point of the process.

MARKETPLACE OF IDEAS

The role of the mass media in a democracy is centered on the right to free speech as articulated in the First Amendment to the U.S. Constitution:

> Congress shall make no law respecting an establishment of religion, or prohibiting the free exercise thereof; or abridging the freedom of speech, or of the press; or the right of the people peaceably to assemble, and to petition the government for a redress of grievances.

The importance of this amendment is not only that people can express their views but also that the public can hear various viewpoints.

In 1644 Milton, in *Areopagitica*, promoted the marketplace of ideas concept where freedom of expression and debate would lead to the discovery of truth. Mill (1859/1956) later stressed the need for debate and an open exchange of ideas so that faulty opinions can be exposed. The marketplace of ideas concept is that democracy is best served by an open exchange of many ideas so that the citizenry has the best possible information with which to make a decision. Without all of the perspectives being offered, potentially valuable information cannot be learned and therefore the best possible decisions on the part of the citizenry cannot be made. Without a system where all opinions and information are exposed, perhaps the most vital information that is necessary to make a decision is what is being concealed. Franklin (1987) argued, "An individual who seeks knowledge and truth must hear all sides of the question, consider all alternatives, test his judgment by exposing it to the opposition, and make full use of different minds" (p. 13).

It is this exchange of ideas that becomes a necessary, core component of an effectively functioning democracy. Gomery (2000) stated, "A democracy needs freedom of expression to make it work and the mass media ought to be open enough to promote debate on all points of view. The marketplace of ideas calls for criteria of factualness, accuracy, and completeness" (p. 523). The marketplace of ideas concept puts much pressure on the mass media but can provide a clear and easy philosophy to content decision making, as the people working in the media can simply evaluate content with a simple question: Is this information that helps the citizenry make an informed decision about an issue or an election? An answer in the affirmative would make it worthy of being a story or part of a story that should be provided to the public. The marketplace of ideas concept begins to bestow a great amount of power to the mass media organizations, as they have the capability to gather the various ideas, select and frame ideas, and distribute these ideas to a mass audience.

Although idealistic, the practicality of achieving the marketplace of ideas utopian concept where there is an open exchange of all ideas is extraordinarily difficult, if not impossible. There are some basic characteristics of a marketplace that appear in the evaluation of the mass media industry. These characteristics illuminate both the strengths and the flaws of the marketplace of ideas concept. Marketplaces have vehicles for distribution and retrieval of products or services. The marketplace of ideas concept needs the opportunity both to disseminate messages by all people and groups, and to provide access for all of these messages to the audience.

Perhaps the key part of the phrase "marketplace of ideas" is that it is a marketplace, and in a marketplace certain products, certain services, and certain ideas become more receptive and simply win out over others and remain in the marketplace. There is competition within the marketplace and, therefore, winners and losers in this competition. Therefore, some content that gets to stay in the marketplace and receives an accepted status was in competition with ideas that were dismissed. In a marketplace, products, services, or ideas are not all of equal value. The marketplace of ideas concept falters in that all information is not created equal, and therefore some ideas do not get equal time and equal staying power in the marketplace. Some sources of ideas have established a high degree of credibility, and the credibility of the source is always a factor in such an evaluation of ideas. Certain organizations also have more resources to deliver products, in this instance messages, into the marketplace.

There is tremendous competition within the marketplace because marketplaces can only be so large; there is only a certain amount of "shelf space." For the mass media industry the practical limits of time and space that foster competition create the size of the marketplace and the amount of ideas that might emerge into the public dialogue at any one time. Because of competition there are stages to entering the marketplace and challenges to remaining in the marketplace. Proper thought formulation and packaging of the idea by the content provider, the ability to persuade the mass media organization to provide it exposure, the interest of the audience retrieving the message, the ability of the audience to believe in the plausibility, and the behavior execution of the idea are all necessary. Then, after an evaluation of the audience response, the process begins again. The initial source or content provider has an opportunity to reshape or reframe the message to obtain media coverage and achieve the desired behavioral response by the audience.

Because the marketplace concept is characterized by the size of the market and what is available, the mass media marketplace is always governed by technological communication advancements. It is the technology that people deem useful that affects society. The changes in technology have created a new communication environment in which unprecedented opportunity exists for gathering, distributing, and retrieving content. In using the terminology of the marketplace of ideas, the market for mass communication is much larger. Cable and satellite technology considerably changed the communication environment, particularly for television. In 1980 only 19.9% of the homes had cable television, whereas in 2002 the number had more than tripled to 69.8% (e.g., Nielsen Media Research, www.mediainfocenter.org).

The Internet has had a profound impact on all mass media industries by altering the possibilities for distributing messages into the marketplace, as many people now can disseminate content through their own Internet sites. With this development, however, there is pressure on the audience to evaluate the source credibility of this information. Kaye and Johnson (2002) explained that "the Internet provides a wealth of political information, including a considerable amount of material that has not been filtered, edited, or scrutinized by traditional media" (p. 66).

The news cycle, which was once dominated by the morning newspaper and the evening news with only important breaking news being reported during the day, has now turned into a 24-hour, 7-day-a-week period with cable news channels and the Internet. Baron (2003) explained that "a news cycle is how long it takes to get information and post it up on a Web site. Once that is done, the process of using the slower methods of distribution can begin" (p. 56). Kaye and Johnson (2002) simply pointed out that "there is little denying that the Web is becoming an important medium that is taking its place alongside television and newspapers. It is becoming an influential medium and one that people are turning towards for serious and reliable information" (p. 67).

The ability to retrieve messages is also a factor in evaluating a technological impact (e.g., Chafee, 1986). Johnson and Kaye (2000) claimed that the Internet increases access to political information, which should create a better informed citizenry who participate more in politics and who then could have a greater influence on the political process. These technological changes allow for the diversity of messages to become content and potentially reach an audience. If a person truly desired to learn about an issue, it would be near impossible in the current technological environment to get some information about it. Kaye and Johnson (2002) did point out that in the current technological mass media environment, political attitudes are shaped by many factors and current studies about political beliefs, and the flow of political information involves respondents who had formed their political beliefs before the advent of the Internet. That, however, will not be the case in the future as generations will not have known life without the Internet, thus increasing the possibility that the Internet will play a major role in how political communication is transmitted and how political beliefs are formed.

Responsibility for a functioning democracy also rests with the citizenry itself to become engaged and make informed decisions about the important issues that could affect their lives. The more information people have about a topic, the more likely it is that they might become engaged or interested in that topic. The more information they have should lead to a better decision about how to view an issue, or which candidate to support. Although the marketplace concept places a huge amount of responsibility for distributing information on the mass media, it also places a tremendous amount of trust in the public to evaluate the many perspectives and make the proper decisions that would benefit society. Burson (1997) added "that invitation to speak out is the basis of democracy. Public opinion is the final arbiter. That idea places a lot of trust in the public" (p. 17).

Trust becomes a critical aspect in a marketplace: trust in the people who are distributing goods, services, and ideas (mass media organizations), and trust in the people who are evaluating these items and behaving in a manner that endorses or rejects them. With the freedom granted through the First Amendment and the trust endowed by the public comes great responsibility for the mass media and the audience—the responsibility on the part of the mass media to provide the necessary information and the responsibility on the part of the audience to do its due diligence and become informed on the relevant issues of the day.

The final, ultimate marketplace characteristic is that the market, the people, decide what remains, what happens to the remaining items, and what gets eliminated. Out of all of the ideas that the mass media organization decides to provide to the audience, the audience then gets to make an evaluation about that content. Even if an idea does get mentioned, if it is quickly dismissed by the audience as irrelevant, that idea might not again receive exposure. In this scenario only certain information remains part of the public dialogue. This is an acceptable outcome so long as it is the citizenry making the final evaluation about an issue after getting exposure to the various ideas. The marketplace of ideas concept becomes problematic, and the critique of the mass media is in their controlling the marketplace.

Trust in the audience is arguably the best characteristic of the marketplace of ideas concept in that it recognizes the ability to make a proper decision when presented with all of the information. This idea of the people's ability to come to a proper decision should convey a feeling of welcome for different ideas rather than a feeling of stagnation for different ideas on the part of the various content providers trying to get a message to the audience in an attempt to influence their opinions and behavior. For example, if, following the marketplace of ideas philosophy, political candidates from the Republican and Democratic parties would desire numerous debates and encourage participants from any other third party to speak, the public will be able to see the value in their respective arguments and correctly dismiss the others. For this to occur, confidence in one's message must be paramount and a fear of being wrong nonexistent, characteristics that few politicians or their strategists are either unwilling or unable to possess.

In a larger nation with decisions about issues that can affect the public, the mass media are invariably an integral part of the marketplace system as gatherers and distributors of information. The complexity of the system is that someone has to make decisions about what information is important and gets exposure in the marketplace. The information that gets the opportunity for exposure is critical. The information must get national mass media exposure, often in many mediums, even to reach the marketplace and be considered in a meaningful way. It is impossible for any issue, national candidate, or product or service to resonate with a national audience without significant mass media exposure. The selection and framing of content decisions by the people of the mass media organizations thus become pivotal factors in the marketplace of ideas and the informing of the democracy. Mass media organizations, particularly those that report on news happenings, are entrusted with the responsibility to provide the many perspectives that would assist the citizenry in making correct decisions that would be based on an informed opinion. Burson (1997) claimed, "The quality of our government, the quality of our society depends on the quality of the public opinion that directs it. And the value of the public's opinion depends on how well the public is informed" (p. 17).

Once the message is distributed, the audience will then evaluate this information and base its opinions not only on the message (the facts presented) but on the source of these facts. The audience is incorporating its own set of beliefs, values, and relationships that have been attained through previous experience with the issue, other information learned through other mass media sources, or any interpersonal communication. Evaluating the audience is difficult because the audience is not a monolithic group receiving and interpreting messages in the same manner. People place different importance on and desire about becoming engaged and learning about certain issues. For example, this disparity of what the audience deems important is indicated in election exit polls when voters are asked, "Which issue mattered most?" The responses vary for many reasons but can provide insight into what the voters care about.

Several authors have made the claim that mass media organizations are only profit oriented, and certainly they have made this statement as a negative reflection on the current practices of the mass media industry as a whole. It must, however, be pointed out that the behavior of the audience is the impetus for any profits. Without the audience behavior and participation in the media content, there are no advertisers, and without the advertisers, there are no profits. The advertisers are essentially going to expose their brands in the locations in the mass media where the audience is attending (the influence of advertisers and their desires in the production of mass media content are discussed in more detail in chap. 8). An argument can be made that being profit oriented is following the will of the people, as expressed by their media use behavior. If the audience's media use behavior is the driving influence of the decision-making process and the mass media environment has created more opportunities to access information and experience different content, an examination into theories of mass media use is vital.

SUGGESTED READINGS

Baker, C. E. (1992). Advertising and a democratic press. *University of Pennsylvania Law Review, 140,* 2097–2243.

Croteau, D., & Hoynes, W. (2001). *The business of media: Corporate media and the public interest.* Thousand Oaks, CA: Pine Forge Press.

Ehrlich, M. C. (1995), The ethical dilemma of television news sweeps. *Journal of Mass Media Ethics, 10*(1), 37–47.

Jamieson, K. H., & Campbell, K. K. (2001). *The interplay of influence: News, advertising, politics, and the mass media* (5th ed.). Belmont, CA: Wadsworth.

Mill, J. S. (1974). *On liberty.* Baltimore: Penguin. (Original work published 1956)

Milton, J. (1644). *Areopagitica.*

Schudson, M. (1995). *The power of news.* Cambridge, MA: Harvard University Press.

Slattery, K., Doremus, M., & Marcus, L. (2001). Shifts in public affairs reporting on the network evening news: A move toward the sensational. *Journal of Broadcasting & Electronic Media, 45,* 290–302.

2

Mass Media Use

The media use behavior of the audience in relation to the marketplace of ideas concept demonstrates that the audience has an important function in mass media content decision making. Different from other industries, and other marketplaces, is the nature of the product in the mass media industry. The cultural products of information and entertainment make the mass media marketplace far different in their impact from the goods and services produced in other industries. The profound impact this industry has on society makes the study of the mass media so important.

The impact of the mass media is through the behaviors of mass media use by the audience and is the result of two primary functions: (a) the mere presence of the mass media and (b) the desire on the part of the audience to experience the content the mass media provide. Both functions make it clear that the mass media draw whatever power they have through the audience's use of the media. Simply put, media use is the main impact the media have on society in that there will always be people using the mass media because their presence makes them easy to access and they provide content that people not only need or enjoy but are willing to pursue and obtain.

The ubiquitous presence of the mass media creates the primary impact of mass communication through easily accessed content. Thayer (1986) contended that the phenomenon of mass communication is not in the technology, the message, or the effect, but rather in "the *social and personal uses* to which people put the media and their fare" (p. 46). The argument that the presence of the mass media is the greatest impact on society is a position often articulated by citing McLuhan

(1964). Through his saying that "the medium is the message," McLuhan thought society was shaped more by technology through the availability of the medium and the way in which people communicated rather than by the specific content itself.

The McLuhan (1964) philosophy is that the various forms of media delivery systems create the primary impact of mass communication. In making the content a secondary characteristic, the focus of McLuhan was on how we experience the world rather than what (the content) we experience. Although the simple access and use of the mass media cannot be overlooked, it would be unrealistic not to acknowledge that in certain circumstances media use can be a purposeful behavior that is driven by the content provided by mass media organizations.

USES AND GRATIFICATIONS

With the most recognizable characteristic that establishes the power of the media within society being audience use, examining how, why, when, and in what manner people use the mass media is vital. People use the media for a variety of reasons, including information, entertainment, or social reasons, including to provide something to talk about with others (e.g., Thayer, 1986). This mass media use can be a purposeful behavior on the part of the audience and can be driven by having access to a particular medium or participating in specific content that is available through any medium. For mass media use that is content driven, essentially, people are turning to the mass media because they know that the content will satisfy their needs.

One media theory that is helpful in explaining the mass media content decision-making process from a more audience-centered perspective and media use as a purposeful behavior is the uses and gratifications literature inspired by Blumler and Katz (1974). The initial idea of Katz (1959) was to synthesize critical work on popular culture and effects studies. Katz questioned what it is that people do with, and what gratifications they find in, mass-produced news and entertainment (e.g., Carey & Kreiling, 1974, p. 226). Katz, Blumler, and Gurevitch (1974) claimed that uses and gratifications "simply represents an attempt to explain something of the way in which individuals use communications, among other resources in the environment, to satisfy their needs, and to achieve their goals" (p. 21). More recently, Rubin (2002) explained that from the uses and gratifications perspective, "communication behavior is largely goal directed and purposive. People typically choose to participate and select media or messages from a variety of communication alternatives in response to their expectations and desires. These expectations and desires emanate from and are constrained by personal traits, social context, and interaction" (pp. 528–529).

McLeod and Becker (1981) identified fundamental characterizations of the uses and gratifications perspective. These characteristics are: (a) the audience is active; (b) media use is goal directed; (c) media use fulfills a wide variety of needs; (d) people can articulate the reasons for using the media; and (e) the gratifications have their origins in media content, exposure, and the social context in which exposure takes place. The most notable characteristic of the uses and gratifications perspective is that of an active audience. Hunt and Ruben (1993) described the uses and gratifications approach as a general perspective rather than a specific theory, claiming "it represents an attempt to understand audience members as active information consumers, and to place the emphasis not on what media *do to* people, but rather what people *do with* the media" (p. 83). The uses and gratifications approach contends that an active audience selects and uses the mass media to satisfy its own needs, attitudes, values, and beliefs. In this media use the audience is acting as people who are volunteering to participate and selecting where they participate based on their own needs and goals (e.g., Levy & Windahl, 1985; Lin, 1993).

Choosing media content thus links with the particular gratifications sought, knowing that the media compete with other sources of need satisfaction. Audience members are aware that mass media use can satisfy some of their needs better than any other resource. The individual uses his or her own experience and perspective in selecting and using media based on expected outcomes of fulfillment of desires and satisfaction of goals. Rubin (2002) explained that "the principled elements of uses and gratifications include our psychological and social environment, our needs and motives to communicate, the media, our attitudes and expectations about the media, functional alternatives to using the media, our communication behavior, and the outcomes or consequences of our behavior" (p. 527). The concept of needs driving behavior indicates that media use can be a purposive behavior on the part of the audience to satisfy its desires. The participation in the media often becomes, thus, a purposeful behavior based on an expectation of the audience member that his or her needs will be satisfied as they have been in previous experiences with that medium and the content they produce.

Rubin and Perse (1987) claimed that the intention of the audience member toward media use is a key factor in evaluating their behavior. Intentionality is described as the extent to which mass media participation is purposive and planned. Similar to Rubin and Perse's ideas of intention, expectancy is defined as a set of beliefs about the various communication media and their content before interacting with the media (e.g., McCombs & Weaver, 1985).

In relation to the variable nature of audience activity, particularly audience intention, Rubin (1983, 1984, 2002) identified two media use orientations toward a medium and its content that are based on motives, attitudes, and behaviors: (a) ritualized mass media use and (b) instrumental mass media use. Rubin (2002) explained that "ritualized and instrumental media orientations tell us about the amount and type of media use and about one's media attitudes and expectations" (p. 534). The ritualized and instrumental uses of media as identified by Rubin are not static or discrete characteristics of individual users.

Ritualized media use focuses on a particular medium, rather than on content. It indicates how people use their discretionary time and which medium they attend to when all of them are available. Ritualized media use is a less intentional and nonselective orientation with a tendency to use the medium regardless of the content. Rubin (2002) explained ritualized use is using a medium more out of habit to consume time as it is the medium the person enjoys. In this situation people are turning on the television and randomly going through different channels during their leisure time attempting to find a program worthy of taking the time to view, as watching is the ritual activity. A similar example could be applied to a random reading of certain articles in a newspaper, going online and simply clicking through various Internet sites, or randomly selecting any particular content during ritualized participation in any medium. Perhaps the better example of where people often engage in ritual media use is driving in a car with the radio on, as listening is the ritual activity.

Instrumental media use focuses on purposive exposure to specific content and is more intentional and selective on the part of the audience member (e.g., Rubin, 2002; Rubin & Perse, 1987, p. 78). It is the content available through a particular medium at a particular time that is dictating behavior. In an instrumental media use orientation, a person turns on NBC on Thursday night because he or she wants to watch *ER* or picks up the newspaper or visits a specific Internet site to find out a stock quote or a baseball score, or read a favorite columnist. The instrumental mass media use could be a factor in the way a person organizes his or her day to be done with any other activities that might need to be accomplished and be available to participate in the mass media content when it is available. This purposeful, content-driven media use remains interesting in that of all the activities people could participate in, they engage in mass media use. For example, there could be a beautiful day on an autumn Sunday, yet millions of people will elect to remain indoors and watch football on television.

Gantz and Zohoori (1982) claimed that accommodation to television changes may be a function of two factors: (a) type of time and activity involved and (b) television content and gratifications associated with it. The element of time deals with the opportunity for media use and is separated into what Gantz and Zohoori referred to as "non-disposable time for required activities such as work or sleep vs. disposable time for leisure activities such as watching TV" (p. 265). They summarized their position claiming:

> The likelihood of accommodation for television is maximized when it involves the rearrangement of leisure activities during disposable time for content sought out and uniquely associated with desired gratifications. The likelihood of accommodation for television is minimized when it involves the rearrangement of non-leisure activities during non-disposable time for content of little interest or value to the viewer or for which there are functional alternatives available. (p. 265)

Accommodation of media use to the other activities people need to do cannot be overlooked. Media use occurs in relation to other media sources and the nature of the other mediums' availability as well as the other activities and responsibilities people need to perform in their daily lives. Mass media organization personnel would like to believe that they produce content whose audience participation is instrumental in nature and that people alter their schedule to participate in the content because of its quality. However, understanding that facilitation of access is also important, mass media organizations develop strategies that relate to ritualistic media use by making certain content can be accessed at a certain time when the audience is available.

Mass media organizations select their content and then carefully situate it to ensure its desired target audience the opportunity to be exposed. Although simple exposure or participating in a medium might produce audience gratifications (ritualized media use), mass media organizations are most hopeful that it is their content that produces the gratification sought and obtained by their target audience (instrumental media use). It is the content being provided on a specific channel or publication that leads to audience gratifications.

However, also understanding that mass media use can be ritualized (e.g., Rubin, 1983, 1984) and based on leisure or disposable time (e.g., Gantz & Zohoori, 1982), mass media organizations try to make quality content available at the appropriate time for the audience. More than simple use, mass media executives must develop and provide content so that people actively select a certain medium at a certain time. For example, a television network might create a compelling programming schedule that also capitalizes on the ritualized nature of television viewing, giving the networks an opportunity for one or both media use orientations to be exercised by the audience. For example, cartoons are placed on Saturday morning when children do not have school, and sports are placed on the weekends when people do not have to work. The Sunday newspaper is the largest, the day when most people are not working. The top talents in radio have their programs during the morning and evening when many people are driving in their cars to and from work and are a captive audience in that they have no access to any other medium and they are able to listen. Simply stated, in an attempt to maximize their business, mass media organizations attempt to align certain programs with the leisure time of their desired target audience and desired advertisers, in essence, align the ritualized and instrumental media use functions.

The uses and gratifications literature indicates that individuals have preferences for a specific type of content, and when needs can be satisfied by that type of content, people actively seek out that type of media (e.g., Rosengren, Wenner, & Palmgreen, 1985). This characteristic is important because it provides an indication to patterns of repeat behavior on the part of the audience. This repeat behavior is a critical factor in the decision making that determines future mass media content through the idea that in the future, people will choose similar types of content (e.g., Webster & Lin, 2002). Webster, Phalen, and Lichty (2000) explained that this audience duplication is relevant to both advertisers and programmers. They pointed out that duplication indicates critical behavior activities such as exposure, frequency, audience flow, and audience loyalty. Choosing content of a similar type is evident in the popularity of reality television, as with a different reality show on every night the audience simply moves from reality show to reality show regardless of which television network the shows are on. Sports provide a similar phenomenon of audience movement as sports fans move from network to network to watch games. Even in news, if people are responding to stories about foreign affairs, health, or religion, there will be more types of stories on those subjects.

In analyzing gratifications based on content, medium availability, and mass media use within the scope of people's day, any new opportunity to access content changes the mass media environment. The Internet has dramatically changed the mass media environment and therefore changed the media use environment, as the audience has a new vehicle to retrieve messages and any type of message at any time they desire. People no longer have to wait until the evening news or the following day's newspaper to learn of the top stories. Even within new opportunities for access, Webster and Lin (2002), claimed that studying Internet use reveals regularities similar to those found in more traditional mass media in that there is still a business component and a need to attract an audience. In pointing out the similarity between the Internet and other forms of the mass media, Webster and Lin stated, "Audience size is critical to virtually all forms of subscriber or advertiser-supported media. Electronic and print media depend upon audience 'ratings' and circulation to sustain their operation. The Internet is no exception" (p. 2). Even for the Internet, the uses and gratifications principles wherein the audience member actively selects the medium and certain content available through that medium to satisfy needs have not changed.

Lin and Jeffres (1998) pointed out that Internet use is goal directed, and users are aware of the needs they are trying to satisfy. Internet users are active in their search for information, clicking on links or using search engines. Perse and Dunn (1998) pointed out that perceptions of the media's ability to gratify needs are influenced by the attributes of the media, particularly the content that is provided and the mode of transmission. Papacharissi and Rubin (2000) indicated that Internet use is more purposeful and instrumental than ritual, as a habit or simply passing time. Kaye and Johnson (2002) found a similar result, stating, "When individuals connect to political sites, it is likely they do so with goal-oriented purposes rather than just for the sake of entertainment gratifications offered by the Web at large" (p. 67).

The Internet possesses characteristics that other forms of the mass media do not, most notably the ability to access at any time, the variety of information available, the interactive nature of choosing the content rather than having the mass media organization simply supply it, and the speed with which new information can be ascertained. It is because these characteristics are beneficial to the audience (and other characteristics such as having no media filter that are beneficial for content providers) that the Internet has had such a revolutionary impact. Rubin and Rubin (1985) claimed that if a "channel is not available, or if the interaction does not effectively fulfill the need, a functional alternative would be chosen" (p. 48). Atkin and Jeffres (1998) explained that similar media may serve similar needs, and replacing the time spent with traditional media could occur if the new technology is perceived to have an advantage over previous technology. If the Internet did not satisfy all of the desires and needs that it does, its impact would be nominal and limited use irrelevant.

ACTIVE AUDIENCE: INTERPRETATION OF MESSAGES

In addition to suggesting the audience is active in choosing media content, the uses and gratifications perspective also contends that the audience is active in interpreting messages (e.g., Katz et al., 1974). Swanson (1987) explained that "media messages are seen as at least partly malleable, capable of being interpreted or taken in somewhat different ways by auditors who seek different gratifications from them" (p. 238). The uses and gratifications approach assumes that different active audience members are oriented to mass media content in different ways and that these orientations are systematically related to different social circumstances and roles, personality dispositions and capacities, different patterns of mass media use, and media effects (e.g., Blumler, 1979). Rubin (1993, 2002) explained that psychological characteristics, social context, and attitudes and perceptions influence people's motives and behavior.

The active audience characteristic in interpreting messages is particularly important in the evaluation of mass media effects. Much research in communication deals with the power of the mass media to influence audience thinking and behavior. The power of the mass media to influence an audience thinking and behavior is often debated (Becker & Kosicki, 1995; Bryant & Zillmann, 2002; Perse, 2001, offer succinct summaries and address the critical issues of the media effects debate). The core of mass media effect studies remains the same, evaluating the impact of the independent variable of exposure to media messages influencing the dependent variable of audience behavior. Gerbner, Gross, Morgan, Signorielli, and Shanahan (2002) described that "traditional-effects research is based on evaluating specific informational, educational, political, or marketing efforts in terms of selective exposure and measurable before/after differences between those exposed to some message and others not exposed" (p. 47).

Several of these mass media content effects studies focus on: (a) the exposure of violent television programming influence on behavior (e.g., Anderson, 1997; Centerwall, 1989; Gerbner, 1972, 1998; Sparks & Sparks, 2002), (b) the exposure of violent programming influence on children's behavior (Huesmann & Eron, 1986; Jason, Kennedy, & Brackshaw, 1999; Kubey & Larson, 1990; Schramm, Lyle, & Parker, 1961; Zillmann, Bryant, & Huston, 1994), (c) news coverage influence on voting behavior (e.g., Bennett, 2000; Graber, 1984; McCombs & Shaw, 1972; McLeod, Kosicki, & McLeod, 2002; Roberts, 1997; Weaver, Graber, McCombs, & Eyal, 1981), or (d) advertising influence on the consumer behavior of purchasing goods or voting (e.g., Stewart, Pavlou, & Ward, 2002).

There are two dichotomous perspectives of mass media effects. A more direct effects perspective contends that mass media messages are powerful in influencing the audience. The indirect, or limited effects, perspective, where the uses and gratifications theoretical model is grounded, contends that mass media messages are not an over-whelming influence and are only one potential factor in influencing behavior as the message is interpreted by the individual audience member. Kline, Miller, and Morrison (1974) claimed the "uses and gratifications model suggests that individual uses for media content act as an intervening variable: mitigating or enhancing the ultimate effects of a media message" (p. 113).

Prominent in the media effects research from a more direct effects perspective is the concept of cultivation, as inspired by Gerbner (1972). Cultivation examines exposure to messages over long periods and was described by Gerbner et al. (2002) as "the independent contributions television viewing makes to viewer conceptions of social reality. The most general hypothesis of cultivation analysis is that those who spend more time 'living' in the world of television are more likely to see the 'real world' in terms of the images, values, portrayals, and ideologies that emerge through the lens of television" (p. 47). From the cultivation perspective, the difference in the amount of television viewing, either light or heavy, is the determination in the cultivation effect, with heavy viewers more likely to take on the reality as expressed by television. People, therefore, essentially have different cultivation levels based on the amount of their media exposure.

Even proponents of perspectives that lean toward a philosophy of a powerful and influential mass media temper their ideas and recognize that the audience through its experiences and interpretive abilities is a mitigating factor in any ultimate effect that a media message might have on an audience. Gerbner et al. (2002) pointed out that cultivation analysis is an ongoing process that takes into account the interaction of messages, audiences, and contexts. They explained:

> From the reception perspective, it seems logical to argue that other circumstances do intervene and can neutralize the cultivation process, that viewers do watch selectively, that program selections make a difference, and that how viewers construct meaning from texts is more important than how much they watch. We do not dispute these contentions. The polysemy of mediated texts is well established. From the cultivation perspective, though, to say that audiences' interactions with media texts can produce enormous diversity and complexity does not negate that there can be important commonalities and consistencies as well across large bodies of media output. (p. 48)

Although the mass media message is selected and framed, a key to the uses and gratifications approach is that the gratifications experienced by the audience are not dictated by the message content, the message producer, or the message conduit, but through the interpretations of the individual audience members. Klapper (1960) questioned a more direct effects perspective by pointing out that several elements interact with the message in producing the person's response to that message. He thought that most media messages reinforce existing attitudes, which, however, can still be argued as an effect. Perspectives of more powerful mass media effects tend to view the audience in a more monolithic nature, but it is a diverse audience of individuals that is active in interpreting the content they are receiving, as described in the uses and gratifications literature. Individual audience members interpret the meaning of these messages they are exposed to based on their own experience, needs, attitudes, values, and beliefs.

Willnat (1997) pointed out that "different people can be exposed to the same message and yet perceive it quite differently, depending on their prior knowledge about the issue under consideration" (p. 58). Budd, Entman, and Steinman (1990) claimed that "whatever the message encoded, decoding comes to the rescue. Media domination is weak and ineffectual, since the people make their own meanings and pleasures" (p. 170). They continued, "We don't need to worry about people watching several hours of TV a day, consuming its images, ads and values. People are already critical, active viewers and listeners, not cultural dopes manipulated by the media" (p. 170).

Evans (1990) pointed out that except for the hypodermic needle model, "no tradition in mass communication research posits a passive audience. Thus, the real difference is not a question of active versus passive, but rather the postulation of one kind of activity versus another kind" (p. 150). Livingstone (1993) believed that researchers should consider audience and text and context together because "text and reader are interdependent, mutually conceived, joint constructors of meaning" (p. 7). I take Livingstone's ideas one step further by considering the producers of the text (the mass media organizations), their resource characteristics, their relationship to the text, their relationship with the constituency groups, the complex process by which the text was produced, and the audience to whom they are presenting that text.

Livingstone (1990) succinctly summarized the problem of analyzing an active audience relating to a mass media organization that is selecting and framing messages, stating:

> If we see the media or life events as all-powerful creators of meaning, we neglect the role of audiences; if we see people as all-powerful creators of meaning, we neglect the structure of that which people interpret. The important questions concern the interrelation between the two: how do people actively make sense of structured texts and events; how do texts guide and restrict interpretations. The creation of meaning through the

interaction of texts and readers is a struggle, a site of negotiation between *two* semi-powerful sources. Each side has different powerful strategies, each has different points of weakness, and each has different interests. It is this process of negotiation which is central. And through analysis of this process, traditional conceptions of both texts and readers may require rethinking, for each has traditionally been theorized in ignorance of the other. (p. 23)

MEDIA DEPENDENCY

Media use is prevalent and purposeful because of the ubiquitous presence and because there are so many needs satisfied through this behavior. If people were able to fulfill their needs elsewhere there would not be as extensive media use and the mass media would not have the powerful role in society they posses. The fact that the mass media consistently satisfy many of these needs creates a situation in which people become dependent on the mass media. Media dependency research as described by Ball-Rokeach and DeFleur (1976), examined media use by the audience with a focus on the critical characteristics of media availability, the type of content, and the purposeful behavior on the part of the audience.

Ball-Rokeach and DeFleur (1976) defined dependency as a "relationship in which the satisfaction of needs or the attainment of goals by one party is contingent upon the resources of another party" (p. 6). From a mass media organization perspective, the resources they possess include the capacity to: (a) create and gather, (b) process, and (c) distribute information (e.g., Ball-Rokeach, 1985, p. 487). It is the capacity to perform these tasks of creating and gathering, processing, and distributing information on a wide range of issues that the audience deems important that creates the dependency. Through these definitions dependency occurs on many levels from both individual and organizational standpoints. The individual dependency on the mass media is through the reception of content that cannot be otherwise obtained. The organizational dependency on the mass media is through the distribution of content and the need for an exposure vehicle to reach an audience. The recognition of both individual and organizational needs on the mass media is a strength of the media dependency model in examining the content decision-making process.

INDIVIDUAL MEDIA DEPENDENCY

Individual media dependency relates strongly to media use and the uses and gratifications perspective. The words *needs* and *dependency* become analogous, as at the core of both streams of research is the purposeful behavior of participation in the mass media because the needs or dependencies of the active audience member will be satisfied. This experience of satisfaction serves as a predictor for future media use behavior with participation being in the same form and with the same type of content that produced previous success for that individual.

Ball-Rokeach and DeFleur (1986) identified three needs where audience members are dependent on the media system: (a) the need to satisfy information goals to understand one's social world; (b) the need to act meaningfully and effectively in the world; and (c) the need to play, satisfy exposure, or escape from daily problems and tensions. Individuals depend on various types of product or service organizations, as well as other individuals, to provide the amenities for everyday life. The need for information, entertainment, and social uses is among these amenities and creates a dependency on the work of mass media organizations. Events happen and people look for an explanation of what it means or a context as to why this event is important. Hunt and Ruben (1993) even described an information dependency on advertising. There is a dependency on certain products to help people in their work and everyday lives, as certain products make life easier or more enjoyable. Through the mass media and advertising, the audience learns about those products that can affect their everyday lives (e.g., Hunt & Ruben, 1993).

Similar to the ritualistic and instrumental mass media use orientations, individual dependencies can be developed for certain content or on a particular medium. Ball-Rokeach, Rokeach, and Grube (1986) provided an example of a media dependency on a particular medium by defining television dependency as "the extent to which the attainment of personal goals is contingent on the information resources of television" (p. 282). They claimed that "when the information television provides in the form of news or entertainment is necessary to people being able to understand, act, and play, we say they have established dependency relations with television" (p. 282). To amplify further the dependent nature of television, considering all of the entertainment options available, although the audience does not watch any one television program (few television shows in a given year have an audience share of more than 50%—the Super Bowl is normally the television show with the highest share, as the game between the New England Patriots and the Carolina Panthers in 2004 had a television share of 63%), the cumulative number of people watching television every night is still significant.

Although at certain times a dependency on one medium might be prevalent, it is having a variety of media forms available and a dependency on all of the media forms that really makes a societal impact. At certain times radio is best; at others, newspaper; and others, the Internet might be the best option for media use. It is using all of these mediums that strengthens the media dependency argument as a whole. For the most part it is not a dependency on only one form; instead, people shift through various mediums. Content providers, therefore, need to be in various delivery systems and locations.

FACTORS OF INDIVIDUAL MEDIA DEPENDENCY

Media dependency takes the behavior of mass media use a step further than the uses and gratifications perspective by introducing factors that strengthen the dependency and increase the likelihood of media use. It is these media dependencies that can predict the behavior of media use. Simply put, the stronger the dependency, the greater is the chance of media use. Because of a diverse and active audience composed of individuals, mass media dependency is not a static condition and can be strengthened or weakened based on a variety of factors.

For individuals, media dependency occurs because the mass media are the only vehicle available for experiencing or learning about events or people they do not encounter through everyday experience. People cannot learn about important issues on a daily basis on their own without participating in some form of the mass media. Individual dependency predicts media use that is driven by experiences that people cannot participate in themselves. Ball-Rokeach et al. (1999) point to the origin of a media dependency, stating, "Media systems develop when interpersonal communication systems no longer can handle the organizational demands placed upon social actors, whether they be societies, organizations, groups, or individuals" (p. 240). McCombs and Reynolds (2002) explained that issues can be categorized along a continuum ranging from obtrusive, issues that people can personally experience, to unobtrusive, issues that people can only learn about through the mass media.

On issues of foreign affairs or following a political campaign, people do not have that type of interpersonal contact necessary to provide information and are therefore dependent on the mass media. In a media context with news occurring all over the world, the mass media are necessary for people to learn some of what is happening. For unobtrusive issues there is potentially a stronger media dependency, as the mass media provide information that cannot be obtained through face-to-face contact alone. Even if people have the ability to learn information through interpersonal communication, they might still opt to learn through the mass media. For example, people could learn about issues of health from a local doctor, but rarely do people speak to their doctor; instead, they get more of their general health knowledge from television or newspaper reports or from searching the Internet. Also, if people were to learn of information through interpersonal communication, it is probable that the person relaying the information learned of it through the mass media.

Halpern (1994) emphasized the availability or lack of a functional alternative to the mass media in creating a dependent relationship. Functional alternatives are simply options that an individual has at his or her disposal to obtain the same content. Functional alternatives are different because the characteristics inherent in the forms of media themselves create disparities. Therefore, some forms of media might not be considered a functional alternative to some members of the audience. For example, there are several events that are covered by every form of media. A presidential state of the union speech is live on television and on the radio. It is highlighted and analyzed later on the television news, video clips of it might appear on the Internet, and articles about it appear in the newspaper and news magazines. Experiencing the event is different through each of these mediums. A similar example can be described for a sports event, but clearly for a fan of a team, reading about the game in the newspaper the next day is not a functional alternative or adequate substitute to watching the game live on television.

The lack of a functional alternative is having access and being exposed to content that the audience desires but cannot ascertain themselves. It is the lack of functional alternatives to the mass media that has created the initial and most vital audience dependency factor. The preferred medium to learn about important issues might be different for each individual, as there are distinct differences to the experience based on the medium, but some form of mass media is used. Rubin and Rubin (1985) claimed that "the more an individual comes to rely on a single communication channel, the greater is the predictability of the outcome of communication. The more functional alternatives available to an individual, in terms of both quantity and quality, the less is the dependency on and influence of a specific channel" (p. 39).

The type of issue can also be a major factor in the strengthening or weakening of a mass media dependency. In analyzing media exposure and media use in relation to media dependency, First (1997) described that the dependency on television increases for issues such as politics that are somewhat remote from personal experience. Fortunato (2001) described a similar mass media dependency on the part of the audience to experience sports, particularly on television. As individuals' motivations differ, their selection of information sources also differs (e.g., Pinkleton & Austin, 2002; Pinkleton, Reagan, Aaronson, & Chen, 1997; Tan, 1980). Reagan (1995) claimed that heightened interest leads to an increased use of information sources.

McCombs and Reynolds (2002) pointed out that individuals orient themselves to certain issues based on their relevancy and uncertainty regarding the issue. Relevancy relates to the importance people place on a particular issue, and uncertainty relates to the knowledge individuals have about the issue. Both relevancy and uncertainty can dictate active audience media use. Individuals with low relevancy about an issue have a low need to orient themselves to that issue, and because they do not deem the issue important, they will not actively seek out information about the issue. A low need for orientation also exists if there is low uncertainty about an issue, as in this case people are confident in their knowledge of an issue and do not have a strong need to retrieve actively mass media content about the issue. Under conditions of high relevance and low uncertainty, the need for media orientation is moderate, as the person deems an issue important but is confident in his or her knowledge of the issue. The situation that most dictates mass media use is when relevance and uncertainty are high. When people deem an issue important but lack sufficient knowledge, their need to learn about the issue increases as does the potential for mass media use. If the conditions of high relevance and high uncertainty exist for an issue defined as unobtrusive by McCombs and Reynolds, a mass media dependency results and active mass media use is likely.

The type of issue also relates to the audience intensity toward that issue, with certain issues featuring intense audience members (i.e., politics, sports). The perceived importance or audience intensity toward issues is another variable that could strengthen or weaken individual media dependency. Intensity was described by Loges (1994) as the extent to which media information resources are perceived as helpful in attaining an individual's goals, with higher intensity indicating that media information is more helpful in attaining goals. In this instance, interest or perceived importance of a topic could cause media dependency for individuals who wish to connect and be familiar with what others might be talking about. People do not want to be left out of conversations about current events, and that could lead to participation in some form of media. People might engage in television programs such as *American Idol* or watch a sports event because they know those programs will be talked about the next day in the office.

Although mass media use might be voluntary on the part of the audience, a strong argument can be made that there will always be volunteers because the mass media provide us with many of the things we "need" or are "dependent" on and cannot experience ourselves. Media use becomes a necessary condition for the majority to experience unique events, but in reality to experience life. The different mass media dependency factors—lack of a functional alternative, interest in the issue, and the perceived importance of the topic—can combine to create an even stronger dependency. The characteristics that can strengthen mass media dependency can perform with each other, as the lack of a functional alternative together with an increase in an interest in the topic, and the perceived importance of the topic lead to a strong mass media dependency and therefore an increase in the likelihood of media use (see Fig. 2.1).

ORGANIZATIONAL MEDIA DEPENDENCY

Because so many people use the media for a variety of reasons, government officials, corporations, advertisers, marketers, public relations professionals, and all content providers vociferously compete for media attention and media time and space. Competition for media time and space is fierce, as explained in the marketplace of ideas concept, as there is only a limited supply but an incredibly large demand on the part of content providers to get their message exposed to the audience. Understanding the relationship between content providers and the people from the mass media organization becomes critical in evaluating organizational dependency. These content providers simply desire to gain exposure and access for their messages in mass media locations where their potential consumers attend. It is analogous to McDonald's wanting to be on a busy highway, a tool company wanting its products available at Sears or Wal-Mart, or an airline creating a hub in a major city. These companies know people are going to be in these locations and can receive exposure for and ultimately purchase their respective brands. Setting up an environment for distribution of goods and services and facilitating the consumers' ability to receive exposure

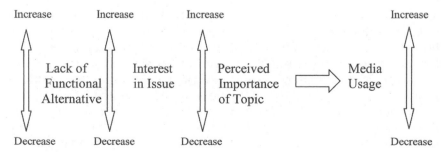

FIG. 2.1. Factors of individual media dependency in predicting media use.

and purchase goods need to be considered in any industry. Content providers have the same challenge of facilitating audience retrieval of their messages and have to develop and implement communication strategies that enhance the possibility of receiving media coverage.

Therefore, in relation to the content decision-making process, mass media dependency research also examines dependency on an organizational level. Dependencies occur for any organization, regardless of the industry, that needs other constituency organizations for its own industry to function. For example, the airline industry is dependent on the fuel industry. Any organizations or persons (content providers) with a message are dependent on the media as the communication vehicle or link for exposure of their messages to the audience. Organizations need the mass media to communicate the features of their brand in trying to persuade consumers to purchase the goods or services that are produced by the organization for their industry to thrive. People or groups compete for their messages to become media content because the mass media provide access to the audience. Without using the mass media, how do content providers get to their audience, particularly if they are trying to reach a large number and wide range of people on a national or global level?

In recognizing both individual and organizational dependencies, two spheres of dependency are created, with the mass media positioned in the middle. Situating the mass media between organizations or content providers, who have a message and are dependent on the mass media as the vehicle for exposure, and the audience, who is dependent on them for information, entertainment, and other social desires, gives the mass media a tremendous amount of power in these relationships. Knowing that there will always be participants using the mass media, the power of the mass media could be in their potential ability to influence the audience, as examined in media effects studies. The power could also emanate from their inherent responsibility to make decisions as the gatherers, evaluators, organizers, and distributors of content.

The decision-making power of the mass media organization to produce content is, however, somewhat devalued if constituency groups external to the mass media organization strongly influence the content decision-making process. The mass media organization has the primary responsibility to produce content. *Time* magazine's primary responsibility is that there will be an issue of *Time* magazine next week. The same way, NBC must fill all 24 of its broadcast hours. Even an Internet site has some limits to the amount of content it can provide. External constituency groups are in a position of power because the mass media organization is dependent on content providers. The quest is not merely to fill the time and space to fill them with quality content that will attract an audience and, in turn, attract advertisers.

At this juncture, an interdependent relationship is a better characterization of the content decision-making process between mass media organizations and content providers. The interdependent characterization of the relationship indicates that the mass media are not autonomous in producing quality content and are very much in need of content providers. Therefore, people such as Tim Russert, moderator of *NBC's Meet the Press*, needs top government officials to come on his program; David Letterman, host of CBS's *The Late Show with David Letterman*, needs the top actors, actresses, comedians, and singers, and sports reporters need access to top athletes. Without quality content, people will watch other television programs or participate in other mediums. McQuail (2000) pointed out one common aim of all media organizations is "to produce something which meets professional or craft standards of quality and has a good chance of success with the audience" (p. 291). Success with the audience for a mass media organization is determined by the initial desired media effect of participation—if the audience watches, reads, listens, or clicks on.

Organizational dependencies can also be strengthened or weakened depending on the circumstances of the situation based on the same criteria as individual dependency. There are instances where content providers desperately need to get a message out to an audience. For example, in a presidential administration if a perspective on an issue really needs exposure the president will conduct a news conference or a prime-time television speech to ensure large amounts of media coverage. The importance of the issue and the potential lack of functional media alternatives to getting the message out, either because a speaker does not have the stature of the president and the media do not pay attention or the president gives a newspaper, magazine, or radio interview that does not have the larger audience reach, create a dependency on television in this instance.

The important component that needs to be considered in an evaluation of media use theory is that dependencies can only be formed and gratifications can only be attained based on the medium and the content that is available. Access and the ability to retrieve content on the part of the audience must always be factored into the evaluation of mass communication processes. Even the early uses and gratifications literature recognized that gratifications and media use are dictated by what is available. McLeod and Becker (1974) pointed out that "the exposure characteristics of the message *combine with* the orientations of the audience member in producing the effect" (p. 141). Important exposure characteristics of the content such as when it is available, how often, and how much time is devoted to a particular topic all become a critical part of the analysis. Although they are active in their media use, audience members are never totally autonomous because they are limited not only by their own psychological and sociological situations or their predispositions to the content but also by the choices they are presented in the media.

In regard to content exposure and mass media effects studies, Shoemaker and Reese (1996) simply stated that "media content is the basis of media impact" (p. 27). They pointed out that media effects studies can only occur on what messages are available to the audience, as it is only these messages that have the potential to affect the audience. Rubin (2002) argued, "By themselves, mass media typically are not necessary or sufficient causes of audience effects, and a medium or message is only a single source of influence in the social and psychological environment, although it is an important and crucial one" (p. 525).

If mass media effects are only a possibility based on what content is available to an audience, learning about the decision-making process of how this content becomes available is critical to understanding the entire mass communication process. In traditional mass media effects studies, the content is often the independent variable acting as the influencing force on the audience. In studying the process of how content is produced, mass media content can be construed as a dependent variable that is a result of the decision making that is being influenced by a multitude of constituency groups (e.g., Shoemaker & Reese, 1996).

If gratifications can be satisfied and dependencies formed, increasing the likelihood of participation in the mass media, it appears that the media would always keep the audience in mind when making critical content decisions. Understanding the audience and its needs is essential to the producers of media messages so they can select and frame the content to meet these needs and achieve audience gratifications through their content decisions. Achieving this success of audience gratification through the content provided greatly help the audience return to that media location.

Mass media organizations try to make decisions in which they match the content being provided with the desires of the audience—perhaps not the total audience, but more important, the target audience that the content is designed to reach and that can be delivered to advertisers. Selection and framing strategies should have the objective of alignment with audience activity. Therefore, it is strongly in the mass media organizations' best interests to understand the sociological and psychological variables of the audience. The difficulty for mass media organizations in producing messages is that audience members are not uniformly active in their media consumption (e.g., Blumler, 1979). Audience members are not monolithic and active in choosing media to satisfy their own particular needs; therefore, often generalizations are made in content decisions.

Regardless of the reason—whether information, entertainment, or social inclusion—media use is where media power is originated and generated. Mass media dependency begins to provide an explanation of media use on the part of the audience and reasons why organizations try to influence the content decision-making process. Media dependency research helps illuminate those reasons from both an organizational perspective and an individual perspective. If people did not use the mass media in the constant and consistent manner in which they do, the institutions of the mass media would not have the relevance or the means to influence the culture in a large, meaningful way. Mass media organizations can capitalize on media use with the power of their inherent responsibility to select and frame messages that will be exposed to the audience. Knowing there will be media use, and some of it will be instrumental and content driven, confers power to mass media organizations that can provide exposure for the messages of content providers to an audience.

SUGGESTED READINGS

Ball-Rokeach, S. J. (1985). The origins of individual media-system dependency: A sociological framework. *Communication Research, 12,* 485–510.

Ball-Rokeach, S. J., & DeFleur, M. L. (1976). A dependency model of mass-media effects. *Communication Research, 3,* 3–21.

Becker, L. B., & Kosicki, G. M. (1995). Understanding the message-producer/message receiver transaction. *Research in Political Sociology, 7,* 33–62.

Blumler, J. G. (1979). The role of theory in uses and gratifications studies. *Communication Research, 6,* 9–36.

Blumler, J. G., Gurevitch, M., & Katz, E. (1985). Reaching out: A future of gratifications research. In K. E. Rosengren, L. A. Wenner, & P. Palmgreen (Eds.), *Media gratifications research: Current perspectives* (pp. 255–273). Beverly Hills, CA: Sage.

Blumler, J. G., & Katz, E. (Eds). (1974). *The uses of mass communication: Current perspectives on gratifications research.* Newbury Park, CA: Sage.

Bryant, J., & Zillmann, D. (Eds.). (2002). *Media effects: Advances in theory & research* (2nd ed.). Mahwah, NJ: Lawrence Erlbaum Associates.

Katz, E., Blumler, J. G., & Gurevitch, M. (1974). Utilization of mass communication by the individual. In J. Blumler & E. Katz (Eds.), *The uses of mass communication* (pp. 19–32). Beverly Hills, CA: Sage.

Kaye, B. K., & Johnson, T. J. (2002). Online and in the know: Uses and gratifications of the Web for political information. *Journal of Broadcasting & Electronic Media, 46,* 54–71.

Rubin, A. M. (2002). The uses-and-gratifications perspective of media effects. In J. Bryant & D. Zillmann (Eds.), *Media effects: Advances in theory and research* (2nd ed., pp. 525–548). Mahwah, NJ: Lawrence Erlbaum Associates.

Rosengren, K. E., Wenner, L. A., & Palmgreen, P. (Eds.). (1985). *Media gratifications research: Current perspectives*. Beverly Hills, CA: Sage.

3

Mass Media Selecting and Framing

The ubiquitous presence of the mass media in the multiple forms that have been created through technological communication distribution and retrieval systems allows for opportunities of unprecedented mass media use. Add in the factor that people use the mass media to satisfy a variety of needs, and a system is created where there is constant and consistent use. Some of this mass media use can become so important for certain issues and information desired through certain mediums that dependencies on the mass media are established. These dependencies can even be strengthened, creating a situation where mass media use on the part of the individual is more likely.

New communication technologies also create opportunities of unprecedented choice of content by an audience. Although people are constantly choosing which radio station, television channel, or Internet site to attend, the concept of their unlimited choice might be misleading in that the choice is only among the mediums to which they have access and the content available to them. Even though the audience is active in its selection of content, Ang (1990), cautions, "Audiences may be active, in myriad ways, in using and interpreting media … it would be utterly out of perspective to cheerfully equate 'active' with 'powerful' " (p. 247).

Decisions are made by people within the mass media organization regarding which content to show and how to present that content to the audience. Although mass media power in terms of content effects are debated, the fact that people use the mass media in the consistent manner they do and that it is the mass media organizations that have the responsibility and ability to select and frame the content they choose to expose to an audience does confer substantial power to these mass media organizations and to the people who are employed by them. However, as the organizational dependency theoretical model indicates, the power in this process of mass media content decision making is centered not only in the mass media organization. In this complex process constituency groups depend on the mass media for exposure, but the mass media organizations depend on content providers for quality content. Thus, making the relationship interdependent and the process one of interaction leaves open for debate the issue of who the power brokers are between mass media organizations and content providers.

Even though mass media effects are questioned, it is imperative to point out that content providers try to influence the process of content decision making because of the potential power the mass media have in accessing the audience and delivering messages that could influence its thinking and behavior. All of these outside constituency groups must still go through the decision makers of the mass media organization. Although the mass media industry draws significant power because it produces a product that people consistently use, it is the ability and responsibility to make decisions about the selection and framing of content that convey much power to people within mass media organizations. Ball-Rokeach and Cantor (1986) claimed that "everywhere mass media exist, the power to decide what is broadcast or distributed ultimately rests with very few people who usually occupy formal roles in bureaucratic structures" and "without understanding how content is controlled (selected and created), by whom, under what conditions, it is not possible to understand what messages finally reach audiences, no matter how creative those messages will be" (p. 15).

Although constituency groups try to influence the process, the members of the mass media organization must use their judgment in making decisions regarding content and can advance or deny any requests made on them. The refusal of a request by a constituency group, however, can be met with consequences for the mass media organization or for a specific media employee, depending on the details of the situation. The process is very much a human process in that there are relationships between people from the mass media organizations and the constituency groups that are trying to influence the process. The employees of these industries are also people with families and other everyday, real-world issues that affect their decisions, perhaps simply to keep a job. This type of capitulation to a boss, or another organization with which the individual's organization has to deal, is not different from other industries except that the output, the content, is witnessed by all and can potentially affect many.

The human element of content decision making highlights the ethics of every person within the mass media organization and how they approach the responsibility of their job. Certainly, people within the mass media organization are cognizant of the legal issues about the content that they can or cannot use. Even if the employee is not sure, larger mass media organizations have lawyers who could clear the use of questionable content. Once the content decision making passes the test for legality, all other decisions can be evaluated on ethical merits. Moore (1999) provided a detailed examination of the legal and ethical issues of the mass communication industry. Mass media organizations are faced daily with making tough ethical decisions, and questions as to where their ultimate allegiances should lie are debated, as evidenced by the literature or the mass media role in a democratic society. The issues of ethics are where human judgment becomes a critical factor in the mass communication process. With each person having his or her own set of ethics, any general standard of decision making regarding content becomes very difficult to establish, as the ethics people apply to a decision are as varied as the number of individuals. Individual ethics certainly factor into content decision making (e.g., Luna, 1995).

Decisions regarding content center around two main criteria: (a) selection: Does the issue have the opportunity for exposure to the audience? and (b) framing: How is the issue portrayed or presented to the audience in terms of both media placement and the facts or perspectives emphasized in the report.

SELECTION

Mass media organizations have to undertake the selection decision-making process, which involves such fundamental questions as: Do we or do we not cover a story? If we do cover the story, does it appear on the front page, or air first on the news, or be what people immediately see when they click on an Internet site? Even for entertainment-oriented mass media organizations questions emerge, such as: Do we put a situational comedy (sit-com), reality show, or drama on the air and in what time slot? Does this movie get made? Does this book get written? Do we give this singer or band air time on the radio?

The initial characteristic that must be considered in selecting of stories is that all mass media decision making is restricted by available time and space. Not all stories can be aired or printed; therefore, selection of content is a necessary condition of the decision-making process. Ettema, Whitney, and Wackman (1987) commented that "far more 'news' is available at a given time than most organizations can reproduce as 'their' news" (p. 766). There are only 24 broadcast hours in a day, and only one thing can be on a television network or a radio station at one time. Therefore, by definition, if one item is being broadcast others are not. For example, a local nightly television news program is scheduled for 30 minutes, but the true content amount that will consist of the hard news of the day is immediately reduced. Commercials might require 8 minutes; 3 minutes each for sports, weather, and perhaps one minute each for other daily segments such as a stock market report or lottery results leaving the total time for all of the news events of that day at approximately 14–16 minutes. Only one item can be on the front page of the newspaper or Internet site or on the cover of a magazine. These decisions reflect a hierarchy of importance on issues. A newspaper or a magazine will only be so large, and even the Internet has its limitations.

The New York Times uses a slogan of "all the news that is fit to print." Under this general standard the newspaper would be huge. There are people who determine what is news, what is "fit to print." The people making those determinations work within a standard format (the idea of formats and mass media routines is expanded in chap. 4). *The New York Times* philosophy exists within a format of a certain amount of space allocated for advertising, sports, comics, television section, stock quotes, and other daily sections before determining the remaining amount of space for which news content decisions can be made. It is these limits of time and space that create tremendous competition for media attention among all of the people or groups with a message (the content providers).

The idea of selection was introduced by Lippmann (1922), who pointed out that reporters could not report all of the happenings of the world; therefore, a selection process is necessary. It is through this initial characteristic of selection that people even have the opportunity to be exposed to only certain content, with other issues having no opportunity to reach an audience, at least at that time through that medium. If there is any consistency through the various mediums, as there tends to be (i.e., stories that appear in the newspaper tend to appear on that newspaper's Internet site, tend to appear on television and the television networks' affiliated Internet site, and tend to be updated on radio throughout the day), there really is only a small opportunity for an issue to receive exposure to the audience. Without mass media exposure for a story there is little chance for it to have a huge national impact. Fishman (1997) simply stated, "Some happenings in the world become public events. Others are condemned to obscurity as the personal experience of a handful of people. The mass media, and in particular news organizations, make all the difference" (p. 210). Regarding the importance of the selection decisions from a mass media organization perspective and the potential value for a content provider, Molotch and Lester (1974) pointed out that events become news essentially because someone notices the event and has an interest in telling about it.

FRAMING

It is not only selection of content and exposure to the audience but also decision making regarding the manner in which the content will be presented to the audience that is critical in the process. Similar to the selection phase of content decision making, once the content is selected the media are limited by time and space in presenting every aspect of a story. Just as some stories will not be covered at all, the nature of news production does not permit even the issues that are covered to be done so with the same standard. Therefore, selection not only includes the content that receives exposure but also includes the facts or highlights that will be presented in that story. The selection of facts is referred to more commonly in the communication literature as the framing the content might receive.

Entman (1993) explained, "To frame is to select some aspects of a perceived reality and make them more salient in a communicating text, in such a way as to promote a particular problem definition, causal interpretation, moral evaluation, and/or treatment recommendation for the item described" (p. 52). He also claimed that frames "call attention to some aspects of reality while obscuring other elements, which might lead audiences to have different reactions" (p. 55). Jamieson and Waldman (2003) pointed out that "just as there are countless events reporters could write about each day, there are many more pieces of information than could possibly fit into a single story. The metaphor of a frame—a fixed border that includes some things and excludes others—describes the way information is arranged and packaged in news stories. The story's frame determines what information is included and what is ignored" (p. xiii).

As was the case with selection, framing decisions are the final determination of the mass media organization production or editorial staff. Framing methods can be separated into two distinct types: (a) exposure and (b) portrayal. Exposure framing methods initially include selection in terms of the stories that get aired, printed, or posted and even have the opportunity of being retrieved by the audience. In addition to mere selection, exposure becomes a method of framing the issue through characteristics such as (a) frequency: how often and how much time a story is given; (b) placement: where the story appears (as the lead story of a broadcast or in the middle, on the front page of a newspaper or on page 5, as what first appears when the Internet site is visited or as a link); and (c) the amount of time or space devoted to an issue within the entire scope of the mass media organization's production. Cohen (2002) explained that the Internet alleviates some of the constraints of deadlines and source availability prevalent in broadcast or print stories, but even the Internet follows similar patterns of selection and framing and prioritizing stories (e.g., Cohen, 2002).

The exposure characteristics of selection, frequency, placement, and amount of time or space devoted to a topic are determined by the mass media organization and can be easily recognizable and consistently identified by independent observers. Whether print media, where frequency is in terms of topic selection, column inches, and placement of an article; or the Internet and what is first viewed when visiting an Internet site and the number of accompanying stories that can be accessed; or television where frequency is in terms of topic selection in its daily reporting, amount of time, and placement of a story, these ideas that are based on issue exposure to the audience alone are present in every major form of the mass media. These framing decisions can be as important as exposure in how a story is perceived.

McCombs and Mauro (1977) pointed out that page placement, story format, and other framing mechanisms influenced the level of readership for a news story. Carroll and McCombs (2003) commented that newspapers communicate a host of cues about the importance of a topic through the placement of a story. They explained, "The lead story on page one, front page versus inside page, the size of the headline, and even the length of a story all communicate information about the salience of the various objects on the news agenda" (p. 4). In speaking of television news, Carroll and McCombs continued, "Even a mention on the evening television news is a strong signal about the salience of an issue, person, institution, corporation, or any other object that is in the news. For all the news media, repeated attention to an object day after day is the most powerful message of all about its salience" (p. 4). They added, "By calling attention to some matters while ignoring others, the news media influence the criteria by which presidents, government policies, political candidates, and corporations are judged" (p. 12).

Portrayal framing methods are how the organization's production staff presents the content about a topic to the audience. Portrayal decision making involves which facts are included and emphasized and how they might be analyzed, and which facts are not included or emphasized in the report. Portrayal framing could involve important questions such as: What type of pictures will accompany the story, who is quoted in the story? What type of language is used in the description and analysis of a story? Just as every story cannot be covered, every aspect of the story cannot be covered.

The pictures and the language used in the framing process can be pivotal in the frame presented to the audience and what might be interpreted by the audience (e.g., Garcia & Stark, 1991; Wanta, 1988; Zillmann, Gibson, & Sargent, 1999). Again, the audience is only able to make a determination about a topic based on the information that is made available. In studying photos of Hillary Clinton, Mendelson and Thorson (2003) found that mere presence of a photo helped in having that story thought of as more interesting, but it did not assist in recall of the items that were contained in the story. They stated, "It appears typical news photos of political actors serve as attention-getting devices, making stories more accessible or available, but are not used as an important informational aid" (p. 146).

The words used in the story are as capable of an impact as are the pictures. Scheufele (2000) commented that framing is based on "the assumption that subtle changes in the wording of the description of a situation might affect how audience members interpret this situation" (p. 309). In analyzing the press coverage of the Clinton–Lewinsky affair, Yioutas and Segvic (2003) pointed to the differences in coverage, with some reports referring to the events as a scandal rather than a story. Similar events attain an elevated status of concern or importance when language such as *crisis* (i.e., energy crisis, health care crisis, education crisis) or *war* (i.e., war on drugs, war on terror) is attached to a story.

Both the pictures and the language could be from the content provider. The language might not be the choice of the media but instead be the words strategically used by the content provider to emphasize a frame. If the report in the mass media quotes a government official, it is the language of the official, but the people of the mass media organization select the quote that is used. Skilled content providers understand the nature of the medium and often provide photographs and video footage as needed with the hopes of their being used. The content providers' intention in trying to influence the framing process is clear—get their perspective to be the dominant frame relayed to the audience to influence the audience to think or behave in some manner (i.e., vote, purchase). Consider some examples in recent political discourse about either events or politicians of language framing:

- the liberation of Iraq versus the occupation of Iraq
- President Clinton was impeached for lying about sex versus President Clinton was impeached for committing perjury

- reductions in an increase in spending versus cutting the budget
- terrorist versus freedom fighter
- soldier versus peacekeeper
- lobbyist versus supporter
- working families versus taxpayer families
- public servant versus bureaucrat
- stubborn versus conviction
- flip-flop on issues versus flexible thinker
- ideologue versus passionate supporter
- attacking an opponent versus drawing contrasts
- conservative versus right-wing conservative versus moderate
- liberal versus left-wing liberal versus moderate

Although similar in their objectives, exposure and portrayal framing methods were differentiated by Lasorsa (1997), who pointed out that newsrooms are concerned with surveillance (exposure), conveying what is going on out there, and correlation (portrayal), interpreting those events. He claimed that "in fulfilling their surveillance functions, the media should agree generally about what is happening and what deserves the most attention now" and "in fulfilling their correlation functions, the media should not agree generally about how the public should respond to what is happening" (p. 164).

Both selection and framing are important because of the potential influence on how the issue might be perceived by the audience. Just as the selection of issues can influence an audience so too can the framing, especially if the issue is unobtrusive and the audience is not familiar with it (e.g., Gandy, 2001; McCombs & Reynolds, 2002; Tuchman, 1978). In these instances, the audience relies on the media to describe and explain the importance of the story. Kaneva and Lenert (2003) stated that "individuals routinely turn to major news outlets, such as local and national newspapers, for information on issues of immediate concern and tips on what action can and should be taken in response to certain events" (pp. 149–150). People are interested in more than simple facts—they seek out analysis of events. This is why people listen to talk radio, read editorials of favorite columnists, and watch news talk shows and choose the shows they watch based on hosts and guests whose opinion they value.

Even more so than selection, these decisions that center around how to frame an issue are where the mass media organizations draw their most power. Nelson, Clawson, and Oxley (1997) commented that "frames influence opinions by stressing specific values, facts, and other considerations, endowing them with greater apparent relevance to the issue than they might appear to have under an alternative frame"

(p. 569). Jamieson and Waldman (2003) added, "Frames tell us what is important, what the range of acceptable debate on a topic is, and when an issue has been resolved. By choosing a common frame to describe an event, condition, or political personage, journalists shape public opinion" (p. xiii). Studies in message framing have demonstrated that excluding information from a message frame can affect how people interpret the message (e.g., Ashley & Olson, 1998; Gitlin, 1980). For example, Kim (2002) posited that "Americans' understanding of other cultures and countries is significantly influenced by the way international news is framed" (p. 431).

Content decision making is inevitable. Selection is inevitable, so too is framing. Some frame will result from the content decision-making process. The frame is the product of the decision and framing is the decision-making process itself. The frame is what is presented to the audience. The audience does not see the alternative frames that were not selected in the presentation of the issue, at least at that time, through that medium. The audience can attend to an alternative medium for more information to learn about alternative frames of the story, if available. The idea that the frame that is presented becomes the dominant reading of the text is where the media effects debate begins to be a point of contention, as an active audience might interpret the story and not accept the provided frame. Even though there is only the potential of the frame to influence the audience, content providers do everything within their power to influence the mass media framing of a story.

AGENDA SETTING

One research area that initiated with mass media content selection and extended into framing is the agenda-setting research inspired by McCombs and Shaw (1972). Agenda-setting research initially questioned mass media effects based on audience exposure (selection), the amount of coverage an issue received, and it evolved to include questions of framing, how the issue is presented (e.g., McCombs, Shaw, & Weaver, 1997). The core idea of agenda setting is that selection by the mass media and exposure of a topic to the audience leads to salience of that issue on the part of the audience. The initial idea of agenda-setting did not, however, emphasize that how people thought about the issue would be influenced by the exposure, but rather that their awareness of the issue and the level of perceived importance of that issue increased. The initial agenda-setting philosophy is often characterized by citing Cohen (1963), who observed that the mass media "may not be successful much of the time in telling people what to think, but it is stunningly successful in telling its readers what to think about" (p. 13). This transfer of salience based on exposure alone has been referred to as Level 1 of agenda setting.

The original agenda-setting hypothesis proposed by McCombs and Shaw (1972) tested whether media coverage influences the public's perception about the importance of issues. This transfer of issue salience from the media agenda to the public agenda was based on selection alone. The mass media can implement the public agenda through their selection of stories or events. Shaw and Martin (1992) pointed out, "The press may, unconsciously, provide a limited and rotating set of public issues, around which the political and social system can engage in dialogue" (p. 903). They added "the media spotlight public events and issues long enough for collective identification and social discourse. That is one major function of mass agenda-setting" (p. 920). Consistent with the work of Miller (1956), who estimated that the information-processing capacity for people's agendas was seven items, plus or minus two, Shaw and McCombs (1977) found that the public agenda typically included five to seven items. McCombs and Reynolds (2002) stated that "establishing this salience among the public so that an issue becomes the focus of public attention, thought, and perhaps even action is the initial stage in the formation of public opinion. Although many issues compete for public attention, only a few are successful in reaching the public agenda" (p. 1).

Shaw and Martin (1992) claimed that "public issues always compete for limited numbers of possible public attention slots" and "public attention is limited. Space is limited. Time is limited" (p. 904). Lasorsa (1997) pointed out that the reality is that the media select and give more attention to some events and issues than to others. These selected issues have the potential to become part of the public agenda. Subsequently, the theory implies the lack of attention given to an event or issue hinders the opportunity for that issue to become an item on the public agenda (e.g., Hunt & Ruben, 1993; Wright, 1986). Wanta and Wu (1992) stated, "If the news media do not devote coverage to issues, individuals will perceive these issues to be less salient than the issues that do receive coverage" (p. 849).

Although transfer of issue salience from the media agenda to the public agenda based on the amount of exposure alone was the original claim to come out of agenda-setting studies, the theoretical framework has evolved as agenda-setting researchers also focused on how an issue gets presented. This second level of agenda-setting research has examined how the framing of an issue by a mass media organization can also affect the public agenda, positing that the mass media may be successful in telling people how to think about an issue. The way an issue is framed could shape public perception of the salience of that issue (e.g., Ghanem, 1997; McCombs & Reynolds, 2002; Schoenbach & Semetko, 1992; Semetko & Mandelli, 1997). In addition to exposure alone, the framing of content offers opportunity for the mass media organization to transfer the salience of an issue from the media agenda to the public agenda. McCombs and Shaw (1993) reconsidered their original agenda-setting hypothesis and extended the agenda-setting function, describing it as a process that can affect both what to think about and how think about it.

It is the second level of agenda setting in explaining decisions about how messages are presented that can influence audience thinking about an issue where comparisons between agenda setting and framing are made. In viewing framing as an extension of agenda setting, McCombs (1997) stated that framing "is the selection of a restricted number of thematically related attributes for inclusion of the media agenda when a particular object is discussed" (p. 6). Other scholars saw the similarity between agenda setting and framing as both dealing with construction of media messages and public perception of those issues (e.g., Semetko & Valkenburg, 2000; Yioutas & Segvic, 2003). Maher (2001), however, drew a distinction between agenda setting and framing, pointing out that "agenda setting has typically not considered the relationships of elements within a text, as they are organized by the text's author" (p. 86). He explained, "Framing scholarship typically concentrates on the communicator's framing, that is, the journalist's framing. Agenda-setting research typically examines the transfer of framing salience between the text (as interpreted by the researcher) and the receiver (public)" (p. 89).

Whether through selection or framing, Protess and McCombs (1991) claimed that "agenda-setting is about the transfer of saliences, the movement of issues from the media agenda to the public agenda" (p. 3). The agenda-setting effect on an audience is measured taking into account the selection and framing that issues receive from the mass media. Any agenda-setting effect is essentially based on the mass media's content decision making. The audience simply cannot make judgments based on information it does not have. For stories in which people have no personal experience for comparison, people might be more willing to accept the perspective offered by the media. If people have experienced the issue, the framing provided through the mass media might not be as influential.

It is also imperative to recognize that the potential media influence on an audience through portrayal framing methods is an extension and not a replacement for the original agenda-setting idea of exposure alone. Agenda-setting researchers now simply recognize that exposure and framing of an issue can both have an effect on the audience. Although the framing of an issue is now recognized in agenda-setting research as a potential influencing factor about how the public thinks about an issue, Ghanem (1997) still emphasized exposure, contending that "the frequency with which a topic is mentioned probably has a more powerful influence than any particular framing mechanism, but framing mechanisms could serve as a catalyst to frequency in terms of agenda-setting" (p. 12). Kosicki (1993) stated that "the amount of space or time devoted to particular issues should be measured, and that this measurement should relate to either the amount of attention people pay to issues or to their judgments of the issues' importance" (p. 105).

Although the results of McCombs and Shaw's (1972) study indicate a very strong relationship between the emphasis placed on various campaign issues by the media and by the public, they are quick to point out that their findings are not discussed in terms of media causality. Critical to their analysis, McCombs and Shaw claimed that the agenda-setting function is "not *proved*" (p. 184) by their correlation data but that the data present evidence that agenda setting does occur. Even in this seminal agenda-setting study, there is a maneuverability and allowance for the audience to be factored into the media effects process. McCombs (1976) clarified any misconceptions regarding direct agenda-setting effects, stating that "no one contends that agenda-setting is an influence process operating at all times and all places in all people" (p. 2). Protess and McCombs (1991), however, pointed out that "placing an issue or topic on the public agenda so that it becomes the focus of public attention, thought, and discussion is the first stage in the formulation of public opinion" (p. 2).

Agenda-setting research has evolved to pose questions of how media agendas are constructed. In recognizing that the mass media might not be acting unilaterally in the selection and framing of content and that the relationships with constituency groups are indeed a vital part of the process, agenda-setting scholars have stressed a need for studying the process of mass media content decision making (e.g., Carragee, Rosenblatt, & Michaud, 1987; Danielian & Reese, 1989; Rogers, Dearing, & Bregman, 1993). Roberts (1997) pointed out that "it is highly doubtful given the growing complexities of contemporary political communication environments that any single medium or entity can solely serve as the agenda-setter. Instead, the individual influence of any particular entity must participate as an agenda builder" (p. 95).

Fortunato (2000) claimed, "The agenda-setting theoretical framework operates from the perspective of the mass media having the power to transfer the salience of an issue to the public. Perhaps, however, too much power is granted to the mass media without the consideration of the processes by which mass media content is selected and framed" (p. 481). He added, "Recognition of other sources having a role influencing mass media content, without accepting the mass media as the only plausible answer, raises the question: who sets the public agenda?" (p. 482). Fortunato concluded, "Simply accepting the mass media as the sole agenda-setting power without recognizing the important role of content providers, the organizations with an agenda to promote and transfer to the public, operating as advocates for their organization is to neglect a critical phase of the creation of mass media content" (p. 497).

FRAMING AND CONTENT PROVIDERS

McCombs and Ghanem (2001) stated, "Agenda setting is a theory about the transfer of salience from the mass media's pictures of the world to those in our heads" (p. 67). They added that the "elements prominent in the media's pictures become prominent in the audience's pictures" (p. 67). The critical question, however, is: Are they the media's pictures, or are others (content providers) simply using the media as the vehicle to announce and promote their own agenda? Maher (2001) raised important questions about any agenda-setting or framing process, recognizing the prospect that content providers or other constituency groups, including the audience, are a prominent part of the process. He asked, "What kinds of issues, causal interpretations, and potential solutions are the news media ignoring that they should not be ignoring? Where do frames originate and how do they spread? Why do reporters adopt a given frame for a social problem and ignore other frames? Which segments of society gain or lose from journalists' framing decisions? Why do different publics accept or reject journalists' frames?" (p. 92).

It is studies of framing and the content decision-making process that provide insight into these complex relationships (e.g., Gamson, 2001; Kaneva & Lenert, 2003). Gamson (2001) pointed out that frame analysis includes "attention to the production process—the ways in which carriers of particular frames engage in activities to produce and reproduce them. A focus on the production process alerts us to issues of power and resources, to the framing process as a struggle over meaning that is ultimately expressed through texts" (p. ix). He added, "Attention to the production process also alerts us to less visible uses of power, those that exclude certain sponsors or marginalize their preferred frames. It leads us to attend to absences and silences in a discourse as well as what is there" (p. ix).

Content providers try to get the mass media to select their stories and frame those stories from their perspective. Why these content providers try to frame an issue is not difficult to discern: They are trying to influence the public, policy, sales, voting, or whatever other behavior might be their desired outcome. The rationale is simple, as Kaneva and Lenert (2003) stated, "The way in which the press discusses an issue can affect the popular interpretation of events and, ultimately public opinion" (p. 150).

Because of the potential influence, the competition that exists for selection is extended to competition for certain frames to be a part of the story. Within each story there are many frames, and some frames will be emphasized and others ignored (e.g., Gamson & Modigliani, 1989; Reese, 2001). All of these potential frames are not of equal value and although the journalist must choose from this array of frame choices, it is at this juncture that the appeals made by content providers are most intense. Gamson (2001) emphasized, "The central importance of the relationship between journalists and sources and the process of selecting sources to quote" (p. ix). Reese (2001) stated, "The power to frame depends on access to resources, a store of knowledge, and strategic alliances" (p. 20). Ryan, Carragee, and Meinhofer (2001) explained that journalistic frames do not exist in a political or cultural vacuum and are "influenced by the frames sponsored by multiple social actors, including corporate and political elites, advocates, and social movements. News stories, then, become a forum for framing contests in which these actors compete in sponsoring their definitions of political issues" (p. 176).

If there is competition for how the issue is going to be portrayed, there is also a winner and loser in terms of whose frame is dominant in the story. Some content providers are better and have more capabilities when it comes to framing messages. Other content providers are so powerful that their perspective will always be included in the text, mainly because these perspectives are desired by the mass media organization and the audience (certainly top government officials fit into this category). Ryan et al. (2001) explained that "the ability of a frame to dominate news discourse depends on multiple complex factors, including its sponsor's economic and cultural resources, its sponsor's knowledge of journalistic practices, and its resonance with broader political values or tendencies in American culture" (p. 176). Jamieson and Waldman (2003) pointed out that in certain situations officials are able to control the frame if they hold a temporary monopoly on the relevant information about a story.

Once an event occurs, the goal of the various stakeholders is to establish a point of view that can be a part of the frame for the event (Miller & Riechert, 2001). All of the stakeholders provide varying perspectives that each stakeholder hopes will be included and gain prominence in the dialogue about the event. Through highlighting certain aspects of the story and downplaying others, Miller and Riechert (2001) explained, "Stakeholders seek to articulate their positions to accommodate journalistic norms and to win support, competing for news media attention. The more a particular stakeholder group is quoted in news articles, the more prominently their particular issue definition is represented in news coverage" (p. 112). They argued, "Stakeholders try to gain public and policymaker support for their positions less by offering new facts or by changing their evaluations of those facts, and more by altering the frames or interpretive dimensions by which the facts are to be evaluated" (p. 107).

If one story could have many frames, even if some frames are not present in one report, many of these frames could still reach an audience, as different frames could be reported more prevalently by various mass media organizations and through various mass media forms. With this many mass media outlets, having only one frame presented by one organization would not seem problematic, as different mass media organizations could focus on and present different frames. Unless all of the mass media organizations use the same frames, multiple frames are exposed and the responsibility to seek them out could be transferred to the audience. In recognizing that there are many mass media outlets and in trying to put forth the frame that supports their position, content providers (government officials, public relations spokespersons, etc.) would make efforts to have their perspective consistently appear in the various reports in the mass media forms.

If journalists use multiple sources, they are inevitably presented with and asked to sift through multiple frames, and there is then pressure to pick the correct frames. Jamieson and Waldman (2003) claimed, "Just as politicians sometimes succeed in deceiving the public, journalists sometimes fail in their task of discovering and describing the knowing, relevant information at play in public discourse" (p. xiv). They pointed out that "the critical variable is usually not the facts themselves but the manner in which they are arranged and interpreted in order to construct narratives describing the political world. Between these two extremes—that there is no such thing as truth, and that there is but a single truth that simply waits to be found—lies the terrain journalists attempt to chart every day" (p. xiv).

Frames can also act as an organizing guide that assists the journalist and mass media organization in content decision making, as there are certain perspectives or frames that need to be included in the story (e.g., Gamson, 2001, Gamson & Modigliani, 1987; Gandy, 2001; Gitlin, 1980). Gitlin (1980) explained that frames are predictable patterns that the people of the mass media organization use to influence the decision-making process. He claimed that media frames serve as working routines for journalists that allow them to quickly identify and classify information. He added that, media frames are "largely unspoken and unacknowledged, organize the world both for journalists who report it and, in some important degree, for us who rely on their reports" (p. 7). Reese (2001) claimed that "framing is concerned with the ways inter-ests, communicators, sources, and culture combine to yield coherent ways of understanding the world, which are developed using all of the available verbal and visual symbolic resources" (p. 11). Reese arrived at the definition of framing as "*organizing principles* that are socially *shared* and *persistent* over time, that work *symbolically* to meaning-fully *structure* the social world" (p. 11).

Even though there are some organizing principles in framing, the jour-nalist is paid for his or her judgment in selecting and arranging the facts of a story. Journalists are in the position they have attained because of their ability to present an acceptable frame of a story. In speaking of the practical application of the people who are actually involved in the fram-ing process, framing can be defined as a philosophy of decision making about what that mass media organization deems important. This philos-ophy of decision making can be extended to the individual reporters, thus making it more difficult to define. Gamson (2001) simply pointed out that "two independent investigators will inevitably slice up the dis-course in different ways," (p. x) as many reporters, or other media deci-sion makers, could represent that many framing philosophies. As Reese (2001) stated, "All frames are not equal in their ability to cause informa-tion to cohere, making sense out of the world. We should ask how much 'framing' is going on?" (p. 13). Jamieson and Waldman (2003) argued, "The frames that journalists adopt are in part a function of the lenses through which reporters view the world and their conception of their roles in the political process at a given moment" (p. xv).

Jamieson and Waldman (2003) summarized:

> Journalists help mold public understanding and opinion by deciding what is important and what may be ignored, what is subject to debate and what is beyond question, and what is true and false. In order to make those judgments, they have to navigate an often confusing thicket of information and assertions. "Facts" can be difficult to discern and relate to the public, particularly in a context in which the news is driven by politicians and other interested parties who selectively offer some pieces of information while suppressing others. (p. xiii)

FRAMING AND THE AUDIENCE

Frames are not equal for a multitude of reasons. Entman (1993) claimed that frames have at least four locations in the communication process: (a) the communicator, (b) the text, (c) the receiver, and (d) the culture. Certain facts are more prevalent than others and certain perspectives more available than others, and journalists have to make judgments about what to include in their stories. Frames are also not equal because of the desires of the audience. The audience is expecting certain frames to be part of a media report. There can be preferred frames to which the audience desires exposure, and those could generally be from the more powerful sources. It is difficult for the reporter not to include certain perspectives or certain frames. How can a reporter justify not putting a comment or the perspective of a top government official into his or her story? The audience might turn to that medium and that content because it is confident that those frames will be part of the story.

Certain frames simply might not be accepted by the audience, which has the ability to interpret actively the messages it is receiving (e.g., Entman, 1993; Gamson & Modigliani, 1989; Goffman, 1974). In coping with the framing of content being produced by the media, audience members orient and perceive media messages by producing their own interpretive frames (e.g., Blumler, Gurevitch, & Katz, 1985). Swanson (1987) explains that audience interpretive frames organize and give coherence to the components that constitute the frame, and direct attention to particular aspects of message content while obscuring other less relevant aspects. Reese (2001) spoke to the interpretive nature of frames, stating, "Frames are never imposed directly on media audiences. The acceptance and sharing of a media frame depends on what understandings the 'reader' brings to the text to produce negotiated meaning" (p. 15).

Audience frames help the audience interpret the content the media provide. The media frames collide with the frames and interpretations of an active audience. Not only does message content factor into individual interpretation, Swanson (1987) claimed that audience motivations are "thought to be capable of playing a significant role in interpretively orienting the audience member to a media message through using an appropriate interpretive frame" (p. 243). He also stated that "audience members are resourceful in the sense that they may construct and apply a diverse repertoire of interpretive frames, shaping particular messages to serve various motivations" (p. 243). Overall, frames have a greater opportunity for persuasive success if they draw on a belief held by the audience (e.g., Binder, 1993).

Just as there are multiple frames to any singular issue, and multiple sources trying to influence the media frame, there are multiple mass media organizations reporting on the same issue. Gamson and Modigliani (1989) described the process in which journalists develop and obtain ideas and language from their many sources; however, "at the same time, they contribute their own frames and invent their own clever catchphrases, drawing on a popular culture that they share with the audience" (p. 3). Gamson and Modigliani further explained that certain frames "have a natural advantage because their ideas and language resonate with larger cultural themes" (p. 5). Certainly, content providers often employ language that will not only be understood by audience members but resonate with them in a meaningful way. Gamson (2001) concluded that framing analysis needs to examine the "complex interaction of texts with an active audience engaged in negotiating meaning" (p. x).

Schramm (1949) noted that news is not the event but the report of the event. It is events that happen, and the various stakeholders react and try to frame how that event should be thought of in the mind of the public. Based on the reactions of the audience, content providers have the opportunity to readjust, or reframe, their messages in the hopes that a new frame might resonate with the audience. Content providers are simply always evaluating the impact of their messages (e.g., Gamson & Modigliani, 1989; Ryan et al., 2001). Framing is thus a continuing process that can evolve daily if the story continues to maintain its presence in the public dialogue. Ryan et al. (2001) explained that frames evolve and "particular frames may gain or lose prominence in the news media. In addition, sponsors may re-structure their framing of particular issues given changing political conditions or given the frames advanced by their opponents" (p. 176).

Miller and Riechert (2001) described what they called a "spiral of opportunity," where content providers carefully evaluate audience response to their messages. They explained, "Stakeholders articulate their positions and then monitor public responses to those articulations. If a stakeholder's articulation resonates positively with the public, then that group will intensify its efforts. On the other hand when an articulation resonates negatively, the stakeholder group will change its articulation or withdraw from debate" (p. 109). Miller and Riechert's position articulates a critical role of the audience and how it will interpret and react to the messages it receives, with stakeholders having the opportunity to reframe the debate. They described the possible strategic options for the proponents of the losing frame, stating, "In this case, they can either adjust their rhetoric to the new frame or concede and withdraw from the policy debate" (p. 113). They concluded through this perspective of the spiral of opportunity that "news media framing of issues as an ongoing process in which journalists and contending stakeholders interact. Thus we must examine the imperatives under which journalists operate and how stakeholders attempt to exploit these imperatives" (p. 120).

Miller and Riechert (2001) summarized:

> Often topics remain on the news agenda for a continuing period, during which time reporters write additional news articles and include comments from people involved in the issue. As stakeholders find access to journalists, they may be able to win visibility for their selective issue definition by exposure in the mass media. Journalists, striving for objectivity, depend on spokespersons as sources for information and comments. This dependence would suggest a win-win situation in which reporters need a quote, and group representatives want to publicize their perspective. As issues become more complex they involve multiple stakeholders or claimsmakers who then compete for access to news reporters. (p. 112)

THEORETICAL OVERVIEW

With so many variables simultaneously at play, the best approach to studying mass communication is to look at the production and reception process in tandem. Studying the process of mass media content decision making does not replace, but rather strongly complements, research on mass media effects and allows for a more complete understanding of the entire mass communication process. Learning about mass communication processes is greatly enriched if the comprehensive literature about mass media effects—that is, questioning what the impact of messages might be—is positioned next to information that describes the complex process of why certain content is produced and how content decisions are made (e.g., Shoemaker & Reese, 1996).

The theoretical frameworks of uses and gratifications, media dependency, framing, and agenda setting assist in understanding the entire mass media content decision-making process. None of the theories, however, can alone explain the process and all of the relationships between the mass media organization and its various constituency groups that influence, or try to influence, decision making. Characteristics from each of these theoretical perspectives are needed because they all contribute to the description of the complex mass media content decision-making process, and without all of these characteristics, any description is not complete.

Media dependency helps explain why relationships between individuals and the mass media and relationships between content providers or other constituency groups and the mass media exist. Individuals depend on the mass media for information, entertainment, or social inclusion. Content providers depend on the mass media for exposure of their message to an audience. Media dependency research also indicates that any dependency can be strengthened or weakened and might not exist if the parties' desires can be satisfied through other means. Factors such as a lack of a functional alternative combine with factors such as an increase in an interest in the topic and the perceived importance of the topic, leading to a strong dependency on the mass media and therefore an increase in the likelihood of media use.

Organizational media dependency relates to the agenda-setting model. Agenda setting helps explain the role of the mass media in selecting and framing stories, thus establishing or potentially increasing the importance of certain issues. Agenda setting influences which issues the public thinks about and how it thinks about those issues. This cognitive thought process as implied in the agenda-setting literature of an audience member relates more closely with the uses and gratifications characteristic of an active audience. The uses and gratifications approach can extend the agenda-setting function of the media by combining the idea that the mass media tell audience members what to think about and how to think about it, with the active audience members choosing mass media and interpreting the content to fulfill their needs. This satisfaction of needs for an audience through experiencing media content can predict future mass media use and future mass media organization or content provider decision making.

The mass media may not have the power to control directly the audience, but the media content does have the potential to influence it. The audience may not be totally active and autonomous, but it can actively select and interpret the meanings of these mass media messages, and behave based on its needs. Even in the ability of the individual audience member to assign his or her own thoughts about an issue, it is imperative to recognize that the audience is always limited in its choices of topic and the amount of information presented on that topic based on the selection and framing decisions of the mass media organization.

McQuail (2000) stated that "there can be little doubt that the media, whether moulders or mirrors of society, are the main messengers *about* society" (p. 63). The comment by McQuail acknowledges the media effects debate but dismisses the question of media effects or at least relegates it to a different area of study. The statement implies that scholars, whatever their position on the media effects debate, would be in agreement that the media are the main messengers about society—the vehicle through which people can learn about social and cultural phenomena. This consensus that the media are the main messengers about society not only encourages inquiry into mass media effects but also emphasizes the remaining question: If the mass media are the main messengers about society, how do they make decisions about their content?

The mass media, however, are not autonomous in selecting and framing content and are constantly being pushed by content providers to provide coverage. Interdependent relationships emerge because the mass media organization needs content providers. Content providers must ask how they can best operate their organization and their business. Inevitably, an integral part of that response includes an association with the mass media to communicate the content providers' message to the audience.

The content decision-making process begins with accepting the general assumptions from each of the theoretical frameworks: (a) the media can be successful in telling the audience which issues to think about (agenda-setting Level 1, selection); (b) the media can be successful in telling the audience how to think about that issue (agenda-setting Level 2, framing); (c) organizations depend on the mass media for communication links (organizational media dependency); (d) individuals depend on the mass media for information and social connection (individual media dependency); (e) mass media organizations depend on content providers for quality content and on the audience to participate in this content; and (f) audiences actively select and interpret media to satisfy their own needs based on their own experience, attitude, and values (uses and gratifications). This selection on the part of the audience is to satisfy needs, and the selection could be based on participation in a mass media source that has previously been successful. In trying to capitalize on this audience behavior, the mass media might try to produce their content in a consistent, patterned way so that the audience knows what to expect from that mass media organization.

SUGGESTED READINGS

Entman, R. (1993). Framing: Toward clarification of a fractured paradigm. *Journal of Communication, 43*(4), 51–58.

Gamson, W. A. (2001). Foreword. In S. D. Reese, O. H. Gandy, & A. E. Grant (Eds.), *Framing public life: Perspectives on media and our understanding of the social world* (pp. ix–xi). Mahwah, NJ: Lawrence Erlbaum Associates.

Gamson, W. A., & Modigliani, A. (1989). Media discourse and public opinion on nuclear power: A constructionist approach. *American Journal of Sociology, 95*, 1–37.

Gitlin, T. (1980). *The whole world is watching: Mass media in the making and unmaking of the new left*. Berkeley: University of California Press.

McCombs, M. E., & Reynolds, A. (2002). News influence on our pictures of the world. In J. Bryant & D. Zillmann (Eds.), *Media effects: Advances in theory and research* (2nd ed., pp. 1–18). Mahwah, NJ: Lawrence Erlbaum Associates.

McCombs, M. E., & Shaw, D. L. (1972). The agenda-setting function of the mass media. *Public Opinion Quarterly, 36,* 176–187.

McCombs, M. E., & Shaw, D. L. (1993). The evolution of agenda-setting research: Twenty-five years in the marketplace of ideas. *Journal of Communication, 43*(2), 58–67.

McCombs, M. E., Shaw, D. L., & Weaver, D. (Eds.). (1997). *Communication and democracy: Exploring the intellectual frontiers in agenda-setting theory*. Mahwah, NJ: Lawrence Erlbaum Associates.

Reese, S. D. (2001). Prologue—Framing public life: A bridging model for media research. In S. D. Reese, O. H. Gandy, & A. E. Grant (Eds.), *Framing public life: Perspectives on media and our understanding of the social world* (pp. 7–31). Mahwah, NJ: Lawrence Erlbaum Associates.

Reese, S. D., Gandy, O. H., & Grant, A. E. (Eds.). (2001). *Framing public life: Perspectives on media and our understanding of the social world*. Mahwah, NJ: Lawrence Erlbaum Associates.

Ryan, C., Carragee, K. M., & Meinhofer, W. (2001). Framing, the news media, and collective action. *Journal of Broadcasting & Electronic Media, 45,* 175–182.

II

The Internal Mass Media Organization

4

Establishing the Mass Media Organization: Routines, Branding, and Promotion

Before examining the complex relationships that mass media organizations have with constituency groups outside of their organization, a description of the complex internal mass media organization environment needs to be considered. McQuail (2000) commented, "The media organization, where media content is 'made' " (p. 244). McQuail's claim that content is made implies the content selection and framing decision-making responsibilities on the part of the mass media organization. The limits of time and space available for media content are the root cause of and necessity for selection and framing decisions. As indicated by some of the literature that defines frames as organizing principles that provide coherence and guidance to the journalist and the mass media organization, selection and framing of content are not so open-ended to the unlimited possibilities as they might first appear. Certain stories are eliminated from the selection process by the very nature of their type of content because they do not fit within the scope of the mass media organization. Even within the stories that are selected, certain frames are eliminated because they lack source credibility or are not deemed as relevant to the audience.

Each mass media organization, even within the same medium and genre type, is different. However, in the greatest similarity among all mass media organizations of needing content to attract an audience and, subsequently, advertisers, selection and framing are conducted in some consistent pattern so that audiences have an idea what to expect when they participate in a medium, network, periodical, or Internet site. These consistent patterns are an important initial step in the content decision-making process of a mass media organization. These patterns help make a complex decision-making process more simplistic. As stories compete for media attention, McCombs and Reynolds (2002) explained that "because the news media have neither the capacity to gather all information nor the capacity to inform the audience about every single occurrence, they rely on a traditional set of professional norms to guide their daily sampling of the environment" (p. 6).

These patterns or professional norms are encompassed in the terminology of media routines. The mass media routines are always a factor in the process of content decision making. The routine assists selection and framing decisions in that these decisions are not as ambiguous as imagined, largely because different mass media organizations focus on different types of content that attract different types of audiences and different types of advertisers. Not all of the possible news events are considered when selecting content, and many stories are eliminated without even being evaluated.

The decision-making process begins on a larger philosophical level, where the mass media organization chooses what type of content it wants to cover. Then, within only one genre, there are still a myriad of stories worthy of becoming content. The relationship between media routines and content indicates the decision-making philosophy and reflects the content priorities of the mass media organization, or more simply, the types of stories the mass media organization will or will not cover. This philosophy could also reflect content decisions they believe will attract an audience. The mass media organization tries to define itself in a manner that resonates with an audience and provides a content that an audience desires; it then attempts to present that type of content in a quality manner.

Shoemaker and Reese (1996) defined routines as "patterned, routinized, repeated practices and forms that media workers use to do their jobs" (p. 105). This definition can be expanded beyond how media workers do their job and recognize the variables that they are constrained by in making content decisions. Each characteristic of the routine is one that facilitates selection for some issues and the framing of the coverage for that issue but also inhibits coverage of some frames and other issues altogether. McQuail (2000) argued that media routines are more of an influential factor in the content decision-making process than any individual or ideological factor involved in the process. He claimed that "in general all phases of media production involve a large volume of work that becomes routinized as a matter of necessity. Even the starting point—a news event or 'creative idea'—is strongly (perhaps most strongly) influenced by convention and prior experience that defines the event as 'newsworthy' " (p. 276).

Shoemaker and Reese (1996) pointed out that prominent in establishing a routine is helping mass media organizations determine what is acceptable to the consumer, the audience. Their point speaks to the types of content mass media organizations could try to acquire. It is probable that the media routines are based on the expectations of the audience and in large part are established by previous audience behavior. Based on audience desires and expectations as explained in the uses and gratifications literature, the media routine helps the mass media organization by allowing it to make quick evaluations whether to dismiss or pursue certain types of content. While helping simplify a complex decision-making process for the employees of the mass media organization, the mass media routine also assists audience members define content expectations from the mass media organization. The routine thus helps audience members select content from the myriad of media choices they are provided. The recognition of the audience by Shoemaker and Reese is important because it points out that at the earliest philosophical stages of decision making by the mass media organization, the audience is a critical component of the process. Content that does not resonate with an audience often ceases to exist in the public domain and does not become part of any future media routine planning.

It appears that the mass media organization should always take the audience into consideration during content decision making. So long as the audience desires the "proper" content, another strong characteristic of the audience as the preeminent media routines feature emerges. For example, if service to democracy is the goal of mass media organizations, that would not be viewed as problematic, as the audience should welcome informative content. In this concept where the audience cannot be "wrong," the system breaks down from its perfect blueprint, as the audience is not always interested in paying attention to information that some would deem important. As the market system allows, organizations rely on only a small portion of the audience to participate in their product to sustain their business. This is particularly true for mass media organizations. Therefore, several types of content remain in the public domain, even without a large audience.

Media routines are an internal decision in which the mass media organization tries to define itself. Being an internal decision, it seems a shift in philosophy and media routine could easily occur. Once a media routine is established, however, changes in the format can be difficult, as the routines have helped establish audience expectations that could lead to a predictable behavior of media use and a media dependency. The predictable behavior on the part of the mass media organization through routine helps predict the behavior of the audience, the very group that its content decisions are trying to attract.

MEDIA ROUTINES:
ALLOCATION OF RESOURCES

In addition to the general philosophy regarding the type of content desired, variables of time and space available, media organization budgets, gathering and distribution technology, and mass media organization genre format are all encompassed within the media routine. Shoemaker and Reese (1996) pointed out that routines are established based on what the mass media organization is capable of producing. Capability speaks to more than a desire of mass media organizations, as they might desire to obtain certain content but do not have the resources to make that acquisition. Capability implies a selection of content based on a careful allocation of the mass media organizations resources in gathering content. Even the largest mass media organization is capable of gathering and distributing only a certain amount of content. The allocation of resources helps demonstrate the content that mass media organizations deem important or that they believe will attract an audience.

Whatever the type of content the mass media organization attempts to provide, decisions about how to allocate their resources have to be considered. The resources are essentially the money, equipment, and personnel that are strategically deployed to gather and distribute content. The allocation of resources leads to questions of: Do the mass media organizations have the time to cover that story? Is that content financially and technically feasible to obtain and distribute?

The mass media resources and the types of content desired by the mass media organization create disparities between all mass media organizations. These disparities indicate that the process of mass media content decision making is not a straightforward recipe followed by all organizations in all circumstances. Although some mass media organizations have substantially greater resources, all mass media organizations must make decisions about the resources they are allocated. The mass media routine helps allocate resources, as certain stories and certain perspectives have to be covered. Ettema et al. (1987) stated, "Uncertainty underlies the generation of news: The organization must make a priori decisions about where news is likely to occur. When news breaks out in unexpected places (e.g., accidents, disasters, conflict) decisions about reallocating staff resources become necessary. Organizations deal with such uncertainties by routinization" (p. 766).

The budget is the major decision-making tool in deciding the type of content to provide to the audience. As Lacy and Niebauer (1995) simply stated, "The process of creating mass communication content cannot be fully understood without considering the economics of the media" (p. 12). As time is limited and always a factor in selection, so too is money. There is not unlimited time and unlimited money to cover every story. As indicated by the framing literature, even the stories that are covered cannot be presented in the same standard, as there will be varying time and resources allocated to the story.

How mass media organizations allocate their financial resources is a strong indication of the type of content they desire and deem important, or simply, the content they believe will attract an audience. For example, if a news organization devotes a large portion of its news budget and deploys a reporter to cover foreign news, one can conclude that this news organization finds that type of content important or that people want to hear those stories, or both. Resources impose restrictions and draw a separation, as some mass media organizations simply cannot afford to pay a reporter to be overseas to cover foreign news or cannot afford to purchase the latest communication technology equipment.

Technology is a function of the equipment being developed and of the budget as a decision of allocation of resources through the types of equipment that the mass media organization decides to or has the ability to purchase. Communication technology greatly alters the news media environment. As the media environment changes through technology (satellite, cable, Internet), the routines of the mass media organization and the content they have the ability to acquire change. The routines of the audience and how, when, and where they experience media and what content they have the ability to access also change.

Cohen (2002) studied how technology and the Internet influence the practices of journalism, questioning the value: "Does the medium that enables interactive and flexible text change the way news producers disseminate information, initiate discourse to cultivate a readership, and satisfy commercial interests?" (p. 532). Arant and Anderson (2001) pointed out that because of the 24-hour newshole and the constant need for updates that online newspapers have to deal with, online editors are more likely than traditional newspaper editors to claim it is important to get news to the public as quickly as possible. The desire to quickly post or update a story could lead to inaccuracies and a lack of balance in reporting (e.g., Brill, 2001; Johnson & Kelly, 2003). Johnson and Kelly (2003) claimed, "Ignoring journalistic values such as accuracy and balance can damage the credibility of online publications and, by association, their traditional newspaper counterparts" (pp. 115–116).

Technological changes in how, when, and where the audience can access content have made entire networks alter their routines. For example, HBO has changed the type of content it offers its subscribers based on the changes in communication technology and what the audience can access. HBO originally focused on first-run movies and often provided the first option to see a movie after the theaters. Today, with the audience able to access movies through home video and DVD rentals or purchases and pay-per-view options, HBO would not keep all of its subscribers if it showed only movies that many have already seen. Instead, HBO has changed its type of content (its routine) and developed several original series to maintain a steady stream of subscribers. HBO must wonder how many subscribers would cancel the network if it did not offer: *The Sopranos, Sex and the City, Curb Your Enthusiasm,* and *Six Feet Under.*

Budgets are not only about what the mass media organization deems important. The decisions regarding the budget and the allocation of resources can essentially be looked at as an investment in attracting an audience. The dilemma is to determine what the media organization can afford to spend while still providing audience members with content they desire. In viewing the budget simply as an investment, like all investments there is the hope of a return, and for the mass media organization that comes in the form of an audience and subsequent advertisers. Shoemaker and Reese (1996) claimed, "Since most media are profit-making enterprises, they strive to make a product that can be sold for more than the costs of production" (p. 109).

Coverage of international news is expensive and requires a large portion of the resource allocation, and therefore it might not be as practical as some other types of news for many mass media organizations. Kim (2002) examined the attitudes and selection criteria of U.S. journalists toward international news, claiming that "television news continues to emphasize local and national events, often at the expense of international news coverage" (p. 431). Of the 31 local and national journalists analyzed, he found that they select international news based on market demands and local relevance. All of the journalists analyzed emphasized timeliness and U.S. involvement in the news story selection. The finding that U.S. involvement is a key variable in whether the issue becomes news content is consistent with other research (e.g., Chang & Lee, 1992; Gans, 1979; Shoemaker, 1999).

Kim (2002) did find a difference between national and local journalists, with national journalists selecting international news with diverse themes but local journalists catering more to business pressures and audience demands, thus choosing stories with a local angle. He recognized that organizational routines such as budget and airtime constrain and limit international news. The decisions regarding international news might not be surprising, as it reflects the audience that is receiving the content, who might desire more local information. Kim described a sense of international news that meets the audience demand, but Graber (1997) cautioned that catering to audience demand could have a spiral effect where the perceived lack of audience interest leads to less coverage, which leads to even less audience interest.

At this point, the routine can best be described as a decision-making philosophy expressed through the practices of gathering, organizing, and distributing media content. A philosophy of decision making is easy to learn through content analysis. Content analysis studies are an easy and effective method for learning about the priorities of a mass media organization. Bae (2000) provided an excellent example of using a content analysis to study the differences in the evening newscasts of cable news networks as compared with broadcast networks. By simply looking at the types of stories the media cover or the type of programming the mass media provide indicates how they spend their resources. In this case, the proof is in the pudding.

The question of who dictates the mass media routines remains. It is a management policy decision, but in whose interests? If the argument is that it is in the business interests, essentially an argument is being made that decisions are in the audiences' interests, as the audiences will create the business through their behavior. That is why media routines often align with the expectations and desires of audiences. If to some extent, as is being argued, media routines are established because of and work in relation to audience routines, the routines of the audience and understanding their behavior during work and leisure time become an important component of the content decision-making process. Understanding the audience is essential to mass media content decision makers so they can establish routines. These routines can simplify a complex process and the selection and framing of content to meet audience needs and achieve gratification and, hopefully, a dependency that will increase the likelihood of use—perhaps not the total audience, but the target audience that the content is designed to reach and the target audience that can be delivered to advertisers.

MEDIA ROUTINES AND BRANDING

Media routines help establish a competitive difference among what mass media organizations offer. Creating and communicating these differences is important with so many communication options for the audience. To try to distinguish themselves in a crowded communication environment and appeal to the audience, mass media organizations attempt to establish themselves as an industry leader by offering different content and higher quality content than their competition. Establishing media routines as an initial aspect of the content decision-making process is a step toward a mass media organization differentiating and defining itself as a brand.

Strategic branding initiatives help clarify expectations for audiences about what to expect when they engage in media use and participate in that mass media organization's content. Much as audience expectations as expressed in the uses and gratifications literature help explain the implementation of media routines, uses and gratifications theory also illuminates the concept of branding and how the audience actively selects content. Many theorists who write about branding comment on audience expectations and desires, terms prominent in the uses and gratifications literature, predicting behavior. Branding aligns with uses and gratifications, as people know which media to attend to satisfy their needs. In this instance, people know which brands have been successful and have satisfied their desires; therefore they once again purchase those brands.

Brand management focuses on the long-term development of a brand (e.g., Keller, 1998; Shocker, Srivastava, & Ruekert, 1994). Bellamy and Traudt (2000) stated that "branding is a form of product differentiation, whereby firms attempt to make their product 'stand out' from competitors by such means as pricing, packaging, and brand image" (p. 132). A brand becomes an implicit contract between a product and a consumer (e.g., Aaker, 1991). Davis (2002) stated, "A brand is a set of promises. It implies trust, consistency, and a defined set of expectations" (p. 3). He added, "A customer cannot have a relationship with a product or service, but they may with a brand" (p. 31).

Branding decisions obviously need to be made in relation to the competition within that industry (e.g., Aaker & Joachimsthaler, 2000). Ries and Trout (1997) described the concept of positioning, where the objective is to place products, companies, services, or institutions in the minds of potential customers in a way that differentiates them from the clutter of the marketplace. Davis (2002) explained, "A strong brand position means having a unique, credible, sustainable, fitting, and valued place in the customers' minds. It revolves around a benefit set that helps your product or service stand apart from the competition" (p. 25).

According to Lacy and Vermeer (1995) in an economic market, "at the most basic level, competition exists when one or more potential buyers consider two or more products to be acceptable substitutes for each other" (p. 50). In a general economic business model, Porter (1980) pointed out that price leadership and product differentiation are two strategies that companies can employ in competition. Redmond and Trager (1998) defined three characteristics of competitive success: (a) product differentiation, (b) niche marketing, and (c) cost control. Hollifield, Kosicki, and Becker (2001) claimed that for the mass media with cost largely absorbed by the advertisers, "product differentiation is almost the only strategy available to news executives seeking to win the attention of the news-seeking audience" (p. 98). They described the scenario where "to succeed they [news executives] must attract the largest possible audience by differentiating their news products from their competitors' offerings. At the same time, however, they also must produce a newscast or newspaper that meets the expectations of the news consumer, which requires some level of adherence to the standards of news judgment, behavior and reporting that traditionally guide journalistic practice" (p. 93).

Through interviewing, writing, photographing, and editing stories, the mass media are in effect producing the news for a particular readership or viewer, and when members of the public buy a newspaper or turn on a news program they are acting as the consumer of what is being produced (e.g., Luna, 1995). Luna (1995) argued that when individuals consume news they offer some type of exchange for it and "this exchange can be made directly through subscriptions to newspapers or cable news channels, or indirectly through advertisers who pay news producers to reach a particular target market" (p. 158). Gomery (1989) explained that product differentiation is standard in industries that are competitive and the more companies in that industry should lead to a greater amount of product differentiation. This perspective relates to the defining characteristic of competitive success—product differentiation—as identified by Redmond and Trager (1998).

Through differentiation from competition, the value of a brand helps attain sales. Bellamy and Traudt (2000) explained, "The fundamental concept is that a recognizable brand will more easily attract and retain customers than an unrecognizable one" (p. 127). Aaker (1991) also spoke to the value of the brand, pointing out that "for many businesses the brand name and what it represents are its most important asset—the basis of competitive advantage and of future earnings streams" (p. 14).

Kapferer (1992) argued, "Products are what the company makes; what the customer buys is a brand" (p. 2). The important distinction is that people will always have a need to use certain types of products, but which companies they support with their behavior (either purchase or in this instance mass media use) is determined by the brand they believe will best satisfy their desires. People need to buy a car, but will they buy a Ford or Chevrolet? People need to fly, but will they fly on Continental Airlines or Southwest Airlines? People need sneakers, but will they buy Nike, Reebok, or Adidas?

A mass media organization competes for consumer attention and advertising dollars and therefore attempts to brand itself. In relation to having to deal with competition, the importance of brand-building strategies is not different in the mass media than in any other industry (e.g., Aaker & Joachimsthaler, 2000). Chan-Olmsted and Kim (2001) wrote about what mass media organizations as brands accomplish, stating that "brands can help media consumers cut through the clutter by identifying the brands that are compatible with their needs and expectations. Developing a sound branding strategy (i.e., business activities that establish a recognizable and trustworthy badge of origin, and a promise of performance) is an essential step for a broadcaster to increase its value for consumers and advertisers" (p. 75).

In a mass media context, a person in New York City will buy a newspaper, but which brand will they buy: *New York Times, New York Post, New York Newsday,* or *New York Daily News*? People will watch the evening news, but will they watch ABC, CBS, or NBC, or will they bypass all of the over-the-air networks and opt for one of the all-cable news networks? For the news media industry the competition exists outside of any one medium, as organizations from all of the distribution forms of media, now prominently including the Internet, have to be considered as competition for audience attention and advertiser dollars.

Brands have established characteristics that can lead to audience behavior. Brands have images and personalities, and the perceptions of these brand characteristics are largely in the mind of the customer (e.g., Aaker, 1997; Blackston, 2000; Keller, 1993). Chan-Olmsted and Kim (2001) claimed, "A viewer's association, perception, and expectation of a television station or network can easily come into play when he or she is making a viewing choice with channel-surfing in an increasingly crowded television environment" (p. 78). The concept of brand associations becomes interactive, where brand messages and images are created and communicated, but the consumer still gets to evaluate the brand.

Blackston (2000) emphasized the relationship between the brand and the consumer, and that relationship requires observation of and analysis about consumers' attitudes and behaviors toward the brand and the brand's attitudes and behaviors toward the consumer. He described two components of a successful brand relationship: (a) trust in the brand and (b) customer satisfaction with the brand. Aaker and

Joachimsthaler (2000) explained that distinctions can be made between what the brand is and what the brand does for customers. What the brand does for customers could touch on more of an emotional appeal for purchase or use on the part of the customer. They contended that "an emotional benefit relates to the ability of the brand to make the buyer or user of a brand feel something during the purchase process or use experience" (p. 49).

A goal of any long-term branding strategy is to develop a series of assets. Mass media organizations have assets such as the trustworthiness of their reporters or anchors, tradition, consistency, and overall reputation. Certainly some people watch NBC's *Meet the Press* because they find Tim Russert trustworthy or subscribe to *Time* magazine because they find the reporting consistently credible. David Westin is the president of ABC News, overseeing its television news properties, *World News Tonight, Nightline, 20/20,* and *Good Morning America*, its Internet news properties, and ABC News radio. He explained that television has an almost inverse branding power to print. He described that in the newspaper industry people might not necessarily read the byline and that the power of the brand is the name of the newspaper itself (*Washington Post, New York Times, USA Today*). For television, people might be dedicated to watching Peter Jennings but not even be sure he is on ABC. Westin explained, for television, that "the brand is the people and their appearance is coming into the home, that does not work in print" (personal communication, May 28, 2004). Westin summarized the idea that powerful brands are built through their people, citing that ABC News as the strongest brand of the ABC company because of the consistency and longevity of the people at ABC News such as Peter Jennings, Ted Koppel, and Barbara Walters.

Assets are essential in building brand equity. The purpose of branding is to create awareness of familiarity with, and a positive image for the brand, which help build brand equity (e.g., Blackston, 2000; Chan-Olmsted & Kim, 2001, 2002; Keller, 1993; Park & Srinivasan, 1994). Brand equity has been characterized as perceived quality, loyalty, and associations, combined with brand awareness (e.g., Aaker & Joachimsthaler, 2000). Brand equity exists through brand knowledge, which consists of high levels of brand awareness and a positive brand image (e.g., Bellamy & Traudt, 2000; Keller, 1993).

Through the use of these assets and a continued excellent performance of the products or services offered, brand equity can be attained. Keller (1998) explained that consumer brand equity is achieved when the consumer is not only familiar with the brand but holds favorable, strong, and unique brand associations. It is these positive feelings toward a brand that then drive consumer behavior. There might be many options available, but only a few brands will dominate the market share in a given industry; therefore, branding strategies strongly relate to consumer use.

Understanding consumer behavior is important in understanding the value of a brand and evaluating its brand equity. Establishing brand equity helps the consumer feel that the products from that company are better than those from a more generic competitor, a trend seen in consumer behavior. Berry and Biel (1992) explained that brand equity reflects the judgment of the consumer, including a willingness to pay for a branded product. Davis (2002) pointed out that 72% of customers say they will pay a 20% premium for their brand of choice, relative to the closest competitive brand; 25% say price does not matter if they are buying a brand that owns their loyalty. Overall, Davis contended, "A brand helps customers feel confident about their purchase decision" (p. 31).

In trying to explain consumer behavior, marketing research has identified the 80–20 rule, which claims that 80% of a brand's sales volume is accounted for by 20% of its buyers (e.g., Anschuetz, 1997b; Hallberg, 1995). In applying the 80–20 rule to mass media use, De Vany and Walls (1999) found that 10% of the movies released in a given year accounted for approximately half of the box office revenue. Compaine and Gomery (2000) found that the top 10 book publishers account for more than 60% of book sales in the United States. For Internet use in studying America Online users, Adamic and Huberman (1999) showed that the top 5% of Internet sites accounted for almost 75% of user volume. Webster and Lin (2002) also found that Internet users are concentrated in only a few sites, with the top 200 sites accounting for roughly half of Internet traffic.

Although the 80–20 rule and other trends might cause a focus on only a portion of the customers, Anscheutz (1997a) emphasized that growth relies on more than only 20% of consumers. He stated, "To increase the number of heavy buyers of a brand, the brand must become more popular in general. Conversely, it will be nearly impossible to increase purchase of a brand among the most profitable 'heavy buyer' group without increasing the brand's appeal to the 'less profitable' lighter buyers as well. Lighter and heavier buyers of a brand go together as two sides of the same coin. The bottom line is that brand popularity leads to brand volume from the full spectrum of buyers" (p. 64). He plainly stated, "The only way to increase the number of frequent buyers of a brand is to increase the brand's overall popularity" (pp. 65–66).

One way of increasing the brand's outreach to different audience segments is through brand extensions. Ultimately, an established brand can create brand extensions, where a strong brand is leveraged to introduce new products (e.g., Bellamy & Traudt, 2000). Bellamy and Traudt (2000) explained that "brand extensions marry an established brand to a new service as a means of establishing instant market credibility" (p. 157). For example, NBC News can leverage its established brand to create a news magazine such as *Dateline NBC*, ESPN can use its established brand name to create *ESPN the Magazine* and *ESPN Radio*, and CBS can capitalize on the brand name of one of its most successful programs such as *60 Minutes* to create *60 Minutes II*. Park, Jun, and Shocker (1996) also described a strategy of composite brand extensions, where two existing brand names combine, for example, MSNBC, which is a composite brand extension of Microsoft and NBC, or CNNSI, which is a composite of CNN and *Sports Illustrated*. In speaking of brand extensions, Davis (2002) pointed out that "more than 50 percent of consumers believe a strong brand allows for more successful new product introductions and they are more willing to try a new product from a preferred brand because of the implied endorsement" (p. 6).

Jeff Webber is the senior vice president and publisher for *USA Today*'s Internet site, usatoday.com. His responsibility is oversight of all business aspects of the Internet site. He explained that as a business manager he is not closely involved in specific editorial decisions as to the newsworthiness of a story but rather strategic business decisions for the newsroom. These business decisions could include targeting a certain audience demographic, determining advertising rates and developing possible advertising offerings, and making any financial decisions relating to resource allocation. Webber explained that the Internet site is currently an extension and a way to increase the *USA Today* brand, but he cautioned that the future could be different, with the Internet site having a status more equal to the print publication. In developing the usatoday.com brand, he stated, "News and information organizations have to understand when, where, and how readers want our information. They have to come to terms with it is about the audience and how they want to access our content" (personal communication, May 25, 2004).

In terms of consumer behavior, certain brands are considered leaders in their respective industry. These brands have a large market share, and whenever a certain product is desired, certain brands immediately come to mind: soup (Campbells), soda (Coca-Cola, Pepsi), sneakers (Nike, Reebok), fast food (McDonald's). In differentiating themselves and striving for the position of brand leadership, certain mass media organizations have attained brand leadership in various categories: *Time* for news magazines and *Sports Illustrated* for sports magazines. Other examples include the dominance of HBO over other movie channels and ESPN over other cable television sports channels.

The difficulty of attaining brand leadership, even brand equality, is difficult for upstart competitors, as evidenced by WB and UPN in trying to be considered on the same level as the more established networks of ABC, CBS, Fox, and NBC. CNN had a long hold on the news cable market until the emergence of Fox News. When leadership within an industry such as this occurs, the brand is itself another critical asset (e.g., Davis, 2002). Anschuetz (1997b) simply explained, "With increased brand popularity comes greater frequency of brand buying, a greater number of heavier buyers in the brand's franchise, a greater level of brand loyalty as measured through repeat buying" (p. 51).

The differentiation between the brand and the content for a mass media organization is, however, a tenuous balance. In speaking of television specifically, Bellamy and Traudt (2000) described, "Networks must walk a fine line between: (1) the need for differentiation in the multichannel era, and (2) the need to maximize audiences in most time periods in order to attract advertisers to pay the total bill" (p. 129). They explained that despite trying to be different, "broadcast television networks remain relatively homogenous as brands because of the need to attract large audiences" (p. 129).

Other mass media organizations are more specialized and offer a single type of content aimed at a niche audience, such as certain cable television or radio stations and certain magazines or Internet sites that only deal with one topic such as sports or music. Even a general topic such as sports could be broken down further, as a magazine or a cable television channel might only be about basketball or golf. Bellamy and Traudt (2000) explained that cable television networks have become niche oriented, which might attract smaller, but very loyal, audiences. The reason cable television networks have been able to offer such specialized content that might not draw a large audience and still function economically is because they receive money from subscriptions in addition to advertising.

Through their basic or tier cable packages people pay for each month, subscribers provide their cable operators with the revenue they need to pass along to the actual networks for the right to include that network as part of a package they can offer their viewers. Obviously, the more popular cable networks cost more per subscriber, but if the cable operators did not offer these networks, they would certainly lose subscribers (see Table 4.1).

Bellamy and Traudt (2000) pointed out another important distinction between a mass media brand and other industries in that "brand and 'purchase/choice' location is the same. The source of the brand is itself the brand" (p. 134). Customers do not have to go to a store to engage with the brand in mass media selection. Bellamy and Traudt also

TABLE 4.1
Monthly Cable Channel Subscription Costs: New York Market

Network	1998	2003	2007 Estimate
A&E	0.15	0.19	0.19
ABC Family	0.15	0.20	0.26
BET	0.10	0.12	0.16
Bloomberg	0.04	0.10	0.11
Bravo	0.11	0.13	0.17
Cartoon	0.07	0.13	0.17
CNBC	0.14	0.23	0.23
CNN	0.33	0.38	0.38
Comedy Central	0.08	0.09	0.13
Court TV	0.09	0.11	0.12
Discovery	0.18	0.23	0.25
Disney	0.74	0.74	0.73
E!	0.11	0.18	0.22
ESPN	0.85	1.93	3.51
ESPN2	0.14	0.20	0.26
Food	0.05	0.05	0.08
Fox News	0.13	0.19	0.29
FOX Sports	0.55	1.16	1.69
Game Show	0.06	0.09	0.09
Golf	0.14	0.14	0.21
History Channel	0.09	0.15	0.18
Lifetime	0.12	0.17	0.24
MSNBC	0.11	0.13	0.15
MTV	0.16	0.23	0.28
Nickelodeon	0.25	0.34	0.41
SCI FI	0.11	0.13	0.14
SoapNet	—	0.08	0.11
TBS	0.18	0.23	0.28
TCM	0.15	0.17	0.19
TLC	0.11	0.15	0.16
TNN	0.14	0.16	0.20
TNT	0.52	0.78	0.95
USA	0.35	0.40	0.39
VH1	0.08	0.11	0.13
YES	—	2.11	2.58

Source: Futterman (2003) and Kagan World Media.

pointed out that price, which is often the most important variable in consumer choice behavior, is rarely a factor in the purchase of mass media brands, with the possible exception of some pay services such as HBO.

Certainly price can be a major factor in automobile purchases, as some brands—Cadillac, Lexus, and Mercedes-Benz—are priced far differently from other brands such as Ford or Chevrolet. Automobile companies even further brand their type of cars within the larger corporate brand name with different style and price ranges. So Ford offers the Taurus family car, Explorer sport utility vehicle, and the Ranger truck. For airlines, although price might be a contributing factor among brands, location is also a critical factor. Several airlines have established major cities as hubs and dominate that market by offering many more flight options from that geographic region.

For behavior to occur the consumer still needs to be satisfied with the brand they are using. To establish brand equity and loyalty over the long term, corporations must emphasize their assets and distinguish themselves from the competition offering a similar product. These corporations also need to outperform the competition, especially in the mass media industries where the competition is only the click of a button away. These distinct characteristics have to resonate with the consumer and prompt behavior. The image distinction and what the brand does for the consumer has to be formed in the mind of the consumer, who ultimately decides about the brand.

BRAND COMMUNICATION AND PROMOTION

The final part of any branding strategy is that the characteristics of a brand and the distinctions from the competition need to be effectively communicated to potential consumers (e.g., Blackston, 2000; Chan-Olmsted & Kim, 2001). Brand assets and features and the overall reasons the consumer should purchase the brand all need to be explained to the audience, especially when initiating first-time use of the brand. In this instance, branding initiatives by a company are analogous to an agenda-setting function that the company is undertaking and trying to achieve, getting the audience to be aware of the brand or, if using agenda-setting terminology, using the mass media to transfer the salience of the brand to the audience.

Brands are obviously best communicated through the performance of their products or services, but performance can only be evaluated after a purchase. Communication of the brand is where the relationship with the mass media and a dependency for a content provider become vital. Blackston (2000) pointed out that brand efforts need to be made in "creating and communicating the correct *attitudes and behaviors* of our brands, because it is these which create *meaning* out of the message" (p. 102).

The brand is communicated through slogans, logos, public appearances by prominent people of the organization, marketing strategies, public relations strategies, and other promotional advertising (e.g., Aaker, 1991; Bellamy & Traudt, 2000; Ridgway, 1998). Mass media organizations announce the brand of future content through promotion on their own network, Internet site, or other print or broadcast locations. Perse (2000) defined audience promotion as "the set of messages directed toward the audience that is initiated by a station or a network" (p. 19). Eastman (2000) explained that this promotion is needed to attract an audience, maintain an audience, and create an image for the mass media organization through communicating the availability of its content. She stated, "At heart, promotion on-the-air, online, and in print is the way that stations and networks announce the availability of their programs" (p. 4).

For the mass media industry, the need for communicating brand promotion is an important strategy. Bellamy and Traudt (2000) stated, "Successful targeting is essential to television, and particularly broadcast television, because creation/generation of audiences for resale to advertisers is the medium's primary (or only) commodity" (p. 131). Promotion is such a necessary strategy that mass media organizations willingly forfeit time and space that could be used to sell advertising to promote their future content (e.g., Eastman, 2000).

Promotion can be an instrumental strategy in facilitating the behavior that the mass media organization is most interested in: media use. If people are not made aware of the content that will be available in the future and presented an opportunity to engage in purposeful instrumental mass media use, the only chance for use is in a ritualistic context if the person happens to stumble across the content. The highest quality content might not be noticed if the audience is not aware of its existence. Creating that awareness is the function of promotion, with the goal being an increase in audience size (e.g., Eastman, 2000; Perse, 2000).

Stephen Ulrich, director of talent and promotion for NBC Sports, stated promotion is "one of the most important parts of television that probably doesn't get the justice it is due" (cited in Fortunato, 2001, p. 77). Ulrich provided a philosophical objective of promotions stating, "You try to match up the audience that is watching as to what they probably will watch in the future. My role is always trying to find that swing audience. You have got to figure there is a core audience that is going to watch no matter what. My job is to try to find those people who might watch if they knew and if they were compelled to watch and that is pretty hard to do" (cited in Fortunato, 2001, p. 77).

Establishing the brand is a process that begins with the promotion of the brand itself. The objective of this promotion through advertising and other communication initiatives is to generate awareness, explain the quality of the brand, and get the audience to sample the product of the brand. Most companies believe in the quality of their product so that if they can merely get the consumer to sample the product they are confident that the performance of the brand will lead to future use. Eastman (2000) explained that, "Program promotion's main goals are to achieve sampling (to get viewers to try an unfamiliar program), to activate interest in upcoming episodes of ongoing programs, to announce changes in the program schedule, and to build viewer satisfaction with the programming" (pp. 8–9). This satisfied use combined with the additional advertising to reinforce the brand image and quality will hopefully lead to brand loyalty.

Eastman (2000) pointed out that promotion can do much more than merely announce when content will be available and that promotion helps establish the mass media organization as a brand by communicating its brand image. Again, the agenda-setting literature is analogous to branding by emphasizing the brand features (framing) that will be communicated to get the audience to think about and how to think about the brand. The promotion helps frame the mass media organization, its content, and how it might be perceived by the audience (e.g., Ferguson, Eastman, & Klein, 1999; Perse, 2000; Scheufele, 1999). Eastman (2000) identified two main types of promotion: (a) image promotion, intended to enhance the brand name and create a positive brand image for the mass media organization as a whole, and (b) program promotion, intended to encourage participation in specific content or induce viewing of a single program, and it may involve newspaper and magazine ads, billboards, radio or television spots, or online announcements, but are primarily on-air promotions.

Image promotions could include a slogan or entire commercials produced about an entire network. In an image promotion, for example, CNN might produce a commercial that features all of its prominent news personalities with its slogan, "The most trusted name in news." HBO produces promotions with all of the characteristics from its many Sunday night original series, with its slogan, "It's not TV, it's HBO." In a program promotion, a promotional spot on CNN announces the content of a specific program, such as a guest that will be appearing on *Larry King Live*. Many television programs also have daily e-mails that are sent to their viewers indicating the guests and topics that will discussed on the show that evening. Bellamy and Traudt (2000) explained that in television both networks and specific programs can be brands, but they contended that the emphasis is largely on the network, which has a longer tradition than certain programs that might only stay on the air for a limited number of years.

Television branding has become necessary because of the media environment and the increased proliferation of the number of television stations, the competitive media environment, and the large amounts of clutter (e.g., Bellamy & Traudt, 2000; Kubey & Csikszentmihalyi, 1990). Bellamy and Traudt (2000) pointed out that a strong brand identity is vital in producing audiences in a highly competitive environment and in expanding markets, either through growing the market for an existing product or developing and distributing new products.

Because of the many choices and a scattered audience, one strategy of promotion is to promote as much as possible within a program so as not to take away from commercial time that can be sold to viewers. Television networks routinely place graphics on the bottom of the screen during one program to announce upcoming programming. This strategy also reaches viewers when they are most apt to be watching rather than changing channels (e.g., Ferguson, 1992; Fortunato, 2001).

With the number of viewers declining because of the mass media environment, promotion has become more important. Self-promotion cannot be the only mechanism for networks to get an audience to learn about upcoming programming. Television networks are creative in promoting their programming, including: TBS putting advertisements for its college football schedule in the bathroom of bars in 12 cities, CBS gave away free interactive DVDs at Blockbuster (also owned by Viacom) that show clips for its 2003 fall lineup, ABC had a premiere weekend at its Disney's California Adventure Park where fans could meet the stars of ABC shows, and HBO bought a magazine insert in *Entertainment Weekly* to promote its latest original series, *Carnivale* (e.g., Elber, 2003).

Through media routines, branding, and promotion strategies, the audiences can develop what essentially become their "go-to" channels, the channels they go-to first for whatever type of content they desire. So the viewer might turn to ESPN for sports; Fox News for news; HBO for movies; and one of the major networks for a dramatic series, situation comedy, or reality show. Bellamy and Traudt (2000) added, "Certain brand names in cable are now so well established that we can assume that: (1) they have a high level of specific image recognition and perception and (2) it is very difficult to compete against them" (pp. 137–138). A similar behavior could take place for magazine purchase if a person is getting on a plane or going to the beach and looking for something to read. Depending on the type of content desired, the prominent brand magazine of that genre might be the choice (*Time* for news, *Sports Illustrated* for sports, *People* for entertainment, or *Rolling Stone* for music). The established branding of these channels and publications and the communication of the brand are especially important when people are engaged in ritualistic mass media use. Eastman (2000) explained that "capturing high ratings is not just a function of program scheduling and appeal, but is also a function of how the audience is told about the programs" (p. 3).

Just as the mass media are difficult to define because there are so many different types and philosophies of media organizations, the mass media routines are also difficult to define. These routines are as varied as the mass media organizations themselves, even among those that produce similar content. Mass media routines are different for every mass media organization, but every mass media organization has a general routine it follows.

Establishing media routines and developing branding strategies help the mass media organization by simplifying the decision-making process about the type of content to provide an audience. These routines also assist in clarifying the expectations of the audience, as people have an idea of the type of content to expect from a certain mass media organization. These routine and branding strategies are still decisions about the overall direction of the mass media organization and the types of content it aims to gather and distribute. These strategic decisions, however, are only somewhat limiting, and content decisions still need to be made within the routine. A closer look at the complex relationships of the people within a mass media organization entrusted with making content decisions thus becomes necessary.

SUGGESTED READINGS

Aaker, D. A. (1991). *Managing brand equity*. New York: Free Press.

Aaker, D. A., & Joachimsthaler, E. (2000). *Brand leadership*. New York: Free Press.

Bellamy, R. V., Jr., & Traudt, P. J. (2000). Television branding as promotion. In S. T. Eastman (Ed.), *Research in media promotion* (pp. 127–159). Mahwah, NJ: Lawrence Erlbaum Associates.

Blackston, M. (2000). Observations: Building brand equity by managing the brand's relationships. *Journal of Advertising Research, 40*(6), 101–105.

Davis, S. M. (2002). *Brand asset management: Driving profitable growth through your brands*. San Francisco: Jossey-Bass.

Eastman, S. T. (2000). Orientation to promotion and research. In S. T. Eastman (Ed.), *Research in media promotion* (pp. 3–18). Mahwah, NJ: Lawrence Erlbaum Associates.

Ettema, J. S., Whitney, D. C., & Wackman, D. B. (1987). Professional mass communicators. In C. H. Berger & S. H. Chaffee (Eds.), *Handbook of communication science* (pp. 747–780). Beverly Hills, CA: Sage.

Keller, K. L. (1993). Conceptualizing, measuring, and managing customer-based brand equity. *Journal of Marketing, 57,* 1–22.

Keller, K. L. (1998). *Strategic brand management: Building, measuring, and managing brand equity.* Upper Saddle River, NJ: Prentice Hall.

Perse, E. M. (2001). *Media effects and society.* Mahwah, NJ: Lawrence Erlbaum Associates.

Shoemaker, P. J., & Reese, S. D. (1996). *Mediating the message: Theories of influences on mass media content.* New York: Longman.

CHAPTER

$$5$$

Ownership

What the mass media organization media routine and overall brand image will be, and how the organization will promote itself are philosophical decisions that can establish the reputation for the entire mass media organization. These decisions are often made at the highest levels of the corporation. Ownership establishes, or at the very least approves, the overall philosophy of the types of content the organization desires and will attempt to acquire. Ownership also makes the critical decisions about allocation of resources. It can be concluded that ownership is thus always affecting content decision making by dictating a fundamental philosophy and controlling the budget resources. This self-defining of the mass media organization itself helps limit the types of content possible. Although facilitating and simplifying content decisions, media routines do not dictate every decision. Even the gratifications and dependencies that can be attained are only formulated based on the medium and content that is available.

The assumption of this book is that each of the constituency groups involved in the process have the potential to influence content and therefore it is important to examine the plausibility and extent of that influence. The relationship between ownership and content is that mass media owners have the power to eliminate the term *potential* in influencing content. The three major ways ownership can influence content decision making are: (a) setting the overall budget and the media routines of the organization, as discussed in the previous chapter; (b) directly ordering news story selection and framing; and (c) hiring and firing employees. Gomery (2000) simply stated, "The ownership of the mass media in the United States is of vital interest. These vast institutions influence what we know, the images of ourselves and the bulk of the way we amuse and entertain" (p. 507).

The controversial question in the role of ownership is not in setting an overall philosophy about the types of content desired but in establishing edicts about specific content decisions that are influenced by ownership that may or may not be in the interests of the larger parent corporation. The recent trends of corporate ownership and conglomeration of many forms of the media have raised concerns. The perspectives of the impact of this corporate conglomeration and the new media environment are varied, but the pivotal question emerging from the discussion raised in chapter 1 remains: Can a mass media organization be a profitable corporation and still serve the democratic citizenry, or are those two positions mutually exclusive?

CONCERN OF CORPORATE OWNERSHIP OF MEDIA ORGANIZATIONS

Mass media content gathering and distributing and access by the audience are very much a function of the mass media environment. The mass media environment characteristic that cannot be disputed is that media corporate conglomeration has occurred. The positives and negatives of this development are what can be debated. What corporations are achieving by merging is obtaining access to every type of media vehicle as well as every other aspect of mass communication from content production to content distribution. One corporation's mass media ownership holdings could include: television networks, cable television networks, cable television system carriers, publishing (books, newspaper, and magazines), radio and recordings, film, television and film production companies, and Internet sites. Substantial media holdings for the larger mass media corporations include:

Disney—ABC (and 10 of its affiliate stations) and ESPN family of television networks and their associated Internet sites; other cable television networks: SoapNet, The History Channel, E! Entertainment, and Lifetime Television; television and film production studios: Touchstone, Walt Disney, Miramax, and Buena Vista; several radio stations and publishing.

Viacom—CBS and UPN television networks (and several affiliates), MTV, Nickelodeon, and Showtime; Simon & Schuster publishing; Infinity Broadcasting radio stations; television and film production studios: Spelling Television, Paramount Pictures, and King World Productions; Blockbuster Video.

General Electric—NBC television networks (and 13 affiliates); cable television networks CNBC, MSNBC, USA Network, and Bravo.

NewsCorp—Fox television stations (and more than 30 affiliates), Fox News Channel, Fox Sports regional networks; HarperCollins Publishers, the *New York Post* and several newspapers in Australia and the United Kingdom; Fox television studios and 20th Century Fox.

Time Warner—CNN and its networks, TBS, TNT, HBO; high-circulation magazines: *Time, Sports Illustrated, People, Money, Entertainment Weekly*, and *Fortune*; television and film production studios: Warner Brothers, Castle Rock Entertainment, New Line Cinema; music recordings: Electra Records, Atlantic Records, Columbia Records; America Online.

It is interesting to note that Disney (ABC), General Electric (NBC), Viacom (CBS), and Fox also own the affiliate television stations in the top four television markets in the United States (New York, Los Angeles, Chicago, and Philadelphia). This is important because it ensures that their prime-time and other essential programming will be shown on those affiliate networks and reach the larger audiences necessary to attract major advertising dollars.

There is also corporate conglomeration within only one industry. In the radio industry, Clear Channel Communications owns more than 1,200 radio stations nationwide. In the newspaper industry, Gannett is the largest owner of newspapers in the United States, featuring *USA Today*, the newspaper with the largest circulation in the United States, and more than 90 other newspapers in 40 states. Knight-Ridder owns more than 30 daily newspapers and more than 20 nondaily newspapers. Its daily newspapers include the major newspaper in cities such as: Detroit (*Detroit Free Press*), Miami (*Miami Herald*), Kansas City (*Kansas City Star*), and both major newspapers in Philadelphia (*Philadelphia Daily News* and *Philadelphia Inquirer*). The New York Times Company owns more than 15 newspapers, including the *New York Times* and the *Boston Globe*. Besides owning the newspaper of the same name, The Washington Post Company also owns *Newsweek* magazine. The Tribune Company has expanded beyond owning the *Chicago Tribune* and owns the major newspaper in Los Angeles (*Los Angeles Times*), Orlando (*Orlando Sentinel*), Baltimore (*Baltimore Sun*), and Hartford (*Hartford Courant*).

The concern of media conglomeration among many scholars is that journalistic principles geared toward the ideal of a better, more informed democracy are secondary to the mass media organization's desire to earn a profit (e.g., Alger, 1998; Bagdikian, 2000; Gitlin, 1972, 1980,

1982; Mazzocco, 1994; McChesney, 1997; McManus, 1994, 1995; Molotch & Lester, 1974; Mosco, 1996; Underwood, 1993; Williams, 2002). Kellner (1990) explained that "centralized corporate control gives these corporations enormous power to decide what people will read, see, and experience" (p. 13). Therefore, according to these scholars the constituency groups with the most influence in the content decision-making process are those that relate to the economics of the corporation, namely, corporate owners, stockholders, and advertisers.

McManus (1994) argued that "investors, publishers/networks, and parent corporations direct capital and shape policies in news organizations to generate profits and increase brand influence" (p. 23). He claimed that media organizations compete for investors and try to convince potential investors of the profitability of their programming and of their relationships with advertisers. McManus concluded that "market norms call for maximizing return to investors. Were purely economic norms to prevail, coverage would center on the least expensively gathered information likely to generate the largest audience advertisers would pay to reach" (p. 35).

Williams (2002) raised another issue regarding large corporate control of the mass media—the size of the corporation owning the media could be a factor in the amount of control exerted on the media portion of the company. He stated, "If pressures come on a news division from outside their walls, the pressure should change in size and scope as the corporation grows. Greater absolute size means that the news division is smaller and likely wields less institutional clout. Greater diversification means that the news division is less and less important, vis-à-vis the other divisions, to the firm's survival" (p. 457). In a large corporate structure, Williams commented, "Instead of the traditional fear of alienating advertisers, an editor might now worry about alienating a powerful executive in another branch of the organization or hurting shareholder equity through inappropriate coverage or non-coverage of a story relating to the corporation's interests" (p. 456).

THE POLITICAL ECONOMY APPROACH TO MASS COMMUNICATION

The political economy approach to understanding the media industry and its organizational relationships is concerned with media ownership conglomeration. The concern is exacerbated by having only a few companies in this powerful position, which is almost immediately assigned to a corporation that has ownership of a major mass media enterprise. To establish and exert their power, communication industries develop critical connections and linkages among their industries and the government and the larger global and national political economies (e.g., Mosco, 1996). Mosco (1996) stated that a central goal of the political economy tradition "is to understand the relationship of government or the state to the communication business" (pp. 91–92). The concern is essentially that having control over many major economic functions and owning the means of communication quickly translate into control over political systems and the flow of information. The movement and integration of capital between the communication industry and the state become pivotal. Mosco explained, "The state has to promote the interests of capital even as it appears to be the independent arbiter of the wider social or political interest" (p. 92). He characterized power as more than a resource, but rather a form of control used to preserve the current status the powerful people and corporations have attained.

The political economy approach contends that in an effort to maintain relationships with other powerful economic and political entities, the mass media will not aggressively pursue stories that could hinder the economic status quo, including harsh criticism of the government and its economic policies. In fact, mass media organizations can serve as advocates for certain policies. Conversely, the government will not overtly pursue policies that could hinder the economic standing and growth opportunities of mass media organizations. Bagdikian (2000) argued, "Media power is political power. Politicians hesitate to offend the handful of media operators who control how those politicians will be presented—or not presented—to the voters" (p. xv). By allowing for media ownership conglomeration and with only a few large corporations involved in the industry, it becomes easier for both entities to maintain the beneficial economic status quo.

A premise of the political economy approach to mass communication industries is that the powerful corporations, through their influence on the government regulatory agencies that allow for corporate expansion of media conglomerates and through their own mergers and acquisitions, limit competition and thus monopolize the publicly owned airwaves. This control hinders democracy by limiting the role of the average citizen (e.g., Mazzocco, 1994). With this control comes two very important by-products of the system: First, there is little challenging of the government, as the mass media organizations need the government for favorable government regulatory policies that help provide an environment suitable for corporate profits and expansion. For example, in describing their coverage of the 1989 Panama invasion and the 1991 Persian Gulf War, Mazzocco (1994) referred to the television networks coverage as "cheerleading" and "glaring examples of how U.S. media companies allow little independent criticism of government policies" (pp. 27–28). Second, ownership control obviously dictates media content decision making. Mazzocco commented, "When you work in broadcasting, it is very hard not to become an agent for the political-economic interests of those who employ you" (p. 27).

It is the drive for profits that turns a democratic process of informing the citizenry into a business enterprise as information becomes a commodity. Commodification is a critical concept in the political economy approach to communication (e.g., Mosco, 1996). As soon as commodification becomes a central idea for an organization, the goal becomes to focus on producing a sellable commodity. In democracy, compelling information might not be sellable. In a mass media organization, the commodity becomes information or entertainment that is sellable to an audience. The audience produced through the behavior of media consumption is then the sellable commodity that the mass media organization has to offer advertisers (e.g., Jhally, 1990; Smythe, 1977). Once content becomes sellable to a large audience, almost by definition it becomes sellable to advertisers. The only messages that get produced are those that are acceptable to the audience and advertisers and nothing extreme that could offend a mass audience.

Theorists of the political economy approach also point out that there is little reporting on the mergers of media companies, as the mass media often do not report on themselves. This behavior becomes problematic in that there is no other entity to report on the media that is not a part of that same mass media system. Reporters do not have the authority to report critically on a merger, especially when it is their mass media organization involved in the merger or their mass media organization that could be the next company that is part of a merger. Citizens, therefore have little knowledge of the system or of the implications of media mergers, and they accept the practice as inevitable (e.g., Mazzocco, 1994).

With virtually no oversight of this economic government and mass media relationship, the political economy approach is concerned that this powerful relationship will exert some form of social control over people and consumption patterns. Mazzocco (1994) stated, "Our perception of the world is largely shaped and guided by the media. It is also true that those who have access to, or control of, those media through personal or corporate wealth have considerably more power than those who do not. Our constitutional right to listen to others and to be heard by enough of our neighbors to make a difference is, in large measure, subject to the desires of those who control the U.S. media" (p. 99).

There are a couple of assumptions about the political economy approach that have to be subscribed to that might be difficult to buy into. Although Mazzocco (1994) contended that the perception of the world is largely shaped by media, Mosco (1996) hedged on this more direct effects perspective stance, claiming, "The political economy approach accepts polysemy and the multiple production of texts, recognizes the need to analyze the full circuit of production, distribution, and consumption, and sees these as central moments in the realization of value and the construction of social life" (p. 261).

There are also major elements of control that are put forth in the political economy approach that are difficult to reconcile. For all mass media organizations, relationships with constituency groups are necessary, as indicated by dependency research. Forfeiting control of the content decision-making process so as to not alienate any of these constituency groups is not, however, necessary to perform their tasks and not necessarily in the interests of the mass media organization. It is a big assumption that media ownership controls every content decision being made. The scenario becomes difficult, as media owners, or their top management employees, cannot be at every location where a critical decision needs to made. Corporations are too big for that level of strict control, and for that control to be implemented everyone in the mass media organization must think in alignment with management and ownership. With the size of the mass media organization, it is also impossible for the top executives to be experts in every area of the industry. For example, the CEO of General Electric might have not have the qualifications to make decisions at NBC overall, let alone all of NBC's divisions (sports, daytime, etc.). These people hire skilled professionals to make decisions in the various media industries that constitute the larger corporation.

NO CONCERN OF CORPORATE OWNERSHIP OF MEDIA ORGANIZATIONS

Other theorists do not see the conflict of corporate ownership of mass media organizations as problematic. Some have pointed out that there is a professional standard among journalists (e.g., Phillips, 1977; Schudson, 1978). Despite his being one of the best known critics of corporate ownership of media, Bagdikian (2000) hedged on his stance by claiming that if General Electric, parent corporation of NBC, experienced a major criminal conviction that "NBC News would probably report it in a straightforward way" (p. 210). He acknowledged that the story would probably not have been covered 50 years ago when newspapers and broadcasters did not publicize bad news about their owner. Schudson (1995) even contended that the practices of fairness and balance have risen over the last century.

In studying the corporate structure of newspapers, Demers (1996, 1998) found that corporate newspapers place much more emphasis on product quality and other nonprofit goals and less emphasis on profits. He contended that "because corporate newspapers are assumed to be profit-maximizers, many critics also believe they place less emphasis on product quality. The assumption here follows a zero-sum formula: If a newspaper maximizes profits, then it has less money to spend on newsgathering, improving the product, or serving the public" (p. 23). He claimed that although corporate newspapers are structurally organized to maximize profits, less emphasis is placed on profits because they: "(a) have a greater division of labor and role specialization, (b) are more financially stable and secure, and (c) are more likely to be controlled by professional managers" (p. 19).

The complex division of labor includes a hierarchy of authority, a staff of highly skilled workers, and a set of formal rules and procedures that helps produce rationality in decision making. Role specialization is described as being an advantageous characteristic of journalistic quality and is a pinnacle of Demers' (1998) argument. He contended that through role specialization journalists have greater autonomy in focusing on gathering and reporting the news. Demers argued that journalists are trying for their own advancement and trying to improve their own monetary situation. He pointed out that journalists place emphasis on product quality, with the goals of winning awards and being innovative in newsgathering, as "these nonprofit goals are revered by journalists, and they—not profits—are the factors that lead to a promotion, an increase in pay, a better job, or greater prestige and power" (p. 26). He pointed out that "professional managers do not benefit as directly from profits as do owners. Managers obtain their primary compensation through a fixed salary" (p. 27). Demers also claimed that large corporate newspapers have many employees, which fosters intense competition among reporters. He stated, "The goal of many reporters, for example, is to publish front-page stories. Such stories enhance the social status of reporters and can indirectly contribute to promotions or better job opportunities" (p. 27).

Demers and Merskin (2000) found that corporate newspapers were also more editorially vigorous and emphasized product quality and innovation. Akhavan-Majid and Boudreau (1995) pointed out that corporate newspapers took a more activist stance toward social change. They claimed that the large organizational size of a newspaper chain may help editors be more activist in their editorial stance toward social change. In a survey of approximately 1,200 daily newspaper journalists from both independent papers and chain-owned papers, Coulson (1994) found that most journalists did not perceive profit seeking as adversely affecting news coverage. Coulson and Hansen (1995) found that when Gannett took over the *Louisville Courier-Journal*, the overall news hole increased, but the stories became shorter and there was less hard news and more wire stories.

One reason for the lack of concern over ownership influence is that there are considerable layers between the corporate ownership and the people who are actually at the scene of a news event. Corporations are so large with so many levels, it is impossible for the CEO and the upper echelons of management to be aware of and consulted on every decision. This is only heightened in the fast-paced decision making necessary in the mass media industry. Westin, president of ABC News, oversees its television news properties, *World News Tonight*, *Nightline*, *20/20*, and *Good Morning America*, its Internet news properties, and ABC news radio. As the president of the news division, Westin has the final say in all content decisions and manages both the editorial side and the business side of ABC News with the goal to "make the two aspects work in tandem" (personal communication, May 28, 2004). He explained that the perception of great conflict between these two areas is largely false. Westin claimed that it is impossible for him to have a final say in every decision overseeing the television, radio, and Internet vehicles.

Alter (1995) claimed, "It's rare for a CEO to call down to a reporter and tell him (or her) to go easy on one of his (or her) subsidiaries. If he (or she) does, the lowly reporter may leak it, and the CEO will look stupid. It sometimes takes a while for executives to figure out that the reporters they think of as little bugs to be squashed or spun can be more powerful than they are" (p. 31). Several reporters and television personalities have become celebrities and are viewed credibly with the American public. These reporters, such as Tom Brokaw, Ted Koppel, Dan Rather, or Tim Russert, earn large salaries and commonly appear on talk shows such as *Imus in the Morning* or even more entertainment-oriented programming such as *The Late Show with David Letterman*. These people have developed a trust with the American people far greater than the CEO of a parent corporation.

In fact, there could deliberately be little or no control coming from the large corporate ownership structure, as the CEO might delegate decisions to employees with more expertise in the mass media industry. The only concern of the corporate ownership could be if that department is earning profits. In speaking about CBS executive Les Moonves, Andrew Heyward, CBS News president, commented that Moonves told him that "as long as you keep me informed, we'll be fine—I'm going to let you run your division," and Heyward stated, "He has totally lived up to that" (cited in Gay, 2003, p. 1). Westin, president of ABC News, indicated that people from Disney do not call him about editorial content; likewise, he does not have to call Disney if he wants to allocate resources in a certain manner. Westin contended that, if anything, media consolidation has led to a lack of sufficient interest in news content. This lack of concern gives the experienced news professional, such as Westin, more autonomy to run his news division. Overall, Westin summarized that the running of a news division in terms of content decision making is more bottom-up than top-down.

Shoemaker and Reese (1996) did, however, point out that the organizational chart reveals that the people responsible for editorial control of content eventually report to someone who is responsible for the economics of the media organization. Lorraine Branham, director of the School of Journalism at the University of Texas at Austin, commented that large newspaper chains such as Knight-Ridder are not normally involved in the day-to-day operations of the newspaper but are still concerned with the bottom line, and if there is a conflict with an advertiser they might inquire as to how it is going to be resolved (personal communication, March 28, 2003).

Webber, senior vice president and publisher of usatoday.com, commented that *USA Today* parent corporation, Gannett, is well managed with its planning and budgeting, and he felt that he is provided the necessary resources (personal communication, May 25, 2004). Webber did contend that part of his responsibility is contributing to a reasonable return for stockholders, but that responsibility does not translate to Gannett's controlling editorial or day-to-day business decisions. Westin claimed that audience levels will determine the allocation of resources, and it is his job to manage the budget prudently (personal communication, May 28, 2004). Westin points out that news divisions do not have to be thought of as loss leaders, as they have in the past, and there is opportunity for profit from a news division.

Jack Welch, former CEO of General Electric, commented, "People would always say to me, 'How can you own NBC? You don't know anything about dramas or comedies.' That's true, but I can't build a jet engine or a turbine, either. My job at GE was to deal with resources—people and dollars. I offered as much (or as little) help to our aircraft engine design engineers as I offered to the people picking shows in Hollywood" (Welch & Byrne, 2001, p. 261). Welch spoke to some of the advantages of a large corporate media structure. He stated, "Most of the shows bomb. Something like one in ten that come out of development make it on the air, and you're lucky if one in five of those are successful. The odds of getting a series that really clicks, like *Seinfeld*, *Frasier*, or *Friends*, is something like 1 in 1,000" (Welch & Byrne, 2001, p. 261). He added that taking chances on certain programming is an advantage of having NBC be part of a larger corporation (General Electric). In talking about the $60 million loss that NBC took by putting the

XFL, a football league partnership with World Wrestling Entertainment and its CEO Vince McMahon, Welch pointed out that "taking those swings is one of the big benefits of GE's size. You don't have to connect all the time" (Welch & Byrne, 2001, p. 272).

To demonstrate their civic responsibility, Westin stated, "If we were simply trying to profit, we would never cover Presidential elections because advertisers do not advertise and people do not watch. We are, however, aware of our civic responsibility and that the news is different and credibility is built up over time and in the long run that does impact if people watch and enhance the value of the asset of ABC News" (personal communication, May 28, 2004). Broadcast networks preempt their programming if there is a major news event, while losing millions of dollars of advertising revenue in the meantime. Moonves, CBS chairman and CEO, commented on breaking news interruptions: "There are tough economic questions every time we do that. Even if it's eleven in the morning and we've got to yank *The Young and the Restless*—we lose *x* amount of dollars on that. We are trying to be good corporate citizens, and we've got to be good public citizens. It's always a tough call" (cited in Gay, 2003, p. 1).

The concern of ownership influence on content decision making is that ownership will directly kill or alter the framing of a story if it would damage the parent corporation (e.g., Williams, 2002). In this instance there is some direct communication, where the owner instructs and pressures a reporter or producer what story to cover and what are the relevant facts (framing) that should be presented or emphasized in that story. In a survey of network news correspondents asking whether they felt any story influence from ownership, Price (2003) found that only 20% felt some pressure from ownership to report or censor stories. Her survey results revealed that 79.4% of national news correspondents from ABC, CBS, CNN, NBC, and PBS responded that they have never felt pressure from ownership to report or not to report a story. In addition, only one respondent claimed that he or she was frequently pressured by ownership to report a story and only four respondents claimed they felt occasional pressure to report a story because of fear of ownership.

Ettema et al. (1987) stated, "News is the product of bureaucratically structured organizations. The work of gathering, assembling, and selecting news is left primarily to workers who are relatively low in the hierarchy, but who, in Western industrialized countries, are considered professionals and given substantial autonomy" (p. 765). Schudson (1997) pointed out "the observable fact that reporters often initiate stories of their own, that editors rarely meet with publishers, and that most working journalists have no idea who sits on the board of directors of the institutions they work for" (p. 10). In describing the newspaper industry, Dreier (1978) claimed that owners are not involved in the daily activities of running the paper, and even in the most ideological areas of the paper there is very little direct contact between ownership and the working journalist. He claimed, "Owners delegate authority to publishers, editors, and managing editors. They, in turn, grant a considerable degree of independence to the news staff" (p. 73).

Syndicated newspaper columnist Kathleen Parker (2003) wrote of the "apparently growing misconception that we in journalism operate as soldiers marching lock step in a sinister army directed by greedy corporate czars" (p. A9). She stated in detail:

> The editorial page of the paper may reflect the publisher's preferences, but not so on the Op-Ed page, where syndicated columns run. Thus, for the record, the editorial content of my columns is my own and only my own. I don't give a rip who likes it, including my editor, publisher, the CEO, Halliburton or Bush. If I cared, I couldn't write. Moreover, my guess is that some of the 300 or so editors who publish my column personally would rather not. The fact that editors run columnists with whom they disagree or don't like is a testament to their professional integrity and their commitment to the marketplace of ideas rather that the marketplace of rack sales. (p. A9)

DIVERSITY OF MEDIA CONTENT

Another reason for the fear of corporate control is that in the marketplace of ideas, people may not be getting all of the information needed to make a proper decision about an important issue when there is corporate conglomeration. That is, in addition to concerns that media organizations operate in the interests of only the economic factions of ownership, stockholders, and advertisers, another prominent concern of corporate conglomeration and subsequent control of the mass media industry is the lack of diversity in the viewpoints provided (e.g., Albarran, 1996; Bagdikian, 2000; Mazzocco, 1994; Mosco, 1996). The fear of consolidated corporate ownership is that much of the market is controlled by only a few voices, which therefore limits the diversity of choices and the diversity of content by blocking out voices from the creative process.

The political economy approach is also concerned with the lack of diversity being produced by mass media organizations because of ownership conglomeration and owners' critical relationships with the government and other major economic industries. Where the relationship between government and mass media industries and the issue of diversity coincide and are considered a threat to democracy is how technology is managed (e.g., Hills, 1986; Hills & Papathanassopoulos, 1991; Mosco, 1996). Any social or technological change becomes important to the media industry, and trying to manage that development is vital.

Garnham (1990) considered reorganizing technological advancement merely to meet market demands and satisfy consumers rather than citizens as a threat to democracy. The government and mass media relationship helps manage technological expansion and telecommunication policy in that by allowing large corporate ownership, only the biggest can afford the best technology and take advantage of the telecommunications laws that allow for even greater expansion. It seems technology that allows for many voices and many channels would be good for democracy and good for the marketplace of ideas. From the political economy perspective, however, there is no equating an increase in the number of channels with diversity, but rather simply more of the same (e.g., Mosco, 1996, p. 261).

The U.S. Federal Communications Commission (FCC) encourages diversity in television programming and assumes competition would create diversity in the marketplace of ideas, especially in media industries where there is little differentiation in price or location for retrieval of the product, the content, as highlighted in chapter 4. Even though there has been corporate conglomeration, there are still five different corporations, six networks, presenting national news on television and competing for market share: Disney (ABC), General Electric (NBC and MSNBC), Viacom (CBS), Time Warner (CNN), and NewsCorp (Fox News). There are few industries that have six brands viably competing for market share.

Bae (2000) studied the content differences between the evening newscasts of cable television and those of the major networks. He concluded that "each network contributed significantly to adding unique news to the daily television news pool and the topics of the unique stories were diverse" (p. 62). In examining similar genres, for example, the nightly news, where the price system for costs and possible advertising revenue are essentially the same, Bae argued that the differentiation among the networks must come in the content they provide. He claimed that this differentiation in turn will provide the diversity of issues being covered.

Bae's (2000) results were that when compared with the other networks, CNN covered more science/technology/computer stories, Fox News covered more diplomacy/foreign relations and social conflict stories, MSNBC reported more government/politics stories, ABC reported more religion/ceremony and war/defense news, CBS reported more crime/court stories, and NBC more health/welfare and education stories (p. 69). Bae pointed out that "the differences in the topics of unique stories across networks also show that each additional network contributed to the increased diversity of the topics of unique stories. Diversity in the topics of unique stories was not the result of a single network's effort, but the result of the efforts of all competing networks" (p. 74). He added:

> Product differentiation in newscasts may operate to the benefit of news viewers by increasing the size of the prime-time television news pool. More news items are in circulation among viewers and come to public attention. In turn, this may affect the public agenda. The diversification of television news sources, and the combined efforts of each competing network to be differentiated from its competitors, has produced diversity, as reflected in unique stories, in line with the FCC's endeavor to facilitate the dissemination of a broad spectrum of information. (p. 75)

Goodwin (1999) commented that online journalists could counter the commercial and political pressures on the more traditional forms of the news media. Although the Internet has provided an incredible capacity for choice, some authors remain skeptical as to the impact of the Internet on an informed citizenry (e.g., McChesney, 1997). The idea is that the dominant corporate mass media organizations continue to control the flow of information, and with the Internet they now simply have a new communication mechanism with which to do it. The Internet site is essentially a brand extension for the more established television network, newspaper, or magazine.

McChesney (1997) pointed out that the large media organizations "have the product and deep pockets to wait it out and establish themselves as the dominant players in cyberspace" (p. 31). He continued, saying that large, established media organizations "can also use their existing media to constantly promote their online ventures, and their relationships with major advertisers to bring them aboard their Internet ventures" (p. 31). Gerbner et al. (2002) argued that "there are no popular Internet or Web-based programs that yet threaten the network-cable alliance; on the contrary, networks and cable channels are working feverishly to drive their viewers to their Web sites, to allow them to obtain more personal information from viewers, and to create another platform for advertising exposures" (p. 62). They also claimed that behavior toward the Internet might be similar to cable television, stating "even with the expansion of cable and satellite channels serving ever-narrower *niche* audiences, most television programs are by commercial necessity designed to be watched by large and heterogeneous audiences in a relatively nonselective fashion" (p. 45).

In terms of examining the future and the impact of the Internet, Cohen (2002) pointed out that "the online commercial news environment increases market pressures at all levels, because news production occurs faster, competition is fiercer, the branding issues are tougher to establish, and media consolidations are what have defined the new media environment" (p. 537). She argued that the Internet itself does little to alter the constraints on journalists presented by media organizations and audiences, stating that "the influence of media conglomerates on news production functions in much the same way as in traditional media" (p. 544). Cohen pointed to the reality that many of the diverse voices available on the Internet will not have the status of the more established mass media brands who are using their Internet site as an extension of their brand. She concluded that the influence on the Internet is not different in the problem of corporate control over content, arguing that "investors, owners, and parent corporations direct capital and shape policies at the level of the media firm to generate profits and increase brand influence of online news" (p. 545). Mulgan (1991), however, claimed that new technologies deconcentrate authority and provide opportunities. More media options created through technology also relates to diversity if one buys into the idea that no two observers report the same (e.g., Roshco, 1975; White, 1950).

Columnist Robert J. Samuelson (2003) wrote on the subject of media ownership, claiming that any fears of media concentration imperiling freedom of speech, diversity, or democracy are "misrepresenting reality" (p. 17). He pointed out the dramatic increases in mass media options as a major piece of evidence in comparing the current media with the 1970s where today there are more major television networks, an explosion in the number of cable channels, close to 6,000 FM radio stations (an increase of more than 3,500 stations), and the Internet. Samuelson stated:

> The idea that "big media" have dangerously increased their control over our choices is absurd. Yet large parts of the public, including journalists and politicians, believe religiously in this myth. They confuse size with power. It's true that some gigantic media companies are getting even bigger at the expense of other companies. But it's not true that their power is increasing at the public's expense. (p. 17)

Samuleson (2003) argued that mass media organizations are simply working within the economic system. He claimed, "It's the tyranny of the market: a triumph of popular tastes. Big media companies try to anticipate, shape and profit from these tastes. But media diversity frustrates any one company from imposing its views and values on an unwilling audience. People just click to another channel or cancel their subscription" (p. 17).

RECRUITMENT AND SOCIALIZATION

The potential for ownership to influence media content is constant, as mass media owners could hypothetically call the newsroom and demand a story be dropped or covered in a certain manner. This scenario puts the person at the other end of the line at risk for his or her job if there is failure to give in to the demand of the owner. Critical theorists claim that ownership relations do not have to be direct, with the overt, obvious situation of an owner calling a day-to-day decision maker to alter or even kill a story. The argument is that if ownership does not control the content per se, they do control the people who will make the decisions regarding content. Media owners, as owners and executives do in any other industry, simply have the power to hire and fire the day-to-day decision-makers responsible for producing the content.

A subtle process through recruitment and socialization in terms of reward and promotion might get the journalists' thinking aligned with the philosophy of the mass media organization. The organization could simply hire only people who philosophically think along with or are willing to capitulate to the ideas and practices of the larger parent corporation to fill the important decision-making positions. Gitlin (1983) offered a seminal piece on the workings of prime-time network television, including hiring practices. He contended that the big three networks, by repeatedly hiring the same type of individuals, reduce their variety and diversity within the organization and do not capture the diversity of the audience. Lauzen and Dozier (2002) stated, "By stubbornly adhering to historically embedded employment practices, older networks place less value on requisite variety, resulting in fewer women on screen and behind the scenes" (p. 141).

Even after hiring a person, there can be further training to develop a clear understanding of corporate goals. Breed (1955) indicated there was a socialization process in the newsroom, where reporters learned about editorial policy indirectly by seeing how stories were edited or placed in the newspaper. He pointed out that these subordinate journalists learn to conform to the policies to succeed. Breed stated, "'Policy' may be defined as the more or less consistent orientation shown by a paper, not only in its editorial but in its news columns and headlines as well, concerning selected issues and events" (p. 70). He added that the slanting of a story "involves omission, differential selection and preferential placement, such as 'featuring' a pro-policy item, 'burying' an anti-policy story in an inside page" (p. 70). More recently, McManus

(1994) explained that journalistic recruitment, training, and socialization practices allow and urge the reporter to work in the interests of his or her employer. Employees are a resource in relation to the overall budget. The reduction of news budgets in the 1980s were highlighted by mass firings at the major networks (e.g., Alger, 1998; Cohen, 1997). Alger (1998) feared these layoffs may have made journalists more sensitive about job security and more likely to work on stories that stress the bottom line rather than those that fulfill pure journalistic functions.

Schudson (1997), however, posited, "If the organizational theorists are generally correct, it does not matter who (the journalists) are or where they come from; they will be socialized quickly into the values and routines in the daily rituals of journalism" (p. 15). Individual judgment is thus devalued, and socialization to the media routines that will be in the interest of the power corporation occurs. In speaking on the issue of socialization as the way that reporters are taught how to make decisions, Soloski (1997) contended that the imposition of elaborate rules and regulations would seem implausible as the rules could not cover all of the possible situations that journalists encounter, the journalists ability for the unexpected would be limited, and it would be an expensive and time-consuming effort to instruct the journalist as to these rules.

Hollifield et al. (2001) studied news directors' and newspaper editors' hiring practices, questioning whether they seek employees with characteristics valued by the organizational culture or those valued by the professional culture of journalism. Although their findings showed mixed support that the organizational culture is the dominant force shaping hiring decisions, they did conclude there has been a trend toward making organizational influences more important to news executives of all types in the past 20 years. Hollifield et al.'s major concern was that this trend in hiring that emphasizes organization culture values would continue, suggesting that "organizational culture is a growing influence in shaping newsroom decisions as compared to the professional journalistic culture. News executives today appear to focus on finding job candidates who will make good employees and who, secondarily, bring with them traditional journalism competencies" (pp. 112–113). They also pointed out that local television news directors are more focused than newspaper executives on hiring people more capable of meeting standards of quality journalism.

Branham commented that the hiring process at a newspaper is not based on overly philosophical thoughts about the newspaper industry on the part of a reporter, but instead deals more with the necessary skills a reporter will need and his or her ability to develop story ideas and cover a beat (personal communication, March 28, 2003). She did, however, point out that when editors are hired, the types of stories they are going to pursue is a consideration in the hiring process.

OWNERSHIP AND PROMOTION

Ownership of many mass media outlets helps provide more locations for promotions to run and increases the chances of reaching an audience that might be interested in that content. Promotion could be an area where ownership and corporate interests are exercised. This strategy of owning all of the aspects from production to distribution and owning a vehicle in each medium type gives owners tremendous cross-promotional opportunities. This cross-promotion is a major reason for ownership of many forms of media and many distribution points within one medium. For example, it is not uncommon for ESPN to air promotions of ABC prime-time programming or MSNBC to promote NBC programming.

The Internet has become another media distribution and promotional vehicle. At the end of a story, news networks often instruct viewers to visit their Internet site for more information about the issue. Webster and Lin (2002) pointed out that "the Internet does not have the same structural characteristics as radio and television, but it does have latent structures. Perhaps the most important are domains. These are families of Web sites, often under common ownership. Because members of the family are typically linked to one another, it seems likely that movement within domains is slightly easier than movement across domains" (pp. 4–5). Bellamy and Traudt (2000) commented that "the continuing consolidation of media companies both domestically and internationally is a reaction to the audience choice, with the rationale being that if the viewer is going to graze, let her/him graze to other channels or, at least, programming controlled by the same company" (p. 130).

The cross-promotional opportunities extend beyond promotion of other media properties to ancillary aspects of the corporation's brand extension businesses, including retail industries. For example, Disney can use ABC to promote its Disney films and theme parks and use its theme parks, to promote its films, musical artists, and ABC programming. ESPN can promote the ESPN Zone restaurants, and the restaurants can promote the networks of ESPN. ESPN television, radio, and magazine all promote the ESPN brand. This cross-promotion occurs in every aspect of the mass media through using the other properties of the corporation. Essentially, one corporation can put the audience member in a box that is surrounded by all of the media vehicles that are owned by the parent corporation, with the promotion leading the audience from one wall to the next, but the audience member never leaves the corporate entity box. A person simply goes from one television station by a certain corporation to a radio station or an Internet site owned by the same corporation (see Fig. 5.1).

Theorists fear that increased corporate conglomeration leads to excessive promotion or "plugola" of corporate properties (e.g., Eastman, 2000; McAllister, 2002). As articulated in chapter 4, promotion is a critical communication strategy for a mass media organization in attracting and maintaining an audience and communication of a brand. Thus, if many media vehicles are owned by one corporation, that corporation constantly promotes its other properties to drive the audience member, and the other media content options will not be in the forefront of people's minds. McAllister (2002) defined plugola as "self-interested news stories that promote entertainment events" (p. 383). He cautioned, "With the increased growth of media conglomerates plugola would also include newscasts featuring stories about a program on a sibling cable or broadcast network owned by the same parent corporation. In addition, news divisions engage in plugola when they create stories promoting movies, CD's, books, and other media products owned by the their parent company" (p. 384).

There are many examples of promotion of programming that is of interest to the parent company. Buchman (2000) pointed out that it is

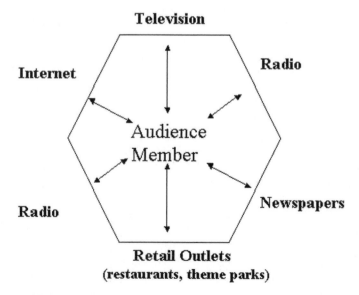

FIG. 5.1.   Media ownership promotion and desired audience movement.

common for a news program to indicate the stories appearing on that network's news magazine show that evening during the broadcast of the news itself (i.e., Dan Rather stating on the *CBS Evening News* what will be on *60 Minutes II* later that night). Buchman explained, "Promotion within a newscast is likely to be perceived as more credible than promotion offered within entertainment programming" (p. 266).

Other examples of promotion of one's own network occur for prime-time programming. Every Friday after a contestant has been voted off *Survivor*, he or she appears on the CBS morning program *The Early Show*, and that same person also makes an appearance the next week on *The Late Show with David Letterman*. A similar tactic has been employed for every person who is fired by Donald Trump on *The Apprentice*. That person will also be on NBC's *The Today Show* the following morning. In the spring of 2004, *Dateline NBC* also devoted entire programs to the season finale of *The Apprentice*, and the series finales of *Friends* and *Frasier*. These interviews or specials are, however, also good "gets" for their respective programs, and those guests would not be appearing if there was not a desire on the part of the audience to see and hear those guests. The desire on the part of the audience is evident in the ratings that these shows consistently receive.

In studying the final episode of *Seinfeld*, McAllister (2002) demonstrated that news organizations with connections to *Seinfeld*, particularly NBC and Castle Rock Entertainment, covered the program's last episode more extensively than those without such connections. It must, however, still be noted that other rival news organizations did do stories on *Seinfeld*'s last episode. It seems that if ownership was in such control, other networks would not do any story promoting a show that would air on another network. McAllister reported that CBS did 7 stories on its morning show the 6 months before the final episode of *Seinfeld* (NBC did 14). He also reported that on their evening news programs during the same period, both ABC and CBS ran one story on *Seinfeld*, with NBC only doing two stories. The coverage of *Seinfeld* is more similar than different, as McAllister pointed out that on December 26, 1997, the day after NBC announced it would be *Seinfeld*'s last season, all three evening newscasts devoted a story to the show, teased the story at the beginning of their newcasts, showed clips from the program, and alluded to the program's success. The differences in length of the respective stories were nominal with NBC's story running for 2:50, whereas ABC's and CBS's stories ran for 2:20 and 2:10, respectively (pp. 389–390).

Williams (2002) studied the influence of parent companies on mass media content, questioning whether this relationship might provide an increase in the quantity and quality of company-related materials mentioned in the news. In using the parent corporation within its nightly news programs for ABC, CBS, NBC, and CNN Headline News, Williams concluded that "none of the four corporations showed a systematic tendency to promote their own products over others' in all fields" (p. 466). He actually reported it was consistent that a network would mention its own product after a competitor's. For example, Disney (*ABC World News Tonight*) mentioned General Electric's (parent company of NBC) products, on average, in the fourth story in its broadcast and its own products in the eighth story. Williams offered a plausible solution, claiming that "it could be that the editors are more aware of who owns what than anyone else, and wish to avoid the appearance of impropriety in this most obvious fashion" (p. 467). Meyer (1987) contended that the market and competition are adequate safeguards against any potential abuse. The audience will recognize that the mass media organization is acting as a shill for the parent company, will not view the report as credible, and will turn elsewhere.

There are numerous other examples where a network has put on programming that in essence promotes the competition and seems to benefit its competition. Again, if ownership were in complete control, this promotional behavior would not be regularly occurring. Consider the following:

- Late night talk shows routinely have guests on who work for a rival network. On January 13, 2003, David Letterman had Jimmy Kimmel on as one of his guests, even though part of Kimmel's show, *Jimmy Kimmel Live*, was about to premiere in the same time slot directly opposite Letterman on ABC in many cities.
- The *Imus in the Morning* radio program is broadcast out of its home station WFAN, which is owned by Viacom. The radio program is, however, also simulcast live on MSNBC, owned by General Electric. In addition to guests from CBS (owned by Viacom) and NBC, Imus also routinely has several guests from ABC, CNN, and Fox News on the program.
- On Monday April 7, 2003, CBS chairman and chief executive Moonves, appeared as himself on an episode of ABC's *The Practice*. The show appeared opposite the championship game of the NCAA college basketball tournament, an event CBS has paid $6 billion for the broadcasting rights to over an 11-year period.
- ESPN every Sunday broadcasts a 2-hour NFL pregame show that promotes the weekend games, of which all but one will be broadcast on its own network and only one other on Disney-

owned ABC, essentially inviting customers to watch other networks for the next 6 hours.

- On Friday March 21, 2003, as war was going on in the Middle East, CBS decided to continue its war coverage and preempt the broadcasting of the NCAA basketball tournament. The interesting aspect of this decision was not to shift the games to another station owned by its parent company but to ESPN, owned by Disney. During the broadcasting of games on ESPN, the crawl on the bottom of the screen indicated for more information about the war, turn to ABC news. The games on ESPN also featured CBS announcers doing promotions for upcoming ESPN programming.
- WABC-TV, the ABC affiliate in New York and one of the ABC stations owned by Disney, televised repeat episodes of *ER* in syndication, even though that program currently is on NBC. WCBS-TV, the CBS affiliate in New York and one of the CBS stations owned by Viacom, televised repeat episodes of *The West Wing*, even though that program currently is on NBC.
- Disney bought commercial time at a cost of approximately $2.3 million for a 30-second spot during the 2004 Super Bowl on CBS to promote its movie *Miracle* about the 1980 U.S. Olympic hockey team.
- In addition to showing same-day episodes of all of its ABC soap operas, The Soap Network, also owned by Disney, features same-day episodes of *Days of Our Lives*, currently an NBC soap opera.
- Tim Russert, moderator of NBC's *Meet the Press*, appeared on rival networks CNN as a guest of the *Larry King Live* program on May 10, 2004; on the Fox News Channel's *Hannity & Colmes* on May 11 and June 14, 2004; and *The O'Reilly Factor* on May 20, 2004, to promote his book.

Guests go on a program of a competitor's network because they want to reach the large audience that some of those programs attain. The point in all of these examples is that each network and each program are trying to put on their best program to attract an audience. The producers for each program need to put the best program they can on the air because if the ratings are not good in that time slot they will be replaced. Therefore, if people will watch Debra Messing, star of NBC's *Will & Grace*, when she appears on David Letterman, the Letterman show has to schedule her as a guest to protect its own rating, even though in having her appear they might also be promoting a prominent actress on a prominent program of a rival network.

SUGGESTED READINGS

Bae, H. (2000). Product differentiation in national TV newscasts: A comparison of the cable all-news networks and the broadcast networks. *Journal of Broadcasting & Electronic Media, 44,* 62–77.

Bagdikian, B. H. (2000). *The media monopoly* (6th ed.). Boston: Beacon Press.

Breed, W. (1955). Social control in the newsroom: A functional analysis. *Social Forces, 33,* 326–355.

Demers, D. (1998). Revisiting corporate newspaper structure and profit making. *Journal of Media Economics, 11*(2), 19–45.

Gomery, D. (2000). Interpreting media ownership. In B. M. Compaine & D. Gomery (Eds.), *Who owns the media?* (pp. 507–535). Mahwah, NJ: Lawrence Erlbaum Associates.

Mazzocco, D. W. (1994). *Networks of power: Corporate TV's threat to democracy.* Boston: South End Press.

McChesney, R. (1997). *Corporate media and the threat to democracy.* New York: Seven Stories Press.

McManus, J. H. (1994). *Market-driven journalism: Let the citizen beware?* Thousand Oaks, CA: Sage.

McManus, J. (1995). A market-based model of news production. *Communication Theory, 5,* 301–338.

Price, C. J. (2003). Interfering owners or meddling advertisers: How network television news correspondents feel about ownership and advertiser influence on news stories. *Journal of Media Economics, 16*(3), 175–188.

Williams, D. (2002). Synergy bias: Conglomerates and promotion in the news. *Journal of Broadcasting & Electronic Media, 46,* 453–472.

6

Day-to-Day
Decision Makers

Through an acknowledgment that decisions are made within the parameters of a media routine and that items such as budgets and the allocation of resources are a function of the routine, the ownership that sets these major policies could emerge as the pivotal constituency group in the determination of the content decision-making process. If after setting budgets, establishing the mass media routine, and perhaps conducting any larger philosophical standards of practice, that is the extent of ownership influence, albeit still very substantial, the day-to-day decision makers become powerful regarding specific content decisions. Often after allocating resources and setting the overall organizing philosophy, the media routine does not dictate all content decisions and there are still many to be made within the parameters of the routine. An argument can be made that routines constrain, but they also enable in that the remaining time and space available for selection and framing of content is open to a multitude of story options and perspectives.

The day-to-day decision makers are in the eye of the storm when it comes to content decision making. The relationship between day-to-day decision makers and content is that they are constantly evaluating all of the items being sent to them and constantly have to make decisions regarding the selection and framing of content. An argument can be made that any time a decision is made some form of agenda setting or framing is taking place. Therefore, anyone who is making a decision about a story, regardless of his or her status within the organization, is performing an agenda-setting function. The hierarchical system of decision making allows for certain agenda-setting decisions to be dismissed or overruled by more powerful editors or producers.

The day-to-day decision makers are the producers, directors, writers, reporters, editors, announcers, and camera and other technological personnel employed by the mass media organization. At some point the people in any one of these capacities could have a say in what does and what does not become content. It can be simply argued that the day-to-day decision makers are the most powerful people in the process, as they always have the responsibility and ability to make decisions regarding the selection and framing (both exposure and portrayal) of content by their job title.

The day-to-day decision makers get paid for their eye and ear, their skills to write and communicate about events in a comprehensive manner, and their ability to make proper judgments in selecting and framing content. Certain reporters and columnists get paid for their analysis of news events. There is complexity simply within the mass media organization among the day-to-day decision makers, who might have varied opinions about whether a story should be selected and if selected what the relevant facts or highlights are that need to be emphasized.

Every person within the mass media organization assigned to cover a certain story at some point has to make selection and framing decisions, from a senior editor or producer selecting which stories to cover to the reporter who is at the scene deciding whom to interview, to a camera person or a photographer who is getting the pictures of the event that are critical in framing an issue. All of these people, at different stages of the decision-making process, can drastically influence the outcome of a story's presentation. Sometimes there is agreement within the mass media organization among all personnel about how a story should be handled, but in other instances there is intense disagreement.

Although opinions are brought forth as to in whose interest the mass media should be operating, it is the day-to-day decision makers that are confronted with this dilemma on a daily basis. These media employees might have varying things occupying their minds as they go through the process of their job and try to determine who is the group they should be trying to please. As previously examined in chapter 1, there are some scholars who think the thought process of the mass media employees in selection and framing should simply be what is best for the people and to hold up social democratic ideals of an informed citizenry. Many of these same scholars, however, strongly believe the decision-making philosophy is only about how to please the economic factions of the mass media organization.

There is another possibility that the focus and the thought process regarding content decisions are on the practical application of their task. This relates to the primary function of the mass media organization—making sure it has enough content to fill its time and space requirements. Within the type of content desired emerges questions of what content is possible to gather and distribute. Because content can only become what information is possible to obtain, and in some cases instantaneously transmit to the mass audience through communication technology, media decision makers have to address practical questions: What is the deadline? Is there access to a camera crew or a photographer? Will there be enough time to obtain footage or pictures and return to the studio to write and edit the story before its airing or going to print?

Another way to determine in whose interest the day-to-day decision makers are operating might be to consider the human element; that is, mass media employees are people with everyday problems. These are people making important content decisions, but they are also people with bills to pay, families to take care of, children to put through college, and any other financial obligations. Their primary allegiance is probably to themselves and their families, and perhaps the first responsibility of a media professional is to keep his or her job. The media professional is no different from any other employee who at times capitulates to his or her boss or any other constituency group to keep a job. Williams (2002) simply commented, "Self-censorship may be a stronger force than direct influence—the danger would not be so much in a corporate head exerting influence, but in reporters and editors anticipating reprisals on their careers for not being team players" (p. 457).

With all of the potential influences from the various constituency groups, there is still the filter of the mass media organization. Kosicki (1993) claimed that "media organizations have considerable autonomy over how a story is constructed, at least at certain points of an issue's evolution" (p. 109). Jamieson and Campbell (2001) explained that "news is gathered, written, edited, produced, and disseminated by human beings who are members of organizations and who have beliefs and values. Organizations such as networks have functions and goals as well as relationships to government, to regulatory agencies, to advertisers, to their parent companies, and to the vast audiences they seek to attract. These beliefs, values, functions, and interests are bound to influence the messages these networks publish and broadcast" (p. 40). Decisions rely on judgment, and judgment has to come from or be influenced by something.

No matter what process went into the decision regarding content, it is the mass media organization and its credibility that are evaluated and receive either the credit or the criticism for how a story is presented. Kim (2002) commented that "although television news is the product of multi-layered decisions, journalists and their news organizations are responsible for the final news product" (p. 431). Accountability rests with the mass media organization. Saying it was influenced by a spokesperson or another constituency group does not become an acceptable defense for a false story that the mass media organization printed, aired, or hastily posted on its Internet site.

GATEKEEPING

With people dependent on information to make decisions about whom to vote for or any other story that could affect their lives where interpersonal contacts are insufficient, decisions made by a news media organization are critical. Molotch and Lester (1974) stated, "Everyone needs news. In everyday life the news tells us what we do not experience directly and thus renders otherwise remote happenings observable and meaningful" (p. 101). They added that the power of needed information and the importance of the process is in the desires and behavior of the audience. They claimed, "News is thus the result of this invariant need for accounts of the unobserved, this capacity for filling-in others, and the production work of those in the media" (p. 101). Molotch and Lester offered a complete definition in that the need for the unobserved and the capacity to fill in others relating to the interpersonal satisfaction represents the audience, whereas the production work of the media incorporates the mass media content decision-making processes.

Some authors have offered a simplistic characterization of news as being essentially what the journalist decides news is (e.g., Cohen & Young, 1973; Fishman, 1980; Gieber, 1964). This perspective is perhaps a little myopic in not recognizing the need for quality content and the acquiescence to cover stories and perspectives the audience desires. Lee (1997) viewed the audience as the group determining what news is, explaining that "news is that which is interesting to the public today," and "news is that which the people are willing to pay to have brought to their attention" (p. 4). In this view, when the mass media present an issue, the audience will determine its importance and whether the issue or a particular perspective remains prominently in the public dialogue. Although audience selection and evaluation certainly occur, this perspective is too incomplete, as the audience behavior can only be based on the content made available to them. Berkowitz (1997) claimed, "News becomes the product of the practicalities and constraints of the process by which it is created. It becomes the product of economic systems and political systems, and the press systems that result from them. And it becomes the product of unspoken cultural values and beliefs by which people manage their daily lives" (p. xii).

The nature of day-to-day content decision making was referred to metaphorically as gatekeeping by Lewin (1947). In a famous essay examining the gatekeeping process, White (1950) described how an editor (White referred to him as Mr. Gates) selects the news by rejecting almost nine tenths of the wire copy in search for the one tenth of news for which there is space in the newspaper. In this study by White, the editing process simply refers to which stories are selected and to which the audience will be exposed. It does not focus on characteristics of framing, other than the important placement frame of where the story is located in the newspaper. White demonstrated that the editing process is highly subjective and reliant on value judgments based on the gatekeeper's own set of experiences, attitudes, and expectations as to what the communication of news really is. He concluded that "theoretically all of the wire editor's standards of taste should refer back to an audience who must be served and pleased" (p. 390). White did point out that there are several gates in the chain of command—from reporter to editor—and the story could have ended at any gate.

White's (1950) essay reveals the individual nature and individual decision-making responsibility at some point of the process for all of the media employees that is such a prominent characteristic of the industry. In that there are many individuals making decisions at many stages of the process, Shoemaker (1991) commented, "One day's news represents the effects of many gatekeepers at many gates" (p. 1). She summarized the gatekeeping process is complex, where "the individual gatekeeper has likes and dislikes, ideas about the nature of his or her job, ways of thinking about a problem, preferred decision-making strategies, and values that all impinge on the decision to reject or select (and shape) a message. But the gatekeeper is not totally free to follow a personal whim; he or she must operate within the constraints of communication routines to do things this way" (p. 75).

At the time of White's (1950) essay, news cycle decision making was a little easier in that there was some time to deliberate whether to include a story and where it should be placed. In the new media environment, issues of when to release information have to be addressed. In this environment where speed and increased competition now constantly have to be dealt with, it is important to point out that there is not always lengthy debate regarding certain mass media content decisions because of time constraints and deadlines. In this rush to be first, sacrificing accuracy could be a consequence.

Kinsey Wilson is the vice president and editor in chief for usatoday.com. In the new media environment and the question of speed versus accuracy, Wilson commented, "The Internet has unquestionably upped the ante in terms of pressures and demands in trying to deal with the pressure and keep pace with the competition, most notably the Internet sites for cnn.com and msnbc.com" (personal communication, June, 14, 2004). With increased competition, Wilson stressed that it is important to be candid about where information is coming from. This is especially important because information from another source is only a click away.

In terms of the 24-hour, 7-day-a-week news cycle, Wilson contended that the mass media organization has to deal in information that the audience knows and be careful not to overreach in terms of offering information too soon. Wilson explained that his philosophy is "to get it right first, get it first second" (personal communication, June, 14, 2004). He commented that you layer or provide additional information as it becomes available and that information is subject to change, and he said you should indicate that what the reader or viewer is seeing might not be the entire or final picture. Wilson explained that what he referred to as "contingent journalism" is an implicit understanding between the journalist and the reader and that what is being reported is the best at this moment and subject to change. He also pointed out that viewers have different expectations for the Internet, as they think of an Internet story as evolving and more information as forthcoming, unlike print media, where a newspaper is labeled as a final edition.

It is becoming evident that several factors combine to influence content and that not merely one single entity dominates the decision-making process even within the mass media organization. The point here is the complexity of the content decision-making process even within the mass media organization on a newsroom level. There are multiple gates and multiple people making decisions throughout the process. The number of individuals within the process raises questions about each individual's autonomy and the convergence or reconciliation between mass media routines and reporter autonomy. Media routines might dictate the types of content on a story-selection level, but the individual reporters create the specific content and select the frames within the story.

Price (2003) pointed out that autonomy is important for reporters and editors to perform their job, but he did not dismiss the business factors that can create a conflict. She explained that "executives are responsible for seeing that the output of the news divisions meet the specified budgets and expectations of the network; producers are responsible for seeing that their own programs conform to budget, quality, and policy guidelines; correspondents are only responsible for the individual stories they create" (p. 177).

With there being several gates within a singular mass media organization, before examining influences from outside the organization it is critical to examine the hierarchy relationships within the mass media organization. These relationships can impact content decision making and question the autonomy of the reporter to make decisions. The reporters are the people at the scene and, although they might have been directed to go cover that story on that day by someone higher in the mass media organization, once at the location the individual reporter uses his or her own judgment and engages in critical aspects of selection and framing of the story by deciding whom to interview, what questions to ask, and what the accompanying camera person shoots. Of all the information gathered, the reporter must decide what to include in the story, which is presented to his or her boss for the next round of decision making. It is critical to point out that the boss can only make decisions based on the material brought back by the reporter at the scene.

Although at the scene there is always some subjectivity in reporting, in that instant decisions have to be made without seeking approval from a supervisor. Perhaps not all reporters would make the same decision. Trying to determine a journalistic philosophy of what is news is as varied as the number of journalists. Although there is consistency across many national mass media organizations of the perceived value of a story (all organizations reporting on the war on terror) or of a framing perspective within that story (i.e., a quote from a senior government official), the story could be reported differently in every news report. This difference and the multitude of mass media organizations providing some form of news help speak to the issue of diversity.

On the topic of diversity in reporting, White (1950) pointed out that the same event "is reported by two reporters in two different perceptual frameworks and that the two men [or women] bring to the 'story' different sets of experiences, attitudes, and expectations" (p. 384). As Cohen (1963) simply stated, the reporter is "a reporter of the passing scene, yet he [or she] is also part of that scene" (p. 19). Each reporter has his or her own interpretation of events, even though various reporters will all be seeing the same event or covering the same story. Objectivity does not reside in the event, but rather the behavior of the journalist does (e.g., Roscho, 1975, p. 55).

The idea of journalistic interpretation raises another important issue: Is the role of the journalist as independent, objective dispenser of facts or is there also a duty to act as an analyst? In speaking of foreign policy, Cohen (1963) contended that the primary role of the press should be to provide factual information so that people could make their own judgments about the issue. Cohen cautioned that "the meaning of particular events is a necessary adjunct of the news about those events and a justifiable function of the news columns of the newspaper, so long as the reporter refrains from expressing his [or her] own judgments about whether those events were good or bad, should have taken place, and so forth" (p. 26). This could be the case for all stories. Cohen added that "there are some important judgments to be made by the reporter about the relative priorities of secrecy as against the public's 'need to know' " (p. 22).

Johnstone, Slawski, and Bowman (1976) identified two types of journalists: (a) neutral journalists who viewed their role as transmitters of information about the real world to the public or (b) participant journalists who provide background information and interpretation to give facts meaning. Weaver and Wilhoit (1996) claimed that reporters with more notoriety are more likely to be a participant type of journalist. Some prominent media people such as Tom Brokaw or Dan Rather have the ability to dictate the coverage of a story, but again, similar to any other occupation, it takes a certain amount of credibility and longevity to attain that type of power. More notoriety brings longevity, credibility, and trust. It simply becomes easier for these reporters to take some chances in story selection.

The utopian concept of the mass media might be service to readers or viewers, with the mass media using their expertise and experience in acting as the filter for the information available. As soon as the mass media act as gatekeepers selecting and framing of information, there is an opening for criticism, and the imperfections of the media system become apparent. Austin and Pinkleton (1999) contended that citizens' cynicism is heightened by the thought that the media hold back information and that there is more to a story than what a reporter is providing. Pinkleton and Austin (2002) argued that "because skepticism motivates information seeking, citizens who do not receive the depth of coverage they desire from traditional media sources may seek information from alternative information sources" (p. 46). Seeking information from various sources and in various forms should be the norm as the audience performs its responsibility in a democracy, as part of becoming an informed citizenry is the citizenry proactively becoming informed.

For all of the similarities discussed between the mass media industry and other industries (i.e., profit-oriented industries whose governance is applicable to the market of audience supply and demand, the necessity for branding and promotional strategies to acquire and maintain an audience), the biggest difference for a mass media organization is the nature of the product itself: content. The acquisition of news content is not static in location or cost. Mass media organizations cannot predict where news is going to occur. Because of this unpredictable nature, there is no cost certainty.

Soloski (1997) offered a comprehensive description of the unpredictable nature of the mass media industry:

> The news department as a subsystem of a news organization must deal with a highly unpredictable environment—news. Decisions about news coverage must be reached rapidly, with little time for discussion or group decision-making. Thus the structure of the news department must be fluid enough to deal with a constantly changing news environment. Reporters and editors must have considerable autonomy in the selection and processing of the news. Controlling the behavior of its journalists could be a difficult problem for management of a news organization, especially since reporters spend most of their time outside the newsroom and out of sight of supervisors. (p. 139)

THE HIERARCHY OF THE GATEKEEPING PROCESS: PRACTITIONER PERSPECTIVE

Trying to learn the philosophies and standard practices of every mass media organization with the responsibility of producing news content is impossible. Some perspective from the people within these organizations can, however, provide insight into the process.

Westin, president of ABC News, explained that the hierarchy of content decisions occurs from two independent routes. The direct route is where executive producers who act as CEOs of each television program or their respective ABC radio and Internet divisions make decisions. The second route is outside of the decision making of an executive producer and is that each employee of ABC News has a copy of written standards and practices of how news will be gathered, vetted, and edited to make sure it is fair. These standards and practices are available on ABC's internal computer system, and seminars are often held to discuss these procedures.

Branham is the director of the School of Journalism at the University of Texas at Austin. In 25 years of newspaper experience, her roles included assistant to the publisher at the *Pittsburgh Post Gazette*; senior vice president and executive editor of the *Tallahassee Democrat*, where she oversaw the newsroom and editorial board operations; and a variety of top editor positions at the *Philadelphia Inquirer* including associate managing editor for features, associate editorial page editor, and New Jersey editor. Branham commented that reporters can bring stories to the table of which they are aware; even if they are covering an assigned beat they have much autonomy and freedom within the beat. She continued that individual reporters bring their own interests and skills to a story and that there is a certain amount of trust given to the reporter once he or she is assigned a story. Webber, senior vice president and publisher of usatoday.com, explained that the usatoday.com reporting staff works for the newspaper and is largely organized through assignment editors and reporters who are given a specific beat to cover on a daily basis.

Giving some trust and autonomy to the reporter is inherent in the task. An executive producer or senior editor cannot be with every reporter on every story. The on-the-scene reporter is thus a vital first stage of selection and framing of content. Control of the story becomes difficult for managers, as they are not at the scene, and once they make the original decision of where to send the reporters they are reliant on what that reporter brings back from the scene. There is, however, a check on whether the reporter is acquiring the best information: the competition. Mass media organizations regularly monitor the content of their competition as one method of evaluating their own decision making. With so many media outlets, not reporting a story could result in embarrassment if it is reported by all competitors. If other mass media outlets are getting information that the reporter is not, that is a critical evaluation of that reporter. By the same token, if the reporter is getting information that competitors are not, that reflects well on the reporter.

Wilson, vice president and editor in chief for usatoday.com, explained that many content decisions and ideas originate from the reporter within a given area of responsibility, generally, a specific beat. These reporters are to stay current with the beat and develop what Wilson referred to as "enterprise pieces"—stories that provide a deeper insight into an area being focused on, either a personality or a trend. Enterprise pieces are pitched ideas from reporters to editors, who evaluate the story ideas. These story ideas are often the preference of the reporter, and Wilson pointed out that reporters generally have more story ideas than there is room or time to write them.

Once the story idea is agreed on and written, it must go through an editing process at multiple levels, with higher level executives getting more involved if it is an important story with a potentially large impact. Wilson described his editorial involvement as "not a second guessing, but the editor is ultimately accountable" for the content posted on the usatoday.com Internet site and therefore wants to review any potentially questionable material himself (personal communication, June 14, 2004).

Wilson explained that a newspaper's content is a mix of both what people want and what the newspaper staff deems important. He explained that a news organization must apply its best judgment to stories that will have the greatest impact on a community. He stressed that for a newspaper, or in this case an Internet site, the two types of stories can live with each other. Both the newspaper and the Internet site can feature important stories and showcase items of interest (i.e., sports, popular culture). People expect both types of stories (established through the media routine) and know where to look for both. Wilson explained that for the usatoday.com Internet site, page views measure audience behavior and the top of the news pages are the most heavily viewed. He indicated that the number of visitors can be equaled for a popular culture event (i.e., the finale of *American Idol*), but the numbers are equal and not disproportionate to those viewing news.

Learning about the process of how content decisions are made can best be accomplished by identifying where day-to-day decision makers originated their stories and the types of stories they initially desire. Peter King is a senior writer for *Sports Illustrated*, covering the National Football League (NFL) beat. He explained that *Sports Illustrated* makes its decisions about what stories to cover as a collaborative effort between the writers and the editors, with story ideas originating from either party. There is, however, a main criterion for a story of which all employees of the magazine are aware. King explained that the main criterion for a *Sports Illustrated* football story is "a story that will be appealing to readers and something that is going to illustrate colorfully" (personal communication, July 23, 2003). Therefore, when King suggested to his *Sports Illustrated* editors that the first article about the 2003 NFL preseason training camps should be about Emmitt Smith, the editors agreed. For this article there was a compelling story about how the NFL's all-time leading rusher left one of the league's most storied franchises, the Dallas Cowboys, and signed with the Arizona Cardinals. The article that appeared in the August 4, 2003, issue also "illustrated colorfully" with a full-page picture of Smith his new white Cardinal jersey and another insert picture in the red uniform of the Cardinals after spending 13 years in the silver helmet and the white-and-blue uniform of the Cowboys.

Once King writes his article, it then goes through an extensive editing process, which includes one of the three executive editors at *Sports Illustrated*, the managing editor, and fact checkers. Again, it is important to emphasize that these editors can only work on the information included in King's original draft. They relied on King's hustle in talking to many people and gathering all of the relevant information needed for a complete, insightful, and accurate story. They would not want to print the story and then have other relevant facts emerge through the reporting of another mass media outlet that would make the magazine's story irrelevant.

Mike Bevans is one of three executive editors for *Sports Illustrated* whose responsibility is to manage all components of a story, from the writing of the story to the photography that will accompany the article. He is also responsible for distributing the workload for the magazine and ensuring that the entire magazine is completed on time. The *Sports Illustrated* week runs Tuesday through Monday, with late Monday evening being the last opportunity to include or adjust a story, as advance copies of the magazine are available Wednesday and subscribers generally receive their issue in the mail Thursday. With most major sports typically occurring on the weekend, short deadlines make for an intense process to complete the magazine on time. Early in the week the editing staff meets to plan that week's magazine as well as to scope out issues for the next 3 or 4 weeks.

Bevans is one of the people who reads and edits a story, but he explained that a senior editor will do the initial edit as well as write the headline and photo captions for the article (personal communication, August 13, 2003). He pointed out that he is merely one step of the editing process for the entire magazine. The managing editor is the highest ranking day-to-day person involved in the decision-making process and oversees all of the content of the magazine. It is the managing editor who ultimately determines what goes into the magazine and budgets the amount of pages for individual stories. The managing editor also has the important task of selecting the *Sports Illustrated* cover.

Bevans explained that there are certain media routines that dictate the content of a *Sports Illustrated* issue. He described that the front and back of the magazine are standard, with the back including a weekly feature, "The Week Inside Sports" (short sections that provide quick storyline updates about three or four sports), and "The Life of Reilly" (the weekly column by Rick Reilly, which is the last page of the magazine). The front portion of the magazine features letters to the editor, "Catching up With" (a profile of an athlete who once appeared on the cover of an issue of *Sports Illustrated*), and "Scorecard" (which features many one-page stories about an athlete or event). Bevans explained that the editors compete for the rest of the space, as the magazine tries to create a good mix of timely sports news and compelling features. These features are the part of the magazine that can be planned in advance. For example, editors know that in 2 weeks a certain number of pages of the magazine are already allocated for a certain feature.

Alain Sanders was a senior reporter with *Time* magazine, where he worked for 21 years covering everything from the Supreme Court to elections to the Congress, and he worked on *Time*'s international issues distributed in Asia, Latin America, the South Pacific, and Canada. Each of the international issues has specific stories and advertisements for its markets. Sanders said stories originate for *Time* in a manner similar to King's description for *Sports Illustrated*, coming from either the reporter or someone in a higher management position (personal communication, August 8, 2003). Both Sanders and King stressed that seniority and reputation of the reporter in making story suggestions carry tremendous weight.

With *Time* coming out on Monday, Sanders explained that the managing editors and senior editors meet on Monday to begin preparing the magazine for the following week's issue. Senior editors then meet with their staffs to discuss potential stories, paying attention to the news cycle and to whether there are any major political speeches or congressional hearings scheduled for that week. This is an early indication that the role of content providers and their events influence coverage and the need for quality, compelling content. If it is congressional hearings that need to be covered, perhaps interviews with the congressional representatives on the committee or people testifying need to be arranged. Comments and reactions from other members of the government might also be needed to provide a complete context for the story.

After these initial meetings, the general theme of a story is established, and once the reporter gets the assignment, he or she has the freedom to call whomever he or she wants and research whatever information desired. The writer assigned to a story then works with field correspondents as well as does some of his or her own reporting and examines other press clippings in the newspaper to come up with all of the information that might be contained in the story. Sanders stressed that the size of the story is a factor in determining the amount of information that needs to be obtained.

The writer then sends a "polished draft" to the senior editor Friday night. The senior editor and one of the top editors both read the article and make corrections and suggestions in a different print font so that the writer knows which person is making the comment. The story then goes back to the writer, who then works with the editors to correct any discrepancies before returning the story to a senior editor for a final review. In the editing process researchers also provide input and check for accuracy, and correspondents receive an edited version to check for accuracy and any omissions. Near the end of the editing process, lawyers from *Time* read the story to check for potentially libelous material.

Karen Blumenthal is the Dallas bureau chief for the *Wall Street Journal* and is responsible for the content output of the bureau, overseeing reporters in eight states. She described that most of the story ideas come from the reporters who are out in the field, but there are instances where the direction of stories does come from the main New York office (personal communication, September 5, 2003). This example depicts the layers of a mass media organization between management and the reporters who are at various locations covering stories. Blumenthal explained that the *Wall Street Journal* has a steady stream of news within its routine, as the scope of its newspaper is that whenever there are financial filings it is in essence a news story.

Mike Emanuel is a correspondent for the Fox News Channel and has reported on the White House, the Pentagon, and other areas of government. In this capacity as a national television reporter, he does both taped segments and live appearances to provide an update on a story. Emanuel stated that his goal as a journalist is to "talk to people on all sides of an issue and to present the story from all sides to provide a well balanced report and let the viewers decide their opinion" (personal communication, January 14, 2004). Although Emanuel described his reports as a collaborative effort with producers, he contended that it is a positive collaborative effort where he maintains a great deal of autonomy and a great amount of input into what gets on the air.

DAVE ANDERSON AND *THE NEW YORK TIMES*

There are, of course, instances when a reporter and upper management disagree over a position on an issue, and the content provided to an audience is compromised. One notable situation was a controversy over the *New York Times*, when it initially rejected two sports columns: one by Pulitzer Prize winning–columnist Dave Anderson and the other by Harvey Araton. The columns by Anderson and Araton opposed the *New York Times* editorial page on the issue of women being admitted to membership of the Augusta National Golf Club, host of the prestigious Masters golf tournament every April. The *New York Times* editorial page had repeatedly criticized the Augusta National Golf Club for having a male-only membership policy and called for Tiger Woods not to play in the 2003 tournament as a form of protest to the policy. The column by Anderson held that the Masters controversy was not the responsibility of Woods and that Woods should play without criticism. Anderson began his article with, "Please, let Tiger Woods just play golf. That's what he does, and does better than anybody else. He's not a social activist. He never has been. And it's unlikely he ever will be. It's not his style. All he wants to do is win golf tournaments, especially the Masters and the other three major tournaments" (Anderson, 2002, p. 1).

The alleged reason the columns did not run, according to Anderson, was the disagreement with the editorial page. Anderson stated, "It was decided by the editors that we should not argue with the editorial page" (cited in Colford, 2002a, p. 50). He commented, "I didn't consider what I wrote an attack on the editorial page, just a difference of opinion" (cited in Singhania, 2002). Anderson also stated, "I was disappointed that they felt that way, but the editorial page is sacrosanct there. I always thought you could still disagree with it. But in this case I couldn't" (cited in Kurtz, 2002, p. C1).

The position of the *New York Times* editors on why the articles did not appear was not that they differed from the editorial page but that they "failed to meet newsroom standards" (cited in Singhania, 2002). The *New York Times* had released a staff memo in which Gerald Boyd, *New York Times* managing editor, stated, "We were not concerned with which 'side' the writers were on. A well-reported, well-reasoned column can come down on any side, with our welcome. One of the columns focused centrally on disputing *The Times*'s editorials about Augusta. Part of our strict separation between the news and editorial pages entails not attacking each other. Intramural quarreling of that kind is unseemly and self-absorbed" (cited in Singhania, 2002). Boyd also stated, "It's not whether he (Anderson) had a different view from the editorial. It's how he [Anderson] executes it" (cited in Kurtz, 2002, p. C1). He added, "I have no problem with columns saying something different than the [*Times'*] editorial stance" (cited in Colford, 2002b, p. 1).

A critical aspect of this story is that the person with the most notoriety in this situation was Anderson and not the executives at the *New York Times*. Other sports columnists demonstrated support for Anderson in their own columns, on sports radio, and on television programs such as ESPN's *The Sports Reporters*. After receiving national criticism for not printing the columns, on Sunday, December 8, 2002, the *New York Times* decided to run both the Anderson and Araton columns beginning at the bottom of the front page of the sports section with the following disclaimer: "The two columns appearing here are revisions of versions withheld by *The Times* about two weeks ago. The columnists have agreed to revisions requested by the editors" (*New York Times*, December 8, 2002, section 8, p. 1). As for the controversy as a whole, Anderson commented, "I've always thought a newspaper should have various opinions. That's what the columns are for, and that's what the editorial page is for. You should be certainly allowed to disagree with editorials. It makes for a better paper" (cited in Singhania, 2002). Anderson added, "When these columns don't appear, they cause more commotion" (cited in Singhania, 2002).

INTERNAL MASS MEDIA SUMMARY

The gatekeeping process is difficult to generalize across all mass media organizations, but there are some commonalities. From a business perspective, all mass media organizations desire quality content that can attract an audience and subsequent advertisers. From a functional performance perspective, all mass media organizations have the ability and responsibility to select and frame messages. Although the selection and framing decisions are simplified through the implementation of routines and an overall philosophy of the type of content desired, several individuals within the mass media organization at some point in the process can influence the content exposed to the audience. Kim (2002) summarized the gatekeeping concept where stories "are accepted or rejected based on various factors, such as journalists' perceptions of a news event, daily working norms, the written and unwritten rules of television news organizations, and extra media pressures as well as societal and cultural influences" (p. 433).

The content decision-making process within the mass media organization can be described through a complex hierarchical progression, where the higher level always has the ability to overrule any lower level, but does not necessarily do so. The selection process begins from within a certain type of story that is established by the overall mass media organization philosophy and media routine of the content desired. This larger philosophical mandate could come from the ownership or the highest executive levels of the mass media organization. The media routines do not account for all decisions, and decisions need to be made within the routine.

Stories are then selected within genre type by the higher ranking day-to-day decision makers who then assign the reporters to cover that story. Certain areas or stories are organized into beats where news generally emerges (i.e., government agencies, sports teams) so that the reporter can learn the area or group and form critical relationships with sources (the media employee and source relationship is explained in more detail in chap. 7). The reporter and photojournalists at the scene then collect the content specific to that story. The evaluation of and decisions about that story are made only from what has been brought back from the scene, giving a tremendous amount of trust and autonomy to the reporters who were assigned to the story (see Table 6.1).

If the day-to-day decision makers are in the eye of the storm, they are surrounded by content providers who are trying to influence content se-

TABLE 6.1
Mass Media Internal Decision Making

Ownership and upper management	Budgets Media routines Brand image Hiring and firing of employees
High-ranking day-to-day executive	Media routine implementation Selection of overall content type Final edit of stories
Mid-level day-to-day management	Assignment of stories Assignment of beats Editing of stories
Reporters and photographers at the scene	Selection of content within that assigned story; framing of elements

lection and framing. The power day-to-day decision makers have in se-lecting and framing content is, however, devalued, as these mass media organizations also need content providers so that they can file a story with all of the necessary perspectives for a complete, accurate report that will appeal to the audience. The interdependent relationship be-tween the mass media organization and content providers is at the core in the evaluation of the complex content decision-making process.

SUGGESTED READINGS

Berkowitz, D. (Ed.). (1997). *Social meaning of news: A text-reader*. Thousand Oaks, CA: Sage.

Kim, H. S. (2002). Gatekeeping international news: An attitudinal profile of U.S. television journalists. *Journal of Broadcasting & Electronic Media, 46*, 431–452.

Kosicki, G. M. (1993). Problems and opportunities in agenda-setting research. *Journal of Communication, 43*(2), 100–127.

Shoemaker, P. J. (1999). Media gatekeeping. In M. B. Salwen & D. W. Stacks (Eds.), *An integrated approach to communication theory and research* (pp. 79–91). Mahwah, NJ: Lawrence Erlbaum Associates.

Soloski, J. (1997). News reporting and professionalism: Some constraints on the re-porting of the news. In D. Berkowitz (Ed.), *Social meaning of news: A text-reader* (pp. 138–154). Thousand Oaks, CA: Sage.

The External Mass
Media Organization:
Constituency Groups

7

Mass Media Organization Interaction With Content Providers

Although there is much to be considered regarding the complex operations within a mass media organization and the structure of its hierarchy on content decision making, the process becomes even more complicated once the potential influence from outside constituency groups is factored into the content decision-making process. Many content providers complicate the process by simultaneously trying to exert their influence on mass media employees. Therefore, the relationship between content providers and the mass media is critical in any evaluation of the decision-making process (e.g., McQuail, 2000).

The major premise of this book is that there are several constituency groups trying to influence, and in some instances are successful in dictating, the content decision making of a mass media organization. Dependency research explains that relationships between the mass media and constituency groups are interdependent, with all entities needing each other. The day-to-day decision makers are always being pulled by people or groups (content providers, advertisers) who are implementing multiple strategies to obtain media coverage. McManus (1994, 1995) pointed out that investors, advertisers, sources, and consumers drive the news production processes at different junctures. Weaver and Wilhoit (1996) found that 34% of journalists thought that forces outside their organization, such as government, a hostile public, or powerful advertisers, were great hindrances to their autonomy. People in different jobs for different organizations all perform their own responsibilities, the efforts of which culminate in the media content the public can see, hear, read, or click onto (e.g., Shaw & Martin, 1992). Some issues or stories receive exposure and become the news and others are never heard, as indicated in the agenda-setting theoretical model.

Content providers are broadly defined as any person or group with a message that needs to be exposed to an audience. They include: entertainment production companies, politicians, companies making news, artists, musical performers, and authors. The content providers are prominent because they are constantly providing news, being asked by the mass media to provide news, or providing comment on news events that have occurred. Content providers try to get exposure for their content because these mass media messages have the potential to influence the audience to behave in a manner that the content provider desires (i.e., purchase, vote).

In trying to achieve these desired behavioral outcomes by the audience, content providers are often represented by professional public relations employees. It is the public relations professionals who have skill and training in crafting messages, carefully selecting their distribution vehicle, and developing relationships with the mass media. External constituency groups, in addition to whatever industry their business is in, need to have communication professionals that deal with the mass media and communicate with any other stakeholder groups with which the organization interacts. Baron (2003) pointed out that other businesses are not in the business of producing news but are experts in their respective industries. He stated, "The public relations industry exists, in part, because companies and organizations that depend on public perception and understanding do not and cannot control the means to gain those perceptions" (p. 39). Although the specific strategies might differ based on the industry or the company, the overall public relations philosophies of representing the employer or client in the most positive light and being proactive on their behalf transcend any industry. Gamson and Modigliani (1989) explained that communication professionals "breed sophistication about the news needs of the media and the norms and habits of working journalists" (p. 6).

THE PUBLIC RELATIONS FUNCTION

The philosophical public relations function begins with the premise that practitioners act as advocates for the clients and organizations they represent. These public relations professionals are entrusted with presenting the person or group they represent in the most positive light to the mass media and audience. Another key public relations philosophical concept is to be proactive in providing information to the mass media before they learn it through other channels. Being proactive is vital, as the alternative is having to explain why the organization or client was not forthcoming with the information, a situation that could create another public relations problem. Public relations is thus essentially about developing and implementing a series of proactive strategic initiatives designed to obtain and frame media coverage on behalf of clients. By presenting the perspective of the client in the news story, public relations professionals hope the audience will learn from that perspective and will be influenced by it.

In explaining the concept of advocacy and client representation, it is important to point out that public relations employees are not under oath and not mandated to provide the truth, the whole truth, and nothing but the truth. This is the most distinct characteristic in separating the public relations professional from the journalist, who is expected to bring a high level of objectivity to the selection and framing of a story. The public relations professional and the journalist perform very different functions in the process. The public relations professionals' objective is in providing honest facts, but their interpretation of facts and events and what they choose to highlight or frame are highly subjective and in their own interests. The journalist must understand that he or she is merely obtaining only one perspective when speaking to a public relations practitioner.

Berger and Park (2003) offered a detailed summary of the public relations function:

> Very broadly, public relations professionals serve organizations by helping them to achieve business goals. Organizations compete with other groups and organizations for attention, sales, markets, employees, favorable policy decisions, and so forth. The goal of such competition may not be to achieve consensus, but rather to survive and win conflicts. Thus, the public relations programs are carried out to attempt to influence stakeholder attitudes, opinions, perceptions, interpretations, ideologies, and choices to achieve outcomes favorable to the organization. (p. 79)

If they are trying to influence opinion with business objectives (i.e., sales) in mind, it becomes incumbent on public relations professionals to do everything within their power to influence the content that could potentially influence public opinion and behavior. A central part of the question as to if and how public relations personnel influence the mass media is to define the goals of public relations strategies. These goals include the managerial function of public relations to help achieve two-way communications with key publics and to balance the interests of the organization and those publics through dialogue, compromise, and conflict strategies (e.g., Berger & Park, 2003; Cutlip, Center, & Broom, 1994; Grunig, 1990; Seitel, 1998).

Although their responsibility is to their employer, the most interesting relationship for public relations practitioners is with the mass media, as their job is to build and capitalize on these relationships to influence content. Bernays (1955) provided a seminal view of public relations, defining it as "the attempt, by information, persuasion, and adjustment, to engineer public support for an activity, cause, movement, or institution" (pp. 3–4). It is more than public support that is necessary or desired; that support needs to turn into a tangible behavior of purchasing, voting, or some other activity that clearly provides a benefit to the content provider. Support becomes too ambiguous a term to identify as the sole achievement desired. To support a candidate for an election does not matter unless the person's tangible behavior of voting for the candidate, or telling and persuading others to vote, or making a campaign donation is performed. Support without engaging in any behavior is almost tantamount to offering no support. At some point behavior needs to occur, and if the desired behavior does not occur the public relations person needs to reevaluate and readjust the message of the communication strategy, either through placement of the message or framing of the message, that might resonate with the audience. The spiral of opportunity perspective of Miller and Riechert (2001) articulated the critical evaluation of media messages necessary by the public relations department to capitalize on the opportunity to craft further messages.

Any power of the public relations practitioner in the content process stems from access to information and people that mass media organizations and their audiences desire. The public relations power emanates from the dependency characteristics inherent in the mass media organization that needs to obtain quality content. If the work of public relations practitioners did not matter and the mass media ignored their tactics, the mass media organizations would become enormously powerful in the relationship. However, that is not often the case, and if public relations practitioners have information or a commodity, in terms of a client the mass media would like to interview, perhaps the pendulum of power in the relationship swings in the direction of public relations.

Public relations people understand their clients' assets in dealing with the mass media and understand the various mass media organizations and which types of stories those organizations desire. They understand that different types of stories will work in different mass media vehicles. First, there are many media outlets, each with different content desires and each with different audiences. For example, for the same issue within the same genre of television, the type of content desired by the evening news, a short sound bite with video, is different from that network's morning show, a sit-down or live interview, and different from that network's prime-time news magazine, a lengthy feature interview that will be heavily produced and edited. For each content provider, knowing which mass media outlet to target with a particular message is important, as it can be a waste of time and effort to target the wrong mass media outlet. One key factor in understanding the media vehicle is for the public relations department to understand the type and size of the audience that mass media organizations and their various forms of content attract.

The changing mass media environment has had an impact on public relations practices, as there are more options for content providers to get their message out into the news. The number of news media outlets, particularly cable television all-news networks and the Internet, have greatly changed the amount of news content that gets into the public discourse. The Internet has reduced the necessity on the mass media to some extent, as now content providers from corporations to music performers can have their own Internet site where people can directly go to learn about them. This is a major advantage for the content provider as it eliminates concerns about whether the content is even selected and how it will be framed. By circumventing the mass media organization, organizations can provide unfiltered content to their audience.

Berger and Park (2003) stated that public relations "practitioners invest in new technologies to gain efficiency, relationship, and control benefits. Practitioners use new technology channels especially to increase the speed and reach of communication. However, they also seek to strengthen and extend stakeholder relationships and increase control over message content and distribution" (p. 77). E-mail has created a new method for public relations practitioners to communicate with members of the mass media and even some select, important audiences (e.g., Henninger, 2001). Mark Beal, executive vice president for Alan Taylor Communications public relations firm, pointed out that the changing media environment, with more media inventory to work with and more people looking for content, is better for his clients because there is more opportunity for exposure (personal communication, January 23, 2004).

Baron (2003) made clear distinctions between the old mass media environment and the new media environment created by communication technologies. He explained that for all of the groups to be successful in the new media environment they must understand the changes that have taken place. Baron offered nine rules for content providers to understand if they are to be successful in creating and dis-seminating messages (see Table 7.1).

In addition to understanding the philosophical approach and func-tion of public relations, all of the characteristics of fostering relation-ships with media members—knowledge of client assets, knowledge of the mass media environment, and knowledge of the mass media organizations and their needs—have to be understood in developing, implementing, and executing an effective public relations communi-cation strategy.

PUBLIC RELATIONS PRACTITIONER PERSPECTIVE

Bob Sommer is an executive vice president with The MWW Group, one of the largest public relations and public affairs firms in the United States. The MWW Group, started in 1986, is headquartered in East

TABLE 7.1
Baron's (2003) Public Relations Rules for the New Media Environment

Rule 1:	Old:	Meet the demands of the media.
	New:	Meet demands of a wide variety of stakeholders who expect immediate and direct information.
Rule 2:	Old:	Follow news cycles.
	New:	There is a new cycle every minute.
Rule 3:	Old:	Bad news usually goes away quickly.
	New:	Bad news can be controlled by opponents and politicians and frequently has a long life.
Rule 4:	Old:	Accuracy above all.
	New:	Speed above all.
Rule 5:	Old:	Legal review optional.
	New:	Legal review required.
Rule 6:	Old:	Provide the minimum needed.
	New:	Provide what the most detail-hungry audience requires.
Rule 7:	Old:	Assume some level of news balance.
	New:	Someone is going to be wearing the black hat.
Rule 8:	Old:	Wait for them to call.
	New:	Credibility depends on getting to them first.
Rule 9:	Old:	Let the media tell your story.
	New:	Tell the story yourself.

Rutherford, New Jersey and has seven national offices located in Chicago, Los Angeles, New York, Seattle, Trenton, and Washington, D.C. Some of the clients for The MWW Group include: Avis, Continental Airlines, Hard Rock Cafe, McDonald's, Nike, Nikon, and Verizon. The values of The MWW Group are, "We are committed to delivering strategic solutions that drive client success" (MWW Group). The public relations mission of The MWW Group is:

> To create smart, strategic and creative communications programs that provide tangible results to help clients achieve their most important business objectives, offer the highest value and ensure clients' return on their public relations investment. To work harder and smarter to ensure that no one has higher expectations to us that we have of ourselves and the work we produce for clients. To constantly set higher standards for our industry—in our strategic approach to public relations, in the innovative programs and campaigns we create for our clients and through the dynamic, energetic and stimulating environment that we provide for our employees. (www.mwwgroup.com)

In his executive role, Sommer manages the public affairs and acts as a liaison to the mass media and to the government for The MWW Group's corporate clients. The responsibilities include helping clients formulate the right message and assisting in getting placement of these messages into the proper media. Sommer stressed that the power in the relationship between himself and his clients (content providers) and the mass media is often only in pitching a story (personal communication, August 7, 2003). His knowledge of the mass media industry and the desires of the various media outlets are critical functions of the job and become apparent in certain circumstances. For example, Sommer conceded that there are times when he can shop around a story on a prominent CEO to the mass media outlet that will provide the best exposure. In this instance, if he can provide an exclusive with a top executive, and one newspaper will only put the story on the front page of the business section but another will put it on the front page of the entire newspaper, the paper providing exposure on the front page of the entire newspaper will get the exclusive story.

Sommer pointed out that it is in times of a crisis for a client when the dynamics of the relationship between the public relations office and the mass media greatly changes. In a crisis, his firm operates within a crisis management plan where the firm and the client operate according to certain protocols. He stressed that during a crisis often he or executives from the client have to talk to the media and merely have to work to get the client's message out, as there is no time to shop around for the best media exposure. In this instance it is important to get a message out on behalf of the client so that the client's perspective is at least part of the dialogue. The alternative is simply having other groups define the news story. Sommer concluded that so much of his tactical strategy and the overall content decision-making process at the interaction level depends on two critical components coming together: "the fostering of relationships with the mass media and the nature of the story that is being dealt with" (personal communication, August 7, 2003). Any variations of these components can vastly alter the nature of the mass media coverage and the tactics used by the public relations department.

Terry Hemeyer is a former communications executive for Pennzoil, handling all of its public relations for 16 years and serving in management in his final 6 years with the corporation. Hemeyer was also a former spokesperson for the U.S. Air Force Academy. He claimed that public relations and the mass media should be a professional relationship, but stressed that underlying all strategies it is important to understand that reporters and public relations practitioners are not doing the same job and do not have common goals. Although the reporter's goals are to be objective, as a public relations person, Hemeyer pointed out that he is there to serve the client and to provide facts that are the most positive, emphasizing on certain facts to assist in the framing of the story. In dealing with the media, Hemeyer explained that his basic philosophy is to not expect favors from members of the mass media but rather to have a simple goal in terms of influencing content by getting his clients' perspective of the story into the article or broadcast. Hemeyer stated, "I'm not looking for egregious breaks, but give me my say in the article. That is all I ask, it could be the last paragraph, but give me my say" (personal communication, August 29, 2003).

In trying to get a perspective into a story, Hemeyer suggested that it is important for public relations professionals to understand the mass media news industry and work to build long-term credibility with the media by knowing their deadlines; being reliable and returning telephone calls; and, if not able to provide comment about a story, telling the reporter why. In establishing relationships with the media, Hemeyer claimed that it is better to "error on the side of being cooperative with the press" (personal communication, August 29, 2003). Similar to Sommer, Hemeyer commented that long-term credibility is helpful when pitching stories, and this credibility can be powerful in helping a client's perspective become part of the story. Providing reliable information in the past helps attain coverage, whereas providing unreliable information will eliminate any trust and hinder future coverage.

Clint Woods is an account supervisor for Pierpont Communications, a public relations firm that assists clients with their public relations, investor relations, and marketing communications. The assistance that Pierpont Communications provides its clients is to help establish an image and help them determine the type of stories they have that are newsworthy to obtain media exposure. Woods explained that his responsibility is to know the clients, their assets, and the mass media outlet possibilities. Matching the interests of both of these groups can result in success and a favorable media placement.

Woods contended that he has little influence over the mass media and although he will pitch stories, he stressed that there has to be a story to tell and he has to be creative in how that story is positioned or the mass media will not cover the story. He importantly stressed that the story has to be of interest to the audience the mass media organization is trying to or has already reached. Although public relations departments pitch ideas, people within the mass media organization develop their own story ideas and simply contact the public relations department to obtain information needed for a story they are already covering. With intense competition for time and space, not assisting or facilitating the press in acquiring all of the necessary elements for a story could ensure a lack of coverage. Woods concluded, "You have to respect the job of the press and work with them. You can't play hardball with reporters and often good public relations involves being good facilitators" (personal communication, September 12, 2003).

Beal, executive vice president with Alan Taylor Communications, a leading sports and fitness public relations agency, defined his responsibility as to generate media coverage for events and initiatives of Alan Taylor's clients, which have included: Adidas, AT&T, Chevrolet, MasterCard, Microsoft, Nabisco, Reebok, Texaco, and the U.S. Postal Service. In terms of generating media coverage, these responsibilities include developing the programs and strategies for client initiatives and calling media and pitching these stories to the media.

Beal also emphasized the common theme critical for the public relations professional to learn not only of the clients' assets but also to learn of the various media outlets and the types of content they desire. He explained that "it is important to identify the right outlet for the right content" and that it is his job to "leverage the assets of our clients and generate media coverage using their assets" (personal communication, January 23, 2004). He provided an example where CNN's Financial Network has a program where everyday it features a CEO of a company. Beal's knowledge of this need on the part of this media organization helps so that if one of his client corporations is about to break news, such as introducing a new product or announcing a strong financial quarter, he can go directly to this media outlet and get the CEO of that company on the air.

Beal explained that stories need to be pitched in a compelling manner to the media, and one effective way to accomplish this is to demonstrate an interest to the audience of that mass media organization. He pointed out that the media are looking for stories too, so the idea is to "create angles and storylines that work for the media in that it will be interesting to their readers, listeners, or viewers" (personal communication, January 23, 2004). He stated there needs to be an explanation to the media professionals of the "strength of what is being pitched to the audience of that mass media organization" (personal communication, January 23, 2004).

Beal claimed that the key is to build relationships with the people at the various mass media organizations. He pointed out that "you can't be lazy" and that "public relations is not about writing a press release or sending a press kit, but getting on the telephone and building a one on one relationship" (personal communication, January 23, 2004). In building relationships, he contended that he will offer exclusives to a particular mass media organization if he has a story that is compelling. Beal explained that they might work hard to give an exclusive to a newspaper such as *USA Today*, noting that broadcast media often take stories from what appears in the newspaper.

Beal explained that another critical factor in pitching a story is the availability of the people from a client. He pointed out the public relations practitioner has to be aware of the timing and understand that appearances on television programs are booked well in advance, and even newspapers or magazines are blocked with stories in advance. If there is ample time for a person to speak with or appear with several media outlets, he will take advantage of the client's time. A more careful selection of the mass media outlet has to occur if the client does not have unlimited time to cater to a variety of mass media outlets. In these situations of limited availability, Beal claimed that generally the pitch will be made to the media outlet that will achieve the highest number of viewers or readers.

Another important aspect that Hemeyer emphasized in the public relations and mass media relationship deals more with the issue of managing internal public relations (personal communication, August 29, 2003). Public relations professionals are cognizant of the workings of the mass media and their desire to obtain a major story. It is the public relations people who have the expertise in answering questions and phrasing responses to assist a desired framing of the story. There are, however, instances where comments from a professional spokesperson are not enough for the situation and the mass media will not put the comments from that person on the air or in a prominent location of a print story. In these instances it is an executive, whose expertise is in running the corporation of that industry and not in media relations, who has to speak to the media.

Hemeyer stressed that when a corporate executive is about to be interviewed, it is imperative that the public relations department learns or estimates what the reporter is going to ask, to prepare the executive as to those questions, and assist in the formulation and delivery of responses. This preparation and training, which could include conducting mock interview sessions, can be vital in what actually becomes part of the public dialogue and influences the perception of the story. An executive saying the wrong thing only creates a further crisis and another element of the story that now has to be addressed by the public relations department. In echoing the sentiments of Sommer, Hemeyer pointed out that this is especially important when dealing with crisis management, as in those cases the story is going to be written (so the issue is not selection) and you have to try to get your message into that story (to try to influence its framing). The public relations people know what the story might look like (how it is going to play in the press), and the internal training of executives is essential.

Hemeyer stated that during a crisis, communication within the corporation is important, and training employees to know and be prepared to execute their roles in a crisis-management situation must be conducted. One important component is for employees not to speak to reporters and allow only one spokesperson to address any mass media inquiries. Achieving this requires great discipline on the part of the employees during the crisis, as it is conceivable they too have relationships with members of the media and have previously been used as sources. It is in this situation that their philosophical understanding of advocacy on behalf of their client must be executed.

To assist the important internal aspects of a crisis, Hemeyer gave all of the key people within the corporation a small card that fits in their wallet and provides instructions about how to handle telephone calls from a media member. Generally, this card instructs the employee to tell the reporter to call the proper spokesperson responsible for talking to the media. The person within the corporation who received the call is then instructed to call Hemeyer, who then returns the reporter's call. The importance of this crisis-management strategy is so there is consistency in the message and various people within the corporation are not providing different viewpoints or damaging statements to the media. Hemeyer claimed that overall "public relations work is more on the defensive rather than the offensive (i.e., pitching stories)" (personal communication, August 29, 2003).

THE NATURE OF THE INTERACTION

Understanding the general public relations philosophies of advocacy on behalf of their clients in presenting them in the most positive light, being honest with the press, and being proactive are essential in the complex interaction between content providers and the mass media. With so many different mass media organizations, examining the relationship between mass media personnel and content providers and establishing general principles are difficult tasks. There are an infinite number of relationships, each with specific organizations, specific people, and a specific set of circumstances (the nature of the story) involved. Inherent in examining the process of interaction between content providers and mass media personnel is to establish that they do need to interact. As described in the media dependency theoretical model, the relationship between content providers and media personnel is interdependent, as the mass media organizations need these content providers to fill their broadcast, Internet site, or publication with quality content that will attract an audience and, subsequently, advertisers.

Curran, Gurevitch, and Woollacott (1982) described that mass media organizations "exist in a symbiotic relationship with their environment, drawing on it not only for their economic sustenance but also for the 'raw materials' of which their contents are made" (p. 20). Content becomes a product of what other people provide and what is accessible. Bagdikian (2000) claimed, "The national news has a major impact on the national political agenda. What the main media emphasize is what politicians attend to. Whatever is not given steady emphasis in the news is more safely forgotten by those who make laws and regulations" (p. xxvii). Content can only be determined from what the mass media organization can acquire. Loevinger (1968) argued in his reflective-projective theory that the media cannot create or project an image that does not reflect something that already exists.

Through all of the public relations initiatives employed in the hopes of obtaining and framing coverage, public relations personnel are, in essence, making the job of the reporter easier by providing them with a viable story, and, at the same time, providing a tremendous benefit to their employer or client by obtaining free, positive publicity. Molotch and Lester (1974) demonstrated that news could be dictated by those in a position to manage publicity about events. They contended that news stories are often promoted as news by the planners of the event.

Cameron, Sallot, and Curtin (1997) spoke to the value of public relations, claiming "public relations efforts increase the probability that an event or issue will be covered, thereby achieving communication objectives for the organization" (p. 112). There is skill to public relations, and certain communities and interest groups are not covered well because they are not good advocates and do not know how to get covered (e.g., Sandman, Rubin, & Sachsman, 1976). Ryan et al.

(2001) pointed out that not all content providers have the same capacity to get their issues or their perspectives about issues into the content of the mass media. They explained, "The lack of resources available to marginalized groups represents an enduring problem in efforts to advance their definitions of political issues through the news media. In contrast, the considerable resources available to those who hold institutional power contribute to their sponsorship of frames and to their ability to have these frames influence public discourse" (p. 179). Ryan et al. added that journalists are often favoring official sources or those holding institutional power or "relying on credentialed experts to provide an analytical understanding of the forces that shape this world" (p. 180).

In examining the *New York Times* and *Washington Post* over a 20-year period, Sigal (1973) found that nearly half of their news stories were based on press releases and other direct information from a content provider. Morton (1992/1993) pointed out that only 3% to 8% of all press releases are published, with some publishers having publication rates as high as 30%. Blyskal and Blyskal (1985) estimated that as much as 50% of the business news in the *Wall Street Journal* originates from press releases or story suggestions by public relations professionals. More recent estimates vary, indicating that news releases influence as little as 25% or as much as 80% of news coverage (e.g., Cameron et al., 1997). Callison (2002) found that out of all the Fortune 500 company Internet sites, those with the more elaborate media press rooms on the web were ranked higher on the *Fortune* list in terms of revenues. Carroll and McCombs (2003) suggested that the findings of Callison indicate "many companies are quite attune to the influence the media have and make significant efforts to cater to the information needs of the media" (p. 14).

Morton (1992/1993) spoke to the necessity of the public relations practitioner having a clear understanding of the mass media industry, knowing the assets of a client in pitching stories to appreciating the desires and needs of the mass media organization and the readers, viewers, or listeners of that media organization's content. Morton stated, "Practitioners who have higher rates for their press releases: (1) write in a simpler style, (2) select different types of information and package information differently than the rest of us. Most importantly, (3) they make their releases relevant to the readers of their targeted newspapers" (p. 9). Shoemaker and Reese (1996) pointed to the negative aspects of simply copying and pasting press releases into the newspaper, claiming "the rise of the press release and press conference reduced the ability of reporters to get scoops and inside stories. At the same time, it made journalists more easily manipulable due to their dependence on the news flow of public relations-generated information" (p. 127).

The mass media can still exert their power by rejecting stories or not accepting interpretations of stories being provided by public relations practitioners. Simply because a story or perspective is provided does not, and should not, mean it has to be printed or broadcast. The mass media employee as the final arbiter is an important factor in giving a sense of freedom of the public relations professional in that he or she is not making the ultimate determination as to what is included in the story's content. Ethically, public relations professionals can be more comfortable with the mandate of their job as there are the mass media gatekeepers with the responsibility to do their job objectively. As Schudson (1997) stated, "Journalists write the words that turn up in the papers or on the screen as stories. Not government officials, not cultural forces, not 'reality' magically transforming itself into alphabetic signs, but flesh-and-blood journalists literally compose the stories we call news" (p. 8).

Bevans, executive editor of *Sports Illustrated*, noted that the magazine constantly receives calls from public relations professionals, not so much to influence a story that is being done but mainly to suggest stories and try to get into the magazine. The editorial staff at *Sports Illustrated* has the ability simply to reject these advances. Pitching stories would largely be for the feature portions of the magazine, as different from news, sports stories are dictated by the sports calendar and the sports audience is aware of what the main sports stories will be. The sports media and sports fans know that late in January is the Super Bowl, March is dominated by the college basketball tournament, the first Saturday in May is the Kentucky Derby, and October brings the World Series. In news, events from the world of politics, business, health, technology, or any other industry can be a major story at any time.

THE NATURE OF THE INTERACTION: SOURCES

Therefore, proficient public relations professionals can assist in obtaining and framing coverage. They understand the audience they desire and the mass media outlets that can reach that audience. Talented public relations professionals understand the mass media organization and the individual reporter as to the types of stories they desire. The interaction between these two groups is based on relationships. From the mass media perspective, this is where the system of beat reporting depends on familiarity, with both the location the reporters are covering and the sources who are providing information. Events happen, and the media employees know whom to reach out to, and as events happen, public relations professionals know whom to reach out to. People within several organizations become valuable sources for media members.

The relationship with sources is where the characteristics of interdependency emerge. Gandy (1982) pointed out that the relationship between a media news organization and its sources is one of mutual need. McQuail (2000) stated that "media of all kinds depend on having a readily available supply of source material" and that "relations with news sources are essential to news media and they often constitute a very active two-way process. The news media are always looking for suitable content, and content (not always suitable) is always looking for an outlet in the news" (p. 287). Bagdikian (2000) claimed that it should be more than a desire on the part of the media to use expert sources but necessary to have experts that challenge the powerful establishment. He stated, "It is a necessary function of the news media to report what the government is doing. But it is equally essential to report reputable authorities who express views and realities that are contrary to the rhetoric of Congress, and to make clear the best known reliable information from independent authorities" (p. xxviii).

It is the need for quality content and access to the organizations that people care about and the sources within these organizations (i.e., government departments, sports teams) that reveals that not all sources are equal. The inequality stems from a couple of factors: the audience's desire to hear about a particular organization (the audience wants to hear officials from within the White House and the presidential administration the same way they want to hear from players on the New York Yankees) and the resources (time, money, and personnel) that these prominent organizations put into getting their message out. The mass media therefore do not and cannot treat each organization they cover and each source within any one organization in the same manner. Simply stated, news is made by the nature of the organization or the person making news (e.g., Schultz, Mouritsen, & Gabrielsen, 2001; Shaw & Martin, 1992).

Gans (1979) defined sources as "the actors whom journalists observe or interview, including interviewees who appear on the air or who are quoted in ... articles, and those who only supply background information or story suggestions" (p. 80). He identified four factors that indicate the performance of a source: (a) the ability of the source to provide a useful and steady flow of information, (b) the media incentive to use the source as the source is eager to provide information or create media events and is credible, (c) source reputation and power, and (d) source geographic location. Sources understand the media function. Sigal (1973) stated that public relations practitioners adjust "their thinking to newsmen's conventions. They talk the same language" (p. 75). Gamson and Modigliani (1989) added, "Smart sources are well aware of the journalist's fancy for the apt catchphrase and provide suitable ones to suggest the frame they want" (p. 7).

Sources must be reliable and credible, as Morton (1992/1993) explained that a successful source will provide information at the right time and in a format geared for that medium. Mass media organizations also look to sources who have provided credible information in the past (e.g., Berkowitz, 1991; Weaver & Elliot, 1986). Gandy (1991) examined how the source of mass media content performs a gatekeeping function. He stated, "Whereas the journalist selects from an array of sources and events on the basis of perceived utility in producing news that will meet organizational requirements, sources select from an even larger array of techniques on the basis of their relative efficiency in the production of influence over the knowledge, attitudes, and behavior of others" (p. 273).

In studying a radio station, Burns (1998) found that of all the material delivered to the station by sources, only 19% of the items collected were used in the broadcast and 20% of the items sent by sources were never opened. Burns indicated that this finding suggests that the credibility of the source is more important than the actual information contained in the item sent. He pointed out that if the package is not opened, what is inside is immaterial and "what is inside appears to not be as important as who, or what organization, sent it" (p. 98). Burns concluded that "what is discarded may be a better indication of the gatekeeper thought process than what is used" (p. 99).

It is the role of public relations personnel and sources influencing media content that raises the question of who sets the agenda. Salwen (1988) claimed that the media agenda is not created within media news organizations as much as it is shaped by the sources that provide them with information. Kanervo and Kanervo (1989) pointed out that when a source succeeds in having its information used in a newscast, it is not only a victory for the source but essentially a loss for others, as time and space have been taken away. The relationship with news sources can be best summed up as the press always wanting to get more information and the content provider always wanting to give only the information favorable to the client.

The role of public relations and the releasing of information are complicated if the issue also has legal ramifications. Conflicts are fought in the court of law and the court of public opinion, and lawyers and public relations professionals might want to approach the situation far differently. The legal perspective might not want to have the client say anything that could be used in court and damage any impending lawsuit. The public relations department might not be as guarded and encourage communication in getting the perspective of the client out to the public to try to sway public opinion.

By not providing the mass media with a story, or as it has been commonly referred, "feeding the beast," journalists are left finding other perspectives to fill their stories. By giving the mass media something to write or broadcast, the public relations department of the content provider can control, or at the very least help manage, the story. Controlling the story and the flow of information is important in any story as a means of swaying public opinion. If the press is not receiving information, a sense of skepticism that the content provider is concealing something can emerge.

The one situation where controlling information and trying to manage public opinion are the most important is military conflict. (The topic of military and press relations is worthy of an entire volume, but a brief comment is introduced here.) Englehardt (1994) depicted how military personnel controlled the information in the Persian Gulf War of 1991 through their daily briefings and press conferences so to act as the final source and always provide the mass media with a story rather than have the media "create" their own stories. He concluded, "The military seemed to have won an adversarial war against the media by marginalizing the hundreds of reporters on the spot and appealing directly to the American public" (p. 82). Although censorship was voluntary, Jacobs (1992) pointed out that field commanders had latitude in controlling the flow of information, and some imposed harsh restrictions (p. 682). In a military situation, Cooper (1996) claimed that many journalists thought the Gulf War restrictions imposed on the press were "a thinly disguised public relations strategy to keep the home front supportive of the war effort" (p. 15). He pointed out that "conflicts are inevitable between the obligation of the press to inform the general public, and the obligation of the military to successfully conduct war" (p. 3).

Military conflict raises the questions of journalistic objectivity. Heyward, president CBS News, commented on the question of journalistic objectivity during a war before the U.S. campaign to liberate Iraq in 2003, stating:

> We are American citizens also. We're rooting for the U.S. to win, with no apology and with as few casualties as possible. That doesn't mean that we are going to distort our reporting, but it's possible to be a citizen and a patriot and also an objective reporter. So this notion that we're indifferent as to the outcome of the war is absurd, and only an idiot would think that. (cited in Bednarski & Higgins, 2003, p. 55)

Heyward added, "We are going to present the facts in a fair way. We're not advocates. The fact that we want the outcome favorable to the U.S. is obvious to anybody." He also stated, "I think the whole notion of objectivity needs to be understood for what it is. It is a function of fairness and open-mindedness to the facts. It means you don't distort what you find out" (cited in Bednarski & Higgins, 2003, p. 55).

Conflict could easily arise in the relationship between content providers, especially major newsmakers, and a mass media organization. Questions are raised of how much a mass media organization should capitulate to a newsmaker to obtain a story or to land a highly sought-after interview. Controversy came to CBS News after obtaining an interview with Iraq dictator Saddam Hussein before the war with the United States in 2003. Veteran CBS anchor Dan Rather conducted the interview that he and the CBS News staff had worked for more than a year to arrange. CBS News did have to give in on certain conditions to obtain the interview: CBS News was not allowed to use its own cameras and had to wait more than half a day for a copy of the tape while the Iraqis edited the interview (e.g., Carter, 2003b).

The interview received criticism from the White House, who wanted to have a rebuttal of Hussein during the Hussein interview broadcast on *60 Minutes II* on February 26, 2003. The White House offered either Ari Fleischer, (then) White House press secretary, or Dan Bartlett, communications director, to present the administration perspective to appear on the *60 Minutes II* broadcast. CBS, however, balked at that option and would only offer the White House a response if President George W. Bush, Vice President Dick Cheney, or Secretary of State Colin Powell, would appear.

GOVERNMENT SOURCES

The importance in the interaction between sources or public relations professionals and the mass media organization is always heightened in dealing with operations of the government. Shaw and Martin (1992) pointed out that "in totalitarian systems, official agendas may be simply delivered to the press," but that in the United States, "the process is more dynamic and pluralistic, with many players from reporters and public relations specialists to government officials to many other institutions and/or key individuals" (p. 905).

Shoemaker and Reese (1996) explained, "The government provides a convenient and regular flow of authoritative information, which reporters find efficient compared with more labor-intensive research" (p. 130). Although this statement is true, the desire of the people to hear from government officials cannot be overlooked in the mass media's always wanting to obtain their perspective.

Fishman (1980) described that the news organization is centered around beats and that reporters get the largest share of their news from official government agencies, as these agencies provide a steady stream of news. Reporters have a beat assignment to cover the happenings at a particular location or agency (i.e., city hall). The White House holds daily press briefings to express its perspective on the events of the day because it knows that that perspective will be covered by many if not all of the mass media organizations that cover the president. The White House's perspective, therefore, gets to become part of the public dialogue. Often news stories contain remarks from the government officials or organization press spokespersons, even when their comments are predictable. Fishman (1997) stated, "Since reporters mainly 'see' events during city council meetings, at White House press conferences, in arrest reports, and through the announcements of public relations officers, news as a form of knowledge is shaped by the contexts in which agencies present and package occurrences for journalists" (p. 226).

Government press secretaries are critical liaisons with mass media personnel, as they provide access to the officials within their organizations who provide content. Press secretaries are vital not only in obtaining coverage for their organization but in providing the interpretations of events and framing content on behalf of their departments. Assisting the framing of coverage is especially important for government organizations that receive coverage on a regular basis.

Rachel Sunbarger is a spokesperson for the U.S. Department of Homeland Security and is one of the people responsible for developing communication strategies for both long-term department policy initiatives and daily dealings with the press. These communication strategies, similar to public relations departments not involved in the government, could include selecting and pitching stories to the right mass media organization or pitching an exclusive story. In dealing with the press responsible for covering the Department of Homeland Security on a daily basis, she could either get calls from reporters for information or perhaps even for a comment from Tom Ridge, (then) Department of Homeland Security director, for a story they are working on. Other beat reporters simply call and ask what is happening on that day within the department. A call of this nature gives a spokesperson a tremendous opportunity to pitch and provide a story that could reflect well on the organization.

One factor that Sunbarger emphasized in terms of the long-term communication strategy is to be aware of the news cycle (personal communication, January 28, 2004). Even all of the public relations strategies to attain media coverage can become victim to other factors in determining what becomes news. Most notably, what else is occurring in the world at that time (e.g., Behr & Iyengar, 1985)? Stories compete for exposure, as selection is a necessary part of the media process. All of the skill of the most talented public relations professionals in trying to obtain coverage will fail if a bigger story occurs. Even the most meticulous handling of the news cycle and arranging for a media event at a certain place and time can find a story trumped by a major event that news media organizations have to cover. Henninger (2001) commented, "Those in media relations don't like to admit it, but they are often forced to follow the rules set forth by members of the press, who frequently are scrambling around to meet deadlines" (p. 12).

Sunbarger commented that she must be aware of the other stories that other government departments might be announcing at a certain time so that any major policy announcement coming out of the Department of Homeland Security will receive the amount of coverage desired. The news cycle in this instance relates more to competing groups and ideas trying to obtain coverage than it does to getting the story to the press to comply with a deadline. She explained that the public relations department is responsible for assisting the communications of Department of Homeland Security Director, Ridge, and her job as an advocate is to "craft a message that shines best on the department" (personal communication, January 28, 2004). Sunbarger also highlighted another interesting variable in working for the Department of Homeland Security in that it is part of the president's Cabinet and it works for the administration and therefore has to work in concert with the White House press office to keep everyone on the same message.

David Wald is the director of communications for New Jersey Senator Jon Corzine and was a reporter for the *Newark Star-Ledger* for more than 20 years. Wald described his responsibility as disseminating and explaining Senator Corzine's perspective on issues to the many media outlets. In knowing that obtaining television coverage is difficult for Senator Corzine because of the competition with the New York news market in the northern part of the state and with the Philadelphia news market in the south, Wald explained that the Corzine communications team still relies heavily on newspapers to reach the audience (personal communication, May 28, 2003).

Wald did, however, concede that in the end it is still the decision of the mass media whether the content he sends them will make the broadcast or the newspaper. He commented that as a former veteran reporter for the *Newark Star-Ledger*, the media do need contacts and there is on occasions pressure to get a story with an elected official. In his role as director of communications, Wald, however, believes he is not in a position to negotiate access to the senator for favorable media coverage. Wald stated, "The worst thing I can do is play games with the relationship [with the press] and hold grudges" (personal communication, May 28, 2003).

Presenting all sides of an issue is important for the viewer to develop the best informed opinion of a story. Wilson, vice president and editor in chief for usatoday.com, claimed that *USA Today* is conscious of the language that could be used in a story and tries to be neutral and objective (personal communication, June 14, 2004). He explained that decisions about language are part of the everyday decision-making process, with higher executive editors providing guidance or dictating phrasing as necessary. Emanuel, Fox News correspondent, pointed out that "everyone in Washington has an agenda so it is critical to balance the voices and give a correct account and a fair representation of the issue" (personal communication, January 14, 2004). He explained that it is a challenge to reach for all perspectives but indicated the importance of this approach in that "a good source has a reason for talking to you and often is very loyal to the cause or the person they are working for. It is the journalist responsibility to determine what is legitimate as you are trusted to report the story fairly" (personal communication, January 14, 2004). Emanuel explained that his philosophy is a reflection of the brand for which he works and that the "fair and balanced" approach of the Fox News Channel "works in a practical way as you think twice to ensure that you examine the other side of an issue and are comprehensive in your reporting" (personal communication, January 14, 2004).

THE OFFICE OF GLOBAL COMMUNICATIONS

The importance of trying to shape the public discourse and influence the news content, which might in turn influence the attitude and behavior of people, is most evident in politics. Politicians always try to make their perspective on an issue part of the dialogue. The White House communications initiatives include daily press briefings, arranging for spokespersons or top Cabinet officials to appear on television news programs or radio programs, and if necessary, the president will hold a prime-time press conference that will certainly be covered. There is an obvious hierarchy in terms of the desire for coverage. If statements from a press official do not guarantee coverage, a Cabinet member might be made available for an exclusive interview. If that does not work and the administration finds the message important and exposure necessary, the vice president or president will make public remarks.

All of these communication strategies have the objective of exposing the administration's perspective to the public. Live speeches covered on television or radio give the president an opportunity to speak directly to the American people and the world without the filter of the mass media. The government, in this instance using the medium as a distribution mechanism, is circumventing the mass media organizations' gatekeeping function instead of having them select only certain quotes from the speech. At this government level of being a content provider, attaining media coverage is easy, as the White House has its own press corps from the respective mass media organizations who cover the White House beat everyday. It is this dependence, as the mass media organizations will always desire and use a quote from the president or a high-ranking official at the White House, that gives tremendous power to any presidential administration and government official in shaping public opinion.

To illustrate the importance of public relations communication strategies in helping explain why certain decisions are made or provide comment on events that are occurring, on January 21, 2002, President George W. Bush signed an executive order establishing the Office of Global Communications. The office was designed to "coordinate strategic communications overseas that integrate the President's themes and truthfully depict America and Administration policies" (Office of Global Communications). The office also "assists in the development of communications that disseminate truthful, accurate, and effective messages about the American people and their government" (http://www.whitehouse.gov/ogc/aboutogc.html). The goal of this communication initiative is stated as "these messages are intended to prevent misunderstanding and conflict, build support for and among United States coalition partners, and better inform international audiences" (White House News Releases).

Section 2 of the executive order provides the mission of the Office of Global Communications stating:

> The Office shall be to advise the President, the heads of appropriate offices within the Executive Office of the President, and the heads of executive departments and agencies on utilization of the most effective means for the United States Government to ensure consistency in messages that will promote the interests of the United States abroad, prevent misunderstanding, build support for and among coalition partners of the United States, and inform international audiences. The Office shall provide such advice on activities in which the role of the United States Government is apparent or publicly acknowledged. (White House News Releases)

In fulfilling this mission, the duties of the Office of Global Communications duties focus on: (a) daily messages, (b) communications planning, and (c) long-term strategy. The office produces a one-page fact sheet, *The Global Messenger*, which is sent worldwide and disseminates key points and daily activities on global issues.

The Office of Global Communications is supported by public affairs offices at many government departments, including the State, Justice, and Defense departments. For example, the State Department has the U.S. Advisory Commission on Public Diplomacy. The bipartisan panel was created by Congress and appointed by the president to "provide oversight of U.S.-government activities intended to understand, inform, and influence foreign publics" (www.state.gov/r/adcompd/).

THE INTERACTION SUMMARY

Ivy Ledbetter Lee is considered to be the father of modern public relations. Lee (1997) offered perspective of public relations and the critical relationship with the mass media, stating, "Nothing is more ridiculous than the idea that anybody can get the papers to print what he [or she] wants them to print" (p. 3). He claimed that "if you want a subject to get on the first page of the newspapers, you must have the news in your statement sufficient to warrant it getting on the first page" (p. 3). Lee summarized:

> Editors of newspapers print what they do print because they have been taught by long experience that certain things, which are said to have news value, are the items which the public will be interested to read. Their estimate of the news value of an article is entirely with reference to the probability of its being read by a substantial number of the leaders of that publication. Now if the trained judgment of these men [and women] does not make them feel that a particular item will be read, what is the use of getting it printed. (p. 4)

All of these public relations strategies have to emanate from a larger philosophy that the work done in public relations can make a difference in the content decision-making process and positively influence the public perception of the organization or client. If people in public relations did not think they could make a difference in the decision-making process, their showing up for work would be pointless.

Fortunato (2000) claimed that "public relations practitioners have the ability to assist the production of mass media content through various proactive public relations strategies that are designed to promote and present the organization they represent in the most positive manner" (p. 481). He added, "Public relations practitioners must operate from an assumption that they have the power to influence mass media content, acting as an advocate on behalf of the organization they represent through the public relations strategies they implement" (p. 482). The idea is that these strategies will help the media select stories that favor the client or frame the content so that it will favorably influence the opinion and behavior of the audience. Fortunato summarized:

> Although many public relations initiatives involve utilizing the mass me- dia to reach the audience, it is imperative for the public relations practi- tioner to understand that they are very much a power broker in the public relations, mass media, and audience relationship. It behooves the public relations practitioner to assist in the gatekeeping processes of selecting and framing mass media content and not simply rely on a mass media interpretation of events. It is the responsibility of the public relations practitioner to develop and implement strategies which do pro- actively advocate the organization they represent in the most posi- tive manner. (p. 497)

McQuail (2000) pointed out that there is "little doubt of the potency of media influence on the 'masses,' when effectively managed and di- rected" (p. 36). Skillful public relations personnel have the ability and skill to generate and frame coverage. Regardless of the industry, there is a public relations communication component to every decision that could provide an explanation for the tactics that a corporation or client has undertaken, and getting that explanation to the people through the mass media becomes important. The questions surrounding the na- ture of the interaction are the degree of influence exerted by the con- tent provider and the degree of objectivity maintained by the mass media. Cohen (1963) stated, "The pressure on the correspondent to re- port 'obvious' news seems more compelling to him [or her] than the fear of being 'used' by policy makers to serve their official or personal ends" (p. 30).

Are the mass media merely the distribution vehicle, the interchange, where the powerful organizations always get to have relatively unfet- tered exposure of their messages? Megwa and Brenner (1988) pointed out that "it is possible that the media may be acting as a channel for the transmission of the priorities of actors and social institutions" (p. 46). Shaw and Martin (1992), however, raised the question: "Why should journalists give away nearly all news space to other news sources?" (p. 920). They argued, "If newspaper journalists aggressively enter the news arena on behalf of the entire community they might revive audi- ence interest in a declining industry. Journalists are professionals, not conduits" (p. 920).

On the relationship between public relations practitioners and re- porters, Branham indicated that although public relations can be a ma- jor player in determining content, some in the public relations field want coverage but hate that they cannot always dictate coverage. She commented, "It is ultimately the journalist responsibility in the relationship to learn who they can trust to provide them with good information and is the journalist responsibility to verify that information" (personal communication, March 28, 2003).

Sanders, former senior reporter for *Time* magazine, commented, "Public relations people never wrote a Sanders story" (personal communication, August 8, 2003). He indicated he was often flooded with calls, which he largely did not return, and mail, which he merely kept in a file for use in case he was to do a story on that topic in the future.

Howard Kurtz, media reporter for the *Washington Post*, wrote extensively about the relationship between the Clinton administration and the press. In his book *Spin Cycle*, Kurtz (1998) stated:

> Clinton's performance had helped create the sense that the country was doing fine on his watch. But it was a carefully honed media strategy—alternately seducing, misleading, and sometimes intimidating the press—that maintained this aura of success. No day went by without the president and his coterie laboring mightily to generate favorable headlines and deflect damaging ones, to project their preferred image on the vast screen of the media establishment. (p. xvii)

The revelation of Kurtz's (1998) book is that the public relations communications staff is going to act in a loyal, advocate, and proactive manner to represent their client in the most positive light. Understanding the reporter and source relationship is crucial, as this is where content is being formulated at its earliest stages. Not putting out the message of their client or not trying to attain favorable mass media coverage would be a dereliction of public relations professionals' duties. However, if the mass media simply accepted the messages of the public relations personnel without questioning those statements, that would be a dereliction of their duties. Public relations professionals will always pitch ideas, but the people within the mass media have to sort through these messages and independently evaluate their veracity before passing them on to the public.

SUGGESTED READINGS

Berger, B. K., & Park, D. J. (2003). Public relation(ship)s or private controls? Practitioner perspectives on the uses and benefits of new technologies. *New Jersey Journal of Communication, 11*(1), 76–99.

Bernays, E. L. (1955). *The engineering of consent*. Norman: University of Oklahoma Press.

Burns, J. E. (1998). Information subsidies and agenda building: A study of local radio news. *New Jersey Journal of Communication, 6*(1), 90–100.

Burson, H. (1997). Beyond "PR": Redefining the role of public relations. In G. R. Carter (Ed.), *Perspectives: Public relations* (pp. 16–22). St. Paul, MN: Coursewise Publishing.

Cameron, G. T., Sallot, L., & Curtin, P. A. (1997). Public relations and the production of news: A critical review and a theoretical framework. In B. Burleson (Ed.), *Communication yearbook 20* (pp. 111–115). Thousand Oaks, CA: Sage.

Fishman, M. (1997). News and nonevents: Making the visible invisible. In D. Berkowitz (Ed.), *Social meaning of news: A text-reader* (pp. 210–229). Thousand Oaks, CA: Sage.

Fortunato, J. A. (2000). Public relations strategies for creating mass media content: A case study of the National Basketball Association. *Public Relations Review, 26,* 481–497.

Lee, I. L. (1997). Publicity and propaganda. In G. R. Carter (Ed.), *Perspectives: Public relations* (pp. 3–7). St. Paul, MN: Coursewise Publishing.

CHAPTER

8

Advertisers

Content providers can also be advertisers who use commercials as part of an integrated communication strategy. The integrated mass media approach is one of targeted communications that could include public relations, advertising, and marketing strategies that feature one consistent message from the content provider being told through a variety of mass media outlets. The integrated communication approach could include circumventing any media through the maintenance of an Internet site or direct mail initiatives to certain audiences. Woods, account supervisor for the Pierpont Communications public relations firm, stressed that in the current mass media environment the strategy is for a more integrated approach. Therefore, advertising is essentially another communication strategy of the content provider, often working in conjunction with public relations strategies to convey messages to their audiences.

Even in the context of news, political advertising is a major communication strategy used to influence audience thinking and behavior. For example, in a presidential campaign a candidate will travel to different important battleground states with the hope of obtaining extra free media time in the local newspaper or on the local television news. That strategy is coordinated with and supported by the purchase of advertising time in that geographic area. To complete the integrated communication strategy, direct advertising mailers, phone calls, or e-mail messages might be sent to critical groups, and an Internet site will be developed where people can go to learn about the candidate.

At its core, any attempt to influence media content by advertisers is similar to that of public relations. The ultimate goal of many public relations campaigns is to influence public behavior (i.e., sales, voting). This goal is no different from advertising and offers the greatest similarities between the two fields. Although the communication strategies might be different, the idea of improving the image of a corporation or an individual client to influence audience behavior is the goal of both advertisers and public relations. Perhaps the corporation will implement public relations strategies that improve its image and make people feel good about their purchase and the corporation or person they are supporting, but the goal is still to try to persuade a purchase.

In public relations, the potential to influence the mass media is debatable and different for every set of circumstances. In public relations, efforts need to be made to gain attention, as stories need to be pitched in a manner that mass media organizations and their audience will find desirable. The public relations objective is in essence to influence the media to obtain coverage and have that coverage be framed in a favorable light to the corporation or client. The advantages of these public relations strategies are that the content provider does not have to purchase broadcast time or space and that the story might appear more credible having passed through the mass media gatekeeping filter. The disadvantage is that the media gatekeeper could choose not to use content or use it in a poor location within the broadcast or publication that has little opportunity of reaching the desired target audience. The framing of the coverage could also include elements of a story not favorable or fail to place an emphasis on the facts desired by the corporation or client.

In advertising, the deal is somewhat cut and dry; the corporation pays a certain dollar amount for a certain media placement location, giving it access to the audience that participates in that mass media organization's content. Advertisers pay large amounts of money because, unlike public relations strategies, their investment guarantees them placement at the time and place desired in the media outlet, giving them the best opportunity to reach the desired target audience. The financial investment for the commercial time or space gives the advertiser control of the content within that time or space. The corporation gets to emphasize the features of its brand that it wants the audience to be most aware of. The disadvantage of advertising is that it is a costly investment and the audience has become fractured with many mass media choices. The audience might not be available for the actual 30 seconds that the commercial broadcast on television or radio, or the audience may have skipped the advertisement in the newspaper or magazine and did not notice it when on an Internet site.

Advertising is an important corporate communication function because the audience gets the idea that advertised products are better (e.g., Carrick, 1959; Sutherland & Galloway, 1981). Much the way and with the same goals that content providers and public relations person-nel try to be agenda setters, so too do advertisers. Sutherland and Galloway (1981) stated, "Products that are advertised heavily have a status conferred upon them—that is, they are felt by customers to be 'the more popular' products. The media are assumed to carry that which is more important, more in demand, more notorious. Just as 'the ordinary person' does not appear on TV, neither does 'the ordinary product' " (p. 27). This is especially important for the first time making a decision about which brand to select in a product category. For ex-ample, if a person needed to rent a car, having never done so before, he or she might immediately think of Hertz or Avis, as those brands are easily recalled because of their repeated advertisements.

Through the mass media and advertising, people learn what these products are and learn which are the reliable brands. There are a cou-ple of caveats to advertising. It is important to note that advertising is not the only message people receive in their evaluation of a brand. In-terpersonal communication with others who have used a certain brand can be a major factor in influencing a purchase decision (e.g., Hunt & Ruben, 1993). People can then experience the brands, and their experience will validate or negate the previously received message. If people have a bad experience with a brand, it will probably negate any advertising that a company might engage in with that customer. Adver-tising can possibly only "fool" the people one time. A bad experience with a brand will cause people not to use that brand in the future, re-gardless of any further advertising attempts. For example, advertising cannot solve an unsatisfactory stay at a hotel, persuading the people who had a bad experience to return to that hotel because they saw a commercial. From all of this information the public makes a determi-nation about which brands to support.

THE ADVERTISING FUNCTION

There are many points between a corporation with a product or service and the final goal of actually putting that product or service in the hands of the consumer and achieving a sale. The initial necessary condition is exposure, getting the audience to learn about the product or service. McAllister (1996) claimed that "advertisers know that the first neces-sary (but not sufficient) condition for persuading a potential customer to buy a product is to force the consumer to notice the message. If the consumer does not see the ad or ignores the ad, then the advertiser's message is wasted" (p. 18). The corporation then provides the cus-tomer with the opportunity to purchase. The location of where the product or service can be obtained is another feature that can be explained in the advertisement. For example, an advertisement for Maytag appliances might include the line "available at Sears." Although the opportunity to purchase might fall equally on product distribution and availability in terms of the ease with which customers can retrieve the product, achieving recognition or product brand recall is an essential function of the advertising department. Overall, each advertising message, whether it is a television commercial, print advertisement, Internet pop-up advertisement, or billboard has three goals: (a) exposure to the desired target audience, (b) increased product brand recall, and (c) increased sales (e.g. Fortunato & Dunnam, 2004).

The strategic advertising function operates on two main criteria to achieve these goals. The first criterion is the proper exposure of the advertisement. Proper media placement relates directly to the initial goal of exposure of the message and getting it noticed by the desired target audience. The second criterion is to put together a creative campaign, which might use humor, feature a celebrity, display a logo, or provide a slogan that could assist in product brand recall. The creative aspect of the advertisement might also feature what the product looks like so that customers can easily recognize it on a store shelf. The optimum condition for the corporation in terms of achieving the ultimate goal of a sale is for its advertisement to be good on both the placement and creative criteria (See Fig. 8.1).

To be successful on only one criterion is to miss out on a critical element that could lead to product brand recall and potential sales. A bad creative advertisement placed in a bad media location might have no chance to achieve the advertising goals, and any purchase made by a customer is due to some other random factor. A good, creative adver-

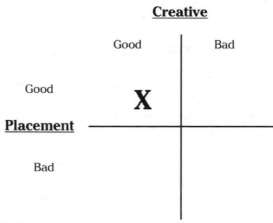

FIG. 8.1. Objectives of an advertising strategy.

tisement might have brand recall, but placed in the wrong media location, it might not obtain exposure to the correct target audience. Conversely, placement in a good media location might gain exposure to the target audience, but if it is not effective creatively the brand might not be recalled. All of these scenarios could hinder achievement of advertising goals.

Tom Breedlove is the managing director of the Ruff, Coffin, and Breedlove advertising agency, overseeing the strategic media and research components of the agency. Breedlove explained that media placement begins with looking at audience numbers from monitoring services and that where the target audience is serves as a starting point for placement decisions. He stressed that he is looking for some association through a media environment or time link to the product that is being advertised. One example of the placement and time link is that movies often buy commercial time on network television on Thursday evening, right before the peak movie viewing period of the weekend. The environment link is more complete if it is an action movie being advertised during an action drama program, trying to match up the audience that is watching the television program with the audience that might be interested in purchasing the product, or in this example, going to see the movie. Breedlove commented, "You need a strong profile of the audience and when and how the message is going to have an impact" (personal communication, August 27, 2003). Breedlove pointed out that the creative elements of the advertisement need to be in sync with the placement. He stated in advertising "you need a sharp that nail [creative] with a big hammer [media placement] to make it work" (personal communication, August 27, 2003).

Sally Brooks is the vice president and associate media director for GSD&M advertising agency, whose client is MasterCard. Her responsibilities include developing marketing strategies and goals, and national media buying for MasterCard. Brooks indicated that any national media buys can be supported with buying time in a specific geographic region (personal communication, May 11, 2004). These purchases in the specific markets might have different creative components, as the advertisement is tailored to the different geographic audiences.

Mandy Bogan, broadcast buying director at GSD&M advertising, oversees all local media purchasing for clients such as Wal-Mart and Macaroni Grill. Her responsibility is to work with clients in establishing overall advertising buying budgets, purchasing media time, and making sure the commercial contract was executed as promised. Bogan works within her clients parameters about how they want their media time purchased, including buying time during certain periods of the day or buying time based on a guideline of a minimum ratings. Bogan stressed that the purchase decision might begin with the audience desired, but she also emphasized that the association between the brand and the media content is something she always takes into consideration in purchasing media time. She offered an example that companies like to purchase time during the news because there is an association where the audience "finds the advertisement more credible" (personal communication, May 11, 2004).

SPONSORSHIP AND PRODUCT PLACEMENT

As the media environment changes and how people experience media changes, so too will the advertising environment. Advertising placement has to be where their potential customers participate to be exposed to the message. Advertisers are always reacting to the audience, and as the audiences move to different media locations, advertisers must recognize this and move with them. The entire sales process breaks down without exposure and consumer knowledge that the brand exists. Thus, with television not producing the large audiences it once did, advertisers have had to implement strategies other than a straight commercial buy.

Mass media organizations have to work with advertisers to create an environment beneficial to both the mass media organization and the advertiser. Meehan (1993) claimed that "media firms and their agents must also develop increasingly sophisticated techniques of selling advertising-desirable audiences" (p. 387). This coordination between advertisers and media organizations is not difficult, as it is in the interest of both entities to create a system and establish relationships that would be successful for both. Advertisers need the mass media for exposure of their products to the audience. Mass media organizations need advertisers for revenue. Ball-Rokeach and DeFleur (1986) pointed out that "the economic system could not operate effectively if the media did not provide massive advertising links between producers, distributors, and consumers" (p. 82).

Grant, Guthrie, and Ball-Rokeach (1991) summarized the relationship among broadcasters, merchandisers, and the public, stating:

> Commercial broadcasting in the United States has been built on dependency relationships between broadcasters and merchandisers. In this system television programs are produced to attract large audiences, with merchandisers buying access to those audiences so they can air advertisements designed to entice viewers into buying their products. Broadcasters depend on the proceeds from the advertising sales to produce their shows. Merchandisers depend on television to reach consumers. (p. 773)

With the difficulty corporations have in getting their brand products exposed to a large number of people, one strategy being implemented is to engage in a sponsorship agreement with a mass media property.

McAllister (1998) distinguished between sponsorship and spot advertising, or buying a single commercial within a program. He defined sponsorship as "the funding of an entire event, group, broadcast or place by one commercial interest in exchange for large amounts and special types of promotion connected with the sponsored activity" (p. 358). He claimed that "from the sponsors' point of view, advertisers have been continually frustrated with the viewer's ability to 'zap' ads, with the fragmentation of the media audience, and with the high cost of spot advertising in different media, and they have turned to sponsorship as a corrective to these problems" (p. 359).

With corporations needing to be in various places to reach all of their demographic groups, Farrelly, Quester, and Burton (1997) pointed out that it is not uncommon for corporations to engage in multiple sponsorship relationships over a given year. This is especially important for corporations whose products have a wide audience. Corporations such as MasterCard, McDonald's, or Coca-Cola that transcend many demographic lines of income, race, gender, or geography need to advertise and sponsor in a variety of locations to reach the many different target audiences that might use their products.

Even for companies with a large general audience, the creative components of the advertisements might be different, in addition to the various placement strategies. For example, a McDonald's commercial on a Saturday morning might feature the Ronald McDonald character, but a commercial in prime time might feature a family or have older people in the commercial. Meanwhile, for corporations with a more narrow target audience, such as Mercedes-Benz or Lexus, sponsorship at golf or tennis, the theater, or any other mass media outlet where the audience participating might be more affluent provides an opportunity to reach that desired niche.

The key advantageous characteristic for a corporation in using sponsorship as a communication strategy to reach its audience is the ability to negotiate with the mass media organization and leverage the agreement to benefit both the media property and the sponsoring corporation (e.g., Fortunato & Dunnam, 2004). The concept of leveraging is taking an already established relationship and expanding on it with new ideas for exposure of the brand. If negotiation takes place between a corporation and a mass media organization, there are unlimited possibilities as to what the agreement might look like and sponsorship thus becomes difficult to define. No two sponsorship agreements are alike, as the negotiated details define the difference.

Meenaghan (1991) did, however, offer one of the more accepted definitions of sponsorship, describing it as "an investment, in cash or in kind, in an activity, in return for access to the exploitable commercial potential associated with that activity" (p. 36).

One of the positive benefits of a sponsorship agreement is the potential for control over the media and advertising environment. Competition for attention is fierce, and corporations need to have their brand exposed at a time and place when their target audience is available. Corporations must present their brand in a fashion that will almost ensure being noticed. Sponsorship advertising through negotiation helps a corporation achieve exclusivity of a particular product genre. McAllister (1998) described exclusivity as a promotional incentive for sponsors, where unlike spot advertisers on commercials, sponsors can now be the exclusive voice of an event. Exclusivity eliminates competition a corporation might receive from a rival for a sponsored event. Therefore, if Coca-Cola sponsors an event or a mass media property and it negotiates for exclusivity with that property, Pepsi will not be allowed to place its brand name in that same location.

Through strategic sponsorship negotiation, in addition to the all-important exclusivity that eliminates product competition, the corporation might also be able to control advertising clutter. McAllister (1996) defined advertising clutter as "the amount of time devoted to nonprogram content on television, including product commercials, program promotions and public service announcements" (p. 24). He pointed out that "advertisers believe that the effectiveness of their messages decreases if their competitors' messages are too close or if too many other promotional messages swallow up their message" (p. 15). Simply, the more corporations that are sponsors of the same property, the more difficult it is to have consumers notice one brand from all of the others. Differentiation of the brand is important but becomes difficult when many other corporations are in the same location and perhaps not possible if other brands from the same product category are consistently mentioned. People might remember that it was a beer company that was being advertised but not be able to recall if it was Budweiser, Coors, or Miller. Being in the right location gives the opportunity for exposure to a desired target audience, but controlling the exposure environment and how brands can be communicated to the audience must also be strongly considered in trying to obtain brand recall.

In addition to the type of audience, choosing commercial media placement and evaluating sponsorship opportunities are about choosing brand associations. Many authors have indicated that brand awareness and brand image through association with a media property are the major sponsorship objectives (e.g., Dean, 2002; Gwinner, 1997; Gwinner & Eaton, 1999). Roy and Cornwell (1999) noted that enhancing corporate or brand image, breaking free from media advertising clutter, and increasing brand awareness rank as the top three objectives of a sponsorship agreement with a media property. Gwinner and Eaton (1999) added that this image transfer would be stronger between brands and properties that had an image-based similarity. Corporations would have their media placement associated with certain types of content. For example, corporations might use placement on a situation comedy or other more family-oriented content but not choose placement and the association with a crime drama. Stipp and Schiavone (1996) pointed out that sponsorship goals assume that the target audience for the sponsorship will transfer from the sponsored property to the sponsor itself.

Although these definitions acknowledge an investment, any desired return should be more than brand association; the desired return should be an increase in sales. Brand awareness and recall are obviously important but are merely a step toward sales. Brand awareness is not an ambitious enough business objective for a sponsoring corporation that needs the consumer to purchase their products. Cornwell and Maignan (1998) correctly described the objectives of sponsorship as including development of goodwill, image, awareness, and increased sales. Dean (2002) claimed that "management objectives for sponsorship may be both economic (increased revenues and profits, increased brand awareness, increased channel member interest in the brand) and noneconomic (creation of goodwill with the community, improvement of corporate image, boosting employee morale, recruiting new employees, pure altruism)" (p. 78).

Research has indicated that achieving brand image transfer through advertising strategies, leading to an increase in sales, is a plausible result. Harvey (2001) argued that "sponsorship changes the consumer's perception of a specific sponsor—which can rub off positively on brands of that sponsor in terms of willingness to purchase those brands" (p. 64). In examining college football fans, Madrigal (2000) pointed out that fan identification can extend from support of a team to support of companies that sponsor and are associated with that team. He stated, "Loyalty toward a preferred team may have beneficial consequences for corporate sponsors. Consistent with the idea of in-group favoritism, higher levels of team identification among attendees of a sporting event appear to be positively related to intentions to purchase a sponsor's products" (p. 21). Trusdell (1997) lent support for this claim, describing one survey that found that more than 70% of NASCAR fans purchase the products of NASCAR sponsors. In this light, sponsorship is not different in its business objectives from any other advertising, marketing, or public relations communication strategy.

Corporations that sponsor media content have a tremendous opportunity for exposure through the way their brand name is communicated to the audience on television. One programming genre that takes advantage of this characteristic is sports (e.g., Fortunato, 2001). In addition to commercial time, sports programming offers the opportunity for a television network to generate advertising revenue within the framework of the program content itself. Unlike sports television, most other programming—prime-time dramas, movies, news magazine shows, or situation comedies—can only offer commercial time to advertisers. The sports format allows for networks to sell advertisers' billboards, still shots when coming out of commercial of a company logo, with a voice-over announcing the company name and slogan against the backdrop of the live event, sponsored pregame or halftime shows, scoreboards, starting lineups, player of the game, and halftime statistics all serving as extra forms of advertising revenue within the context of the program itself. Other prime-time programming, notably, reality-based programs, use this type of sponsorship and product placement, as Ford Motor Company and Coca-Cola have paid millions to have their logos appear in a prominent location on *American Idol* (e.g., Carter, 2003a).

Sponsorship of a media property, such as sports, reality programming, or perhaps a major event like the Academy Awards, also normally comes with purchased commercial time within that television broadcast. For example, to become a sponsor of major league baseball a company has to make a commitment to buy commercial time during games and buy commercial time during prime-time programming that might help promote the game. Forcing sponsors to buy commercial time helps the television network sell a substantial portion of the commercial inventory for that broadcast and allows it to increase the price of the remaining commercial spots, as the supply has been limited for a media location that might have strong demand.

This sponsorship within the program is more closely aligned with product placement strategies. Much like sponsorship strategies, negotiation is pivotal in product placement. It can be negotiated how the brand is seen or whether the brands get mentioned by any of the characters. Moonves, chairman and CEO of CBS, described product placement initiatives as the future, stating, "There's going to be much more product placement. We did it with *Survivor*, obviously. They're doing it with *American Idol*. I saw *Minority Report*, Steven Spielberg's movie—that had more product placement than any TV show I've ever seen" (cited in Gay, 2003, p. 1). Moonves added, "You're going to see cars incorporated into shows, and instead of Ray Romano, sitting there with a can of nondescript soda, he'll be drinking a Diet Pepsi. That is going to happen" (cited in Gay, 2003, p. 1).

In speaking of product placement, Hemeyer, former communication executive at Pennzoil, added that Pennzoil had people who worked in Hollywood who were out on studio production lots and going to events to get to know producers and look for opportunities to get the Pennzoil brand name and product into television programs and movies (personal communication, August 9, 2004). One product placement strategy of Pennzoil was to sponsor a car on the NASCAR racing circuit that was painted a bright yellow that would be easily noticed by television cameras and the crowd. The Pennzoil car also did not have many other advertisements to eliminate any advertising clutter.

People might change channels during commercials, but if they tuned in to watch a game or any television program they virtually cannot escape certain brand name exposure. Thus, advertisers simply move to sponsorship and product placement to put their brand name in a position where it is virtually impossible to be ignored. Breedlove pointed out that the goal is to develop a strategy that will break through and be noticed by the consumer, but that being noticed is becoming increasingly difficult to achieve (personal communication, August 27, 2004). He contended that movement of sponsorship and product placement on the part of advertisers is thus prevalent in trying to get noticed.

Corporations invest in sponsorship and product placement just like traditional advertising strategies because there is a perceived and expected return on the investment. With the increase of media diversification and multiple media options available to the audience, all indications are that in the future sponsorship will continue to be part of the strategic communication plan of many corporations (e.g., Miyazaki & Morgan, 2001; Parmar, 2002).

Moves toward sponsorship and product placement do not, however, mean the end of the broadcast commercial spot or print media purchase. Although having the advantage of brand product exposure within the program, there are potentially two major disadvantages to these sponsorship and product placement strategies. The first disadvantage is that the brand may not be noticed, as people could be so engrossed in the plot of the program that they do not notice it was a Coca-Cola Ray Romano was drinking. This problem could be solved by having the character repeatedly state the name of the brand so it is noticed. The film *Castaway* with Tom Hanks is one example where Federal Express and Wilson made their brand names such a prominent part of the movie that it was virtually impossible for the audience not to notice the product placement and recall the brand.

The second disadvantage is that the corporation often cannot talk about the features of the product through product placement or sponsorship. People could see the Lexus automobile in a movie but learn nothing about the product. The 30-second commercial or magazine advertisement explains the features of the Lexus brand. Sponsorship and product placement are thus not often the only advertising strategies implemented, but rather are another tactic of an integrated communication strategy.

There is another danger to any brand association in that the media property or person with which a relationship was fostered could become involved in a scandal and come under public scrutiny. In conducting research on celebrities, Till and Shimp (1998) stated that marketers "hope their target audience's positive feelings toward a chosen celebrity will transfer to the endorsed brand or will otherwise enhance the brand's standing" (p. 67). They, however, cautioned that "activation of negative information about a celebrity can have an adverse effect—through lowered brand evaluations—on the endorsed brand with which that celebrity is associated" (p. 72). Such was the case when National Basketball Association (NBA) superstar Kobe Bryant from the Los Angeles Lakers was arrested for felony sexual assault in 2003. In addition to his $13.5 million dollar salary from the Lakers, Bryant had lucrative sponsorship agreements with Nike, Upper Deck, Sprite, Spalding, Nutella, and McDonald's, totaling more than $10 million (e.g., Reilly & Futterman, 2003). The Ferraro U.S.A. Company that manufactures Nutella decided it would phase out any Bryant promotions despite another 5 months remaining on his endorsement contract. Sprite decided not to renew its association with Bryant, opting instead to sign and feature Lebron James. Nike, too, has made James the focal point of its basketball advertising campaigns.

In speaking on the difficulty of a brand association with a celebrity, T. J. Nelligan, founder of sports marketing company Nelligan Sports Marketing, commented, "There is high risk and high reward with doing endorsements with professional athletes. If they get in trouble, it's going to hurt your product. Any major company is taking a huge risk by having any athlete or celebrity endorse their products or services" (cited in Reilly & Futterman, 2003, p. 42). The Bryant case and many others speak to the importance for a corporation to select wisely the media properties and people they want to associate with their brands before making a major financial investment. The negative public reaction might not only be toward the person or program involved in the scandal but also toward the corporation that continues to support that person or program, with people deciding not to purchase that corporation's products.

ADVERTISER INFLUENCE ON CONTENT

The relationship between advertisers and media content is economic in that advertisers provide mass media organizations with their largest source of revenue, and they are the only source of revenue for broadcast. Although advertisers may use direct mail, the mass media are often the necessary source for any national or wide-ranging exposure to the audience. The exchange is simple: The mass media organization offers an audience and the advertisers pay for exposure of their brand to that audience. Advertisers constantly make decisions about where to put their monetary resources and sponsor media content perhaps not necessarily because of the content but because of the audience who watches, reads, or listens to that content. Wenner (1989) pointed out that "the content per se is not what is being sold; rather it is the audience for that content that is being sold to advertisers" (p. 22). In addition to reaching an audience, advertisers implicitly express support for certain content through the purchase of time or space, but questions remain: Do advertisers desire to influence content? If there is a desire, can advertisers influence content? If advertisers can, to what extent do they influence content? Do advertisers simply desire access to the audience that is watching, reading, listening, or clicking onto that content? The pivotal question is whether the achievement of the advertising goals—(a) exposure to the desired target audience, (b) increase product brand recall, and (c) increase sales—necessitate a control of the media content. Do advertisers desire or need to influence content or mainly need access for exposure of their brand.

Some believe that because advertising pays the mass media organizations, the organizations might be more willing to capitulate to the demands of advertisers. Altschull (1995) found that media content is often directly correlated with the interests of those who finance it and that influence is exerted by advertisers' demands for a suitable environment for their commercial messages. Cohen (2002) claimed that as "advertisements are placed in a newscast, magazine, or newspaper, advertisers can negotiate a commercial environment supportive of their interests" (p. 535). From an advertising perspective, a suitable environment could simply mean acquiring a large amount of viewers, listeners, or readers to participate in the content. Shoemaker and Reese (1996) raised another issue in that mass media organizations only produce content that is "safe" in drawing a large audience or that will not offend a large number of viewers and therefore scare off advertisers who would not want to be associated with the controversial content. They stated, "Television networks react to their perceptions of what advertisers will tolerate" (p. 197).

Richards and Murphy (1996) described the potential problem: "The inherent danger is that advertisers might use their economic influence to set as unofficial censors of 'the press,' thereby barring media from publishing or broadcasting certain material" (p. 21). In a survey of 147 daily newspapers, Soley and Craig (1992) found that more than 90% of editors were pressured by advertisers and that more than 33% claimed advertising had succeeded in influencing news at their papers. In these ideas, advertisers have the power to prevent certain voices and certain content from being heard.

Schiller (1989) wrote extensively about the emergence and continued dominance of American corporations and their influence in the societal culture. The influence goes beyond that of simple economic support, but this economic support translates into support for ideas and images and, more importantly, for who controls these ideas and images. Schiller contended that there are only two main choices for control of ideas and images—either big government or big business—and that corporations have emerged as the proliferators of culture and images, largely through advertising and the media. Schiller stated that "the private corporate sector in the American economy has widened its economic, political, and cultural role in domestic and international activities" (p. 3). He also claimed that corporate speech, advertising, is the "loudest in the land" (p. 4).

Schiller (1989) explained that economic activity produces symbolic as well as material goods, and together they represent the totality of a culture. Corporations must find a way to influence or control the culture, and this is achieved through advertising and supporting what Schiller referred to as the culture industries such as publishing, the press, film, television, radio, recordings, photography, and sports. To a large extent, according to Schiller, economic support becomes tantamount to support for that entity and its existence within the culture. The corporate power as a cultural influence is in validating certain performers, or even entire industries, through economic support—advertising. Validation occurs not solely through talent but, perhaps more important, through marketability. Schiller stated that "if a creative project, no matter what its inherent quality, cannot be viewed as a potential money-maker, salable in a large enough market, its production is problematic at best" (p. 43). Without receiving economic support, individual expression and creativity are only available to those who can afford it and have the means to put out their messages on their own. With this expression limited to people or groups with monetary resources, other individuals need the support of corporations to get out their messages and then, eventually, the support of the market through its behavior to maintain their status.

The influence of corporations goes beyond that of financial support to the individual or industry, extending to the public as a whole who see their advertising as a degree of validation in that there will be continued exposure of those ideas and images. Schiller (1989) operated from a "strong assumption that social imperatives channel individual expression" (p. 6). He explained:

> Individual expression occurs each time a person dresses, goes out for a walk, meets friends, converses, or does any of a thousand routine exercises. Expression is an inseparable part of life. It is ludicrous to imagine that individual expression can be completely managed and controlled. Yet, no matter how integral to the person, it is ultimately subject to social boundaries that are themselves changeable but always present. These limits have been created by the power formations in society, past and present. I have tried to trace how some of these defining conditions have been established or reinforced in recent decades and what impact they have. The growth of private corporate power is seen as the prime contractor in the construction of contemporary boundaries to expression. (p. 6)

In acting as a validation for cultural ideas and images, personalities, and industries, Schiller (1989) explained that "the corporate history machine has at its disposal the means by which it becomes the national narrator of record. Television, which takes its screening orders from corporate marketing furnishes the history (such as it is) that is seen by millions, be it through the news, drama, sports, or historical narratives" (pp. 7–8). He also claimed that "television is now one of the most influential, largely unacknowledged educators in the country. One reason why television is heavily discounted as a powerful educational force is the distinction made between 'educational' and 'entertainment' programming. This artificial separation seems to mesmerize many into believing that entertainment shows are not educational" (p. 106).

For broadcast networks, the recruitment of advertisers, and therefore validation of their programming content, is a never-ending endeavor, as it remains their only revenue source. In this regard, it appears that corporations have all of the power and that there is a one-way dependency from the media to advertisers. However, advertisers also depend on the media to reach their potential customers, in particular, their target market, and to gain exposure for their products and services available. In this regard, broadcast networks regain some power in the relationship, as they ask for a higher price for commercials during their better programming.

Mass media organizations, however, do not want to hurt relations with any advertiser they might need in the future and will often work with them in a manner suitable to both entities. The interdependent nature of this relationship between advertisers and mass media organizations becomes evident in how they deal with one another. Once it is realized by both the mass media and corporations that their relationship depends on one another, mutual support and relationships are fostered to make the advertising endeavors in the media successful. There is a willingness to develop strategies so that advertisers' products get noticed (i.e., sponsorship, product placement).

Another perspective is that advertisers simply follow the behavior of the audience and are merely responding to their desires. Advertising, or any marketing or public relations communication strategy, is designed to influence behavior (i.e., sales, vote). The extent to which advertisers are going to attempt to influence content is only in relation to an increase in sales for their brand. The key element is thus the audience, and what the advertiser most desires is not necessarily to influence content but simply to reach the largest possible numbers of its desired target audience as often as possible to increase sales. As the desire to influence content relates to sales, it would then seem that the influence largely extends to increasing chances for exposure—offering initiatives such as sponsorship of entire segments of a broadcast, newspaper, or magazine, or product placement strategies in television or film. In this philosophy, control or influence of media content is not a necessary condition for achievement of advertisement goals.

Sutherland and Galloway (1981) claimed that "advertising does not create needs; it merely reflects those needs that are already existent in society at the time" (p. 25). They stressed the desire for product brand recall, stating "the major goal of advertising may be to focus consumers' attention on what values, products, brands, or attributes to think about rather than to try to persuade consumers what to think about" (p. 26). In his study of CBS, NBC, *Time*, and *Newsweek*, Gans (1979) did not find evidence of pressure from advertisers at the national level to run or kill a story. In addition to studying the influence of ownership, Price (2003) asked network news correspondents to determine whether they felt any story influence from advertisers. Price found that only 7% reported some advertiser pressure. Her survey results revealed that 93.1% of national news correspondents from ABC, CBS, CNN, NBC, and PBS responded that they have never felt pressure from advertisers to report or not report a story. No correspondents responded that they were frequently pressured by advertisers to report or not report a story, and only one respondent reported occasional pressure from advertisers.

For mass media organizations there would not be fear from advertisers if they produce quality content that draws an audience. If the media content produces an audience that advertisers need and cannot attain through other methods, chances are they will have to return to that media location to reach that audience. Any fear from advertising diminishes if mass media organizations produce content that attracts a large audience the advertisers covet in that another advertiser will gladly fill that location. There is intense competition for advertising locations, and the mass media do not have to capitulate to advertisers if another corporation is available with its dollars. This is particularly the case on a local level where businesses might not have many other advertising placement options. For example, many communities only have one newspaper, and classified, real estate, or automobile dealerships in the area, all of whose advertising dollars are big money makers, simply do not have many media options other than the local newspaper.

Breedlove, managing director of Ruff, Coffin, and Breedlove advertising agency, stated that smaller advertisers are relatively helpless in trying to influence content and must simply look for the content that is going to capture the advertiser's target audience and then try to build a connection between the content and the product that helps achieve the advertising goals. This speaks to what advertisers most desire—not controlling the editorial content of the mass media organization with which they are advertising, but exposing their message to the audience that the content of a particular mass media organization provides. Breedlove claimed that trying to become part of programming is "as far as most advertisers are willing to take an influence into content" (personal communication, August 27, 2003). Breedlove also pointed out that he has "never seen a situation where a journalist was so biased we wouldn't advertise there" (personal communication, August 27, 2003). He explained it can be shortsighted not to continue advertising with that media outlet if that is where your audience is.

Sanders described instances when *Time* magazine would do a special issue where a corporation would pay for the entire publication of the magazine to place an advertising circular in the middle of the magazine. Often this was done when the corporation was trying to introduce a new product. Even in these circumstances where the corporation was paying the entire bill for producing the special issue, the desire was not editorial control but access to the readers of *Time* magazine and its demographic. The special issues of *Time* that were produced would also be about a topic of no relevance to the advertiser. For example, a special issue on a foreign country might be funded by a motor vehicle corporation. Sanders stated, "There was no advertiser pressure whatsoever" and "no one ever told me to change a story, a point or an angle based on advertisers—to be kind to an advertiser" (personal communication, August 8, 2003).

Other employees for mass media organizations agree with Sanders' assessment of the lack of advertiser influence. King, senior writer for *Sports Illustrated*, added that when taking on an assignment he has no idea who the advertisers are going to be in the magazine (personal communication, July 23, 2003). Blumental, Dallas bureau chief for the *Wall Street Journal*, commented that there is no advertising influence on the newspaper and that "even the advertising people understand the separation (between the editorial and advertising departments)" (personal communication, September 5, 2003). Emanuel, correspondent for the Fox News Channel, pointed out that he has no contact with advertising people and is "proud that he has never been asked by anyone at the Fox News Channel to give a little favorable light to a story so we can get an advertising contract" (personal communication, January 14, 2004). He claimed that he is thankfully far removed from the business side and that if he is doing a report for a particular program he has no clue who is advertising on that program. He also pointed out he has no idea who is advertising on the local level during Fox News Channel programming.

Westin, president of ABC News, explained there are instances where advertisers sponsor entire segments on a particular broadcast. For example, Sears is the official sponsor of the 2004 summer concert series on *Good Morning America*. Westin offered his philosophy for allowing this type of sponsorship as "would we have editorially done this story anyway, and the advertiser has no editorial control over the content" (personal communication, May 28, 2004). In the *Good Morning America* example, the summer concert series is something ABC was going to do regardless of corporate sponsorship and Sears does not pick the musical guests.

Regarding overall influence, the argument is that advertisers could apply pressure to the mass media organizations to have coverage framed in a manner that helps the sponsoring corporation. There are many examples of advertisers pulling out of shows (e.g., Richards & Murphy, 1996). It is important to note that often it is not a complete pull-out and cancellation of the advertising contract with a mass media organization. Often, the result of a conflict regarding content is to shift the location of the advertisement. If there is a conflict, an arrangement is made where there is a location or time shift and the advertiser will merely move its commercial to another segment of the program or possibly to the next week. Brooks, vice president and associate media director for the GSD&M advertising agency, offered an example of the location-shifting process by describing that when purchasing time on a television news magazine, the content of the program can be an issue for an advertiser as there is certain content with which advertisers do not want to be associated (personal communication, May 11, 2004). For example, if a news program was doing a story on airline safety, any airline that might have had a scheduled commercial will move its commercial to the next week or another segment of the program. Most airlines also have a standard rule where if there was a plane crash, they immediately pull all of their advertisements and run them at another time when the crisis is receiving less attention.

Brooks pointed out that because there is some unpredictability about what the content will be on a television news magazine, whereas there is generally some predictability on scripted television, some clients avoid media placement in these locations altogether. With the purchase of time as much as 1-year in advance for national network television, it is impossible even for the clients who bought time to know the topical content of that television news magazine on that night. This also makes it difficult, if not impossible, for day-to-day decision makers to tailor a story to fit the needs of an advertiser who they probably do not know has commercials planning to air during the segments they are producing.

Television news magazines are screened by the advertising agencies and their clients, and if there is a controversial topic that the advertiser does not want to be associated with, arrangements are made between the network and the advertiser. If there is a possibility that advertisers would not want to be associated with certain content, the networks might even call ahead to alert the advertiser. The fact that the financial commitment does not change, only the placement of the advertisement, is an important point when evaluating the influence that advertisers have or even desire to have on the content decision-making process. There was a reason the advertiser bought time on the program in the first place: primarily its the audience in both numbers and demographics, and secondarily the association of the brand with that media content.

Time shifting is also common in the print industry, echoing the idea that what advertisers frequently desire to control is the placement of their advertisement within the magazine, not the editorial content. Sanders provided an example that if there was a story in *Time* about tobacco litigation, a cigarette company who bought an advertisement in that issue would probably not want it placed near that story and would have it shifted to another part of the magazine (personal communication, August 8, 2003). Similar to television, with the advertisements sold well in advance of knowing what the content of the magazine would be in terms of the exact stories, this shifting of the advertisement within the magazine or even the shifting of a story is a minor violation, and the editorial content of the magazine is not affected at all.

The advertisers at *Sports Illustrated* pay more for a full-page color advertisement than any other magazine. Bevans, executive editor of *Sports Illustrated*, contended that advertisers do not dictate the editorial content of *Sports Illustrated*, stating, "Nobody tells us how to write a story" (personal communication, August 13, 2003). He stressed that the editorial personnel of the magazine are aware of any possible perceptions of advertiser influence and work even harder to avoid even the slightest hint of improper behavior and maintain the credibility of the magazine.

Bevans also contended that advertisers' influence is more an issue of placement, as some corporations might not want to be associated with certain articles that deal with criminal or controversial issues. Corporations that do not want to be associated with a certain story have their advertisements shifted within the magazine. One characteristic of time shifting that advertisers desire and that magazines try to accommodate is page separation between brands of the same product type. For example, there will at least be a six- or eight-page separation between automobile advertisements.

Some corporations desire to be part of certain popular sections of *Sports Illustrated*, such as opposite Reilly's article, or adjacent to the "Catching up With" feature at the beginning of the magazine. *Sports Illustrated* also features special sections that do not go to all subscribers. One example is the "Golf Plus" section, which Bevans described as an advertising-driven part of the magazine that provides an opportunity for the niche golf advertiser to reach a specific targeted audience. This provides a great source of revenue for the magazine even though the advertisers for this special section pay a lower rate because it does not go to all subscribers. The advertisers reach their core niche audience, and it becomes a great combination of matching up a niche audience with a niche advertiser.

Kelley Gott is a sales managing director for *Time* magazine for the southwest region of the United States. She is the liaison between *Time* and the clients and their representative advertising agencies in that geographic region, including Dell Computers, Shell Oil, and Southwest Airlines. Her responsibility is to sell the advertising space in the magazine by calling on existing clients and prospecting new clients. In prospecting new clients Gott explained that she has to convince them of the benefits of using the print medium, as well as describe the benefits of advertising with *Time*, which includes 22 million readers and a 44% market share of all news magazines sold (personal communication, May 20, 2004).

Time is very accommodating to its advertisers by creating specific programs to meet their many needs. There are more than 400 ways to buy advertising space in *Time*: "*Time* specializes in customizing programs for the unique needs of each advertiser." And, "nearly every issue includes targeted editorial to a specific demographic of *Time*'s audience" (Time Magazine Online). By having a large subscriber base, *Time* can segment its audience through many demographic variables. In addition to the national edition of *Time*, the magazine has different editions based on subscriber interest and geographic region. The special editions based on interest are: *Time Business/Inside Business*, *Time Global Business*, *Time Women/Connections*, *Time Gold/Generations*, and *Time Luxury/Style & Design*. Certain consumers can receive a version of the magazine that has extra or different editorial content and advertisers. Gott stated, "It is possible that a person can receive a different *Time* magazine from their neighbor" (personal communication, May 20, 2004).

Advertising rates are determined by the size of the audience. The advertising system that *Time* sets up allows for efficiency of advertising dollars, which helps strengthen the relationship between *Time* and its advertisers. Through this system advertisers are not paying to get exposure to audiences outside of their target (see Tables 8.1 and 8.2).

USA Today has the largest circulation of any newspaper in the United States, with a weekly national circulation of more than 2.2 million and a daily readership of 5.4 million readers. Pricing for the newspaper's advertisers is based on whether it is a weekday or weekend edition that is available every Friday (the weekend edition of *USA Today* sells approximately 500,000 more copies), the size of the advertisement, whether the advertisement is in black and white or color, and whether placement is guaranteed (see Table 8.3).

Gott explained that it is her job to keep the advertisements of her clients where they are editorially comfortable with the content. She stated, "All advertisers want to be in the front of the magazine on the right hand of the page" (personal communication, May 20, 2004). This location strategy makes sense for the advertiser, as the stories that ap-

TABLE 8.1
Advertising Rate in *Time* Magazine: Interest Editions

	Black and White Full Page	Color Full Page
Time National Edition	$167,250	$223,000
Time Business/Inside Business	$103,500	$138,000
Time Global Business	$73,500	$105,000
Time Gold/Generations	$54,000	$72,000
Time Luxury/Style & Design	$47,250	$72,000

TABLE 8.2

Advertising Rate in *Time* Magazine: Geographic Editions

City	Black and White Full Page	Color Full Page
Boston	$16,958	$22,611
Chicago	$16,958	$22,611
Detroit	$16,958	$22,611
Los Angeles	$20,862	$27,816
Miami	$16,958	$22,611
New York	$27,692	$36,923
Philadelphia	$16,958	$22,611
San Francisco	$16,958	$22,611
Washington DC	$16,958	$22,611

Source: www.timemediakit.com

TABLE 8.3

***USA Today* Advertising Rates**

Ad Size	Monday–Thursday	Monday–Thursday	Friday	Friday
	Black and White	Color	Black and White	Color
Flexible Placement: Day/Section				
Spread	$166,020	$262,750	$200,790	$317,830
Half spread	$107,740	$171,000	$130,420	$206,860
Full page	$82,900	$125,100	$100,290	$152,600
1/2 page	$53,870	$85,500	$65,210	$103,430
1/4 page	$33,230	$51,480	$40,140	$62,280
1/8 page	$19,190	$29,710	$23,170	$35,970
1/16 page	$11,110	$17,240	$13,490	$20,800
Guaranteed Placement: Day/Section				
Spread	189,730	$300,280	$229,730	$363,630
Half spread	$123,120	$195,440	$149,220	$236,680
Full page	$94,740	$143,900	$114,740	$175,50
1/2 page	$61,560	$97,720	$74,610	$118,340
1/4 page	$37,970	$58,840	$45,920	$71,260
1/8 page	$21,900	$33,960	$26,500	$41,160
1/16 page	$12,700	$19,700	$15,430	$23,800

Source: www.usatoday.com

pear earlier in *Time* magazine have a connotation of being more important. Gott described that advertisements are sold as packages, and placements generally operate on a split where six of the advertisements are placed in the front of the magazine and three are placed toward the back. She explained that because of the close editing time no advertisement placement is guaranteed for any issue aside from the table of contents and cover advertisements. Only a general location in the front or back of *Time* can be promised.

People who are responsible for laying out the magazine have specifications of where advertisers desire to be. Gott explained that the people responsible for laying out the magazine understand the location parameters that advertisers desire. She contended that they are sensitive to location shifting to another part of the magazine or another issue altogether, and they attempt to satisfy advertiser desires for page separation for brands of the same product type. To complete the magazine and make up for any missing space due to location shifting, *Time* sells what are referred to as remnant advertisements. The structure of a remnant advertising agreement is that *Time* agrees to run the advertisement of a company at a reduced rate, but *Time* runs the advertisement at its discretion within a 3- or 4-week window with no location guarantee provided to the advertiser.

Gott explained that even though advertisers provide *Time* with revenue, being sensitive to advertisers "does not affect the editorial process in the slightest" (personal communication, May 20, 2004). With *Time* selling its advertising space more than 6 months in advance of when the actual issue will appear on the newsstand, Gott claimed, "Advertisers have no idea what is going to be in the magazine and the buy is based on *Time*'s demographic, the *Time* brand, and *Time*'s relationship with its readers" (personal communication, May 20, 2004).

Westin, president of ABC News, said that advertising is much less involved than many people perceive it to be. He explained that at ABC, the selling of advertising time is a networkwide function and no salespeople report to him and no salespeople meet with any of the executive producers out of concern that any type of ongoing dialogue between these two entities could lapse into stories that advertisers do and do not like. Westin explained that there are situations where, after a story is completed, ABC might call an advertiser and offer them the option of shifting to another placement location. He commented that "you do not want to embarrass the advertiser" (personal communication, May 28, 2004).

There is a big leap from not wanting to offend or embarrass a business partner, an advertiser, to turning over decision-making control of your product, the content, to them. Much as influencing editorial content is not a necessary condition for achievement of advertising goals, accommodating measures by a mass media organization toward an advertiser do not lead to their influencing editorial content. Both Brooks and Bogan from GSD&M advertising pointed out that mass media organizations do not want their editorial practices compromised but do not want to lose advertising dollars so it is in their best interest to alert the advertisers, and it is in the advertisers' best interest not to be associated with that content so arrangements in time shifting are not difficult, as it is in both groups' interest. Brooks stated, "The last thing networks want to do is offend the advertisers" (personal communication, May 11, 2004).

Webber, senior vice president and publisher of usatoday.com, commented on any potential conflict with advertisers, stating "you have to maintain editorial integrity with the audience. The audience is smart and they can tell if you are writing for the advertiser. It is critical to present the news in a totally unbiased way" (personal communication, May 25, 2004). Webber added that losing integrity merely erodes the audience and credibility as a trusted news and information Internet site is lost. Webber contended that advertisers do not try to influence content because if the audience does not view the publication as credible the audience is going to go to another location, particularly in an environment with many options. The advertisers then do not get the exposure to the large audience that they desired. Webber stated that even if advertisers ask for special treatment, his philosophy is the same: "We report good or bad on companies." He added, "You have to be respectful of the First Amendment privilege and the news organizations special place and obligation to the government and the audience" (personal communication, May 25, 2004).

Time shifting is one example where mass media organizations work with advertisers. More often than not, the mass media organization and the advertiser work together to rectify any conflict. The relationship between these two groups is often not adversarial, as both entities understand the others' needs. It is a give and take by both groups, where at times both ask for favors and both are accommodating.

In purchasing television time, especially when buying in the upfront period, which could be several months in advance, networks provide audience guarantees where if a program does not obtain the expected audience rating, the network will provide the advertiser with "make-goods," or extra commercial time to make up for its underdelivery of an audience. Audience guarantees are part of the negotiation process. Although television ratings might be difficult to predict, magazine and newspaper circulation can be easier to discern. To increase subscriptions, magazines offer incentives to subscribe such as a price lower than the newsstand cover price or a free gift. The increase in subscribers is needed so that the magazine can say a larger, guaranteed number of readers receive the magazine. This guaranteed audience can then be offered to advertisers and increase the advertising rate, which easily offsets any subscription incentives of a lower price.

When offering advertising time, mass media organizations often provide something extra, referred to as added value. Buying commercial time might come with the added value of sponsoring that night's closed caption or weather segment of the broadcast. Added value is an incentive to advertisers and has become a standard part of doing business, as media vendors know to make added value part of the advertising negotiation process. Bogan offered an example that added value for advertising in print might be a banner headline on the newspaper's accompanying Internet site (personal communication, May 11, 2004).

Although time shifting, audience guarantees, and added value are things mass media organizations do to accommodate advertisers, there are instances when advertisers accommodate mass media organizations. For example, television networks often package different programs in selling advertising time. In knowing that it would be hard to sell commercial time during low-rated programming and that advertisers want to be on the network's most popular and highest rated program, the network will package a commercial spot during the highest rated program with commercial spots on programs not as popular. This common practice is an accepted part of the industry, and advertisers simply try to match the popular program with a similar type of programming. For example, the advertiser might desire to be on a highly rated situation comedy, and the network might package that purchase with time on another situation comedy rather than forcing the advertiser to buy time on a drama or a reality show.

THE ADVERTISING SUMMARY

The role of advertising in the mass media industry is clear from an economic standpoint, as advertisers provide the revenue that allows the mass media organizations to earn a profit. For many scholars, this arrangement allows for a clear connection between advertisers and influence over content decisions. Evaluating advertisers' influence on the content decision-making process, however, is more complicated. If advertisers are most interested in selling a product, what they most desire is exposure of their brand to the audience, not control of the content. The relationship between mass media organizations and advertisers is not contentious, and often these groups work closely together to help each other achieve the goals of their respective industries. This close relationship does not, however, necessitate interference into the editorial aspects of content decision making, as that level of influence is not a prerequisite to advertisers' achieving their goals of: (a) exposure to the desired target audience, (b) increased product brand recall, and (c) increased sales. The tactic of time shifting, rather than completely pulling out of a program, is evidence that advertisers are not necessarily trying to intrude on the editorial process but are merely trying to use that media vehicle to reach the audience and obtain a positive association for their brand. Influence occurs more in time shifting because this arrangement does not conflict with the advertisers' need of exposure and does not conflict with the editorial decision making and the mass media organizations' need for revenue.

The desire for exposure to a target audience points to the audience as the pivotal constituency group in the content decision-making process. Advertisers will follow the behavior of the audience in developing their communication strategies in terms of placing ads where the audience is participating and developing a creative strategy that enhances brand recall.

SUGGESTED READINGS

Fortunato, J. A., & Dunnam, A. E. (2004). The negotiation philosophy for corporate sponsorship of sports properties. In B. G. Pitts (Ed.), *Sharing best practices in sports marketing: The Sports Marketing Association's inaugural book of papers* (pp. 73–86). Morgantown, WV: Fitness Information Technology.

Gwinner, K. P., & Eaton, J. (1999). Building brand image through event sponsorship: The role of image transfer. *Journal of Advertising, 28*(4), 47–58.

Meenaghan, T. (1991). The role of sponsorship in the marketing communications mix. *International Journal of Advertising, 10*(1), 35–47.

Price, C. J. (2003). Interfering owners or meddling advertisers: How network television news correspondents feel about ownership and advertiser influence on news stories. *Journal of Media Economics, 16*(3), 175–188.

Richards, J. I., & Murphy, J. H. (1996). Economic censorship and free speech: The circle of communication between advertisers, media, and consumers. *Journal of Current Issues and Research in Advertising, 18*(1), 21–34.

Schiller, H. I. (1989). *Culture, Inc.: The corporate takeover of public expression.* New York: Oxford University Press.

Sutherland, M., & Galloway, J. (1981). Role of advertising: Persuasion or agenda-setting? *Journal of Advertising Research 21*(5), 25–29.

9

Audience

In each chapter of this book, the behavior of the audience has been referred to in some capacity. The theoretical foundations of uses and gratifications and media dependency speak to the desires of the audience and their needing certain mass media systems to satisfy multiple needs. It is this consistent satisfaction of needs by media sources that leads to the conclusion that although participation in the mass media is voluntary, there will always be volunteers. It has also become clear that mass media organizations align their content decision making with the expectations, desires, and ultimately the behavior of an active audience seeking certain media outlets.

Agenda setting and framing deal with content providers and media relationships using the many communication vehicles to reach an audience and in many instances, persuade an audience. Transfer of salience is at the core of agenda-setting research, but messages need to be in certain locations and presented or framed in a certain manner to resonate with an audience. The audience has the ability to reject any agenda-setting efforts being made toward them.

At every point of the decision-making process the audience is a factor and is potentially influenced by the relationships and decisions of others, but likewise, the behavior of the audience influences future content decision making. For example, if a film does well at the box office or in video rentals, there is a good chance that movie will have a sequel. If a musical artist has a compact disc sell, there will surely be more recordings from that person or band. The behavior of the audience, both in terms of simple medium use and specific content, is monitored by mass media organizations and other critical constituency groups such as content providers and advertisers.

The initial audience behavior evaluated is mere use in terms of the different mediums in which they are participating. The quantity of mass media use is easy to ascertain as television and radio ratings, newspaper and magazine subscriptions, movie attendance and rentals, Internet sign-ups, and Internet site visits indicate behavior patterns. Once the type of medium use is learned the challenge for people in mass media industries is to get the audience to engage in the specific content they are offering. Medium use and the specific types of content people are participating in are common knowledge for mass media organizations, content providers, and advertisers.

For a television network, the audience feedback measure is ratings. Webster and Lichty (1991) defined ratings as "estimated percentages of the population that see a program or listen to a station" (p. 3). The rating estimation is based on the number of television households in comparison with any other activity in which people might be involved. Ratings data provide the network with the number of people who watch the program and their demographic characteristics, such as geographic location, income, race, and gender. With so many mass media options, television ratings have been on the decline compared with previous generations. For example, the number one prime-time entertainment show for the 2003–2004 season, *CSI*, had an average rating of 15.9, whereas the top program in 1983–1984, *Dallas*, had an average rating of 25.7, and the top show in 1963–1964, *The Beverly Hillbillies*, had an average rating of 39.1.

Atkin and Litman (1986) pointed out that "the broadcast industry is unique in that there is a 'short circuiting' of the program market: consumers express their preference through ratings rather than explicit patronage of market products" (p. 33). They noted that the "ratings game is worthy of academic study because, for better or worse, it subsumes important elements of the public interest in broadcasting" (p. 34). Ratings data are vital because these numbers have such a tremendous impact on the economics of a television network. Webster and Lichty (1991) described ratings as "a fact of life for virtually everyone connected with the electronic media. They are the tools used by advertisers and broadcasters to buy and sell audiences" (p. 3). Whether correctly or not, network personnel and advertisers treat ratings as the ultimate audience feedback measure. These ratings numbers are so accepted in the practical industry that they are often the basis for content decision making on the part of a television network and advertisers.

As much as learning how content is produced, understanding the mass communication process entails knowledge of how, when, and where the audience experiences content. The emerging communication technologies have had a huge impact on audience behavior and have created the capability to access multiple forms of media and information at various times in various locations. The technological change has been in the practical usage and expectations of the audience. People now expect and demand news instantly. They no longer have to wait until the evening news or the next day's newspaper. Some people prefer to go to the Internet and retrieve the information desired at a time convenient to them. Others still prefer to receive their information through traditional media in the packaged, linear fashion that it is presented.

Baron (2003) emphasized that news can now be direct, personalized, and essentially at a person's hip through text pagers. He did point out that people still demand credible information and in a communication environment that is dictated by speed, maintaining accuracy and credibility remains important. The audience expectation of both speed and accuracy puts pressure on the mass media organization and content providers in developing and distributing messages. Baron stated, "In an age of extremely high-speed expectations, those providing information need to understand that there is considerable tolerance for error, providing the errors are acknowledged and explained, and it is clear that there is a strong desire and intention to provide the best and most accurate information then available" (pp. 57–58).

Westin (2004), president of ABC News, wrote an editorial about the changing technological media environment and its impact on the news industry, stating:

> The days are largely gone when the three broadcast networks could decide what the American people watch—and then get them to watch it. With the advent and expansion of cable and, more recently, the Internet—including streaming video that looks a lot like television—there are just too many alternatives available to the audience at all times. Now you'll attract an audience only if what you have to offer is seen to be better than hundreds of alternatives. We've moved from a media oligarchy to a media democracy. We've gone from a few programmers in New York and Los Angeles deciding what people will watch to the people themselves voting with their remote controls every night. This changes fundamentally the decision a news division makes about what it covers. (p. 15)

THE AUDIENCE FUNCTION IN RELATION TO CONTENT PROVIDERS AND ADVERTISERS

As audience media behavior shifts, content providers and advertisers must recognize this movement and strategize to receive exposure for their brand and their message in those locations. Content providers and advertisers simply need to be where the audience is. Through their monitoring of media use, both have a strong idea where their content might receive maximum exposure to the audience. Advertisers, marketers, public relations practitioners, and all content providers know there is going to be mass media use in many diverse forms, and therefore they implement multiple, integrated strategies to get their message exposed to an audience. It is more than just location, as the interpretive behavior of the audience causes content providers and advertisers to evaluate their message and readjust their messages if necessary to one that resonates with the audience.

The mass media organization closely monitors the behavior of the audience, as they are essentially the revenue source. Although advertisers actually pay the bill, they are only going to be in media locations that attract an audience. As is being argued here, more than trying to control editorial content, if advertisers are only seeking exposure of their brand products to a desired demographic to establish brand recall and eventual sales, the relationship between audiences and their participation in content becomes the most crucial. The audience, therefore, becomes the most influential constituency group in the process.

Schiller's (1989) argument claimed that advertising serves as the ultimate validation that allows for messages to exist in society. Validation, in the form of advertising, might guarantee a continuing presence (exposure) of that industry. However, validation does not guarantee, or equate to, public acceptance of the endorsed industry. An audience member can express his or her opinion through media participation in certain content. Audience behavior through watching a television program, listening to a radio broadcast, purchasing a print periodical, or signing up for an Internet service acts as the ultimate validation and acceptance. Schiller made valid points that advertisers act as the validating agent in supporting content and that advertisers try to associate with certain content. A question can be raised if validation and support of content by an advertiser will continue if that content cannot draw an audience. It seems that any validation on the part of advertisers will quickly dissipate without an audience, and what the advertisers ultimately want is the audience in terms of demographics and size they were promised when they agreed to buy the time or space.

Richards and Murphy (1996) stated, "Most contemporary media have chosen to finance their businesses by selling ad space or time. And that space or time is worthless without readers, listeners, or viewers, which means these businesses serve two groups of customers: advertisers and consumers" (p. 29). For many scholars, however, those two constituencies are not equal and the advertisers are always the group being catered to (e.g., Baker, 1992; Croteau & Hoynes, 2001; McChesney, 1997; McManus, 1994). Baker (1992) argued, "Of course, the medium's attempt to obtain advertising revenue leads it to tilt media content toward what advertisers, not readers or viewers, want" (p. 2180). Croteau and Hoynes (2001) claimed, "The consumers that media companies are responding to are the advertisers, not the people who read, watch, or listen to the media" (p. 27). This thinking seems flawed in that how does a mass media organization operate in the interests of the advertiser to the detriment of the audience if choosing content that advertisers desire would not draw an audience? It seems that advertisers would want content produced that is in the interest of the audience and attracts a large audience. Richards and Murphy stated that "a medium is only beneficial to advertisers if consumers use it, and consumers will not use a medium if they are unhappy with its content. Consequently, a smart advertiser will never make demands of a medium that will reduce audience satisfaction" (p. 30).

Buying the products of advertisers who support, or validate, that content can also be construed as approval of that content. Richards and Murphy (1996) pointed out audiences engage in advertiser boycotts. They cautioned: "Advertisers, like politicians, want to alienate no one. Where they suspect consumers will be offended by media content, advertisers will avoid placing their ads in that context, even if no one threatens a boycott" (p. 28). They also contended that "an effective boycott of the medium or program would reduce ratings and therefore make the medium less attractive to advertisers" (p. 29). Although people can choose simply to change the channel or not buy a publication, Fahey (1991) claimed, "Boycotters are not trying to change the media they use, but rather restrict what other people see and hear in the media" (p. 654). This form of protest is on an individual level and it requires similar behavior from large aggregates of the essential targeted demographic to have a major impact.

Although some advertisers clearly would not want to be associated with certain content, it seems highly doubtful that there would be some form of media content, no matter how controversial, that would receive a large audience that some sponsors would not support with their advertising dollars. Conversely, media content, no matter how much it should be in the public interest, that does not receive large amounts of audience participation will probably not attract many advertisers. If there are problems with certain content, this is when time-shifting arrangements for advertisers are made.

The movements to include strategies of sponsorship and product placement are simply movements to locations where the audience is and where the brands exposed hope to be noticed and recalled. The challenges of the mass media environment and advertising clutter are to get the message into the location where the audience is, and for some of these locations, competition between content providers can become very intense. Bernays (1955) commented, "Competition for attention of the public has been continually broadened and intensified because the public decides whether an enterprise is to succeed or fail" (p. 5).

At this point the content is being governed by the laws of supply and demand and the similarity between the mass media and other industries is the strongest. Gordon and Kittross (1999) contended that the business influences of the mass media are irrelevant, as the market will determine what customers want. The caveat is that for any type of content, majority participation on the part of the audience is not necessary and often a majority is not achieved. Therefore, content that obtains largely recognized cultural status is not supported by the majority of the population. There simply needs to be enough participation on the part of the audience to sustain the place of that content within the market. There is not one single media entity, television program or Internet site, in which half the country participates, although the Super Bowl comes the closest in gathering the largest share of the television audience each year.

In not obtaining a majority, each mass media organization and the content it produces (i.e., each television program or magazine) have "their" audience, as all of this media content comes with its own set of audience demographic variables. An audience can be segmented based on common behavior, interest, and occupation, and common demographic characteristics of age, gender, or income. The objective is to get these specific audiences to continue to behave in a certain manner (e.g., Hunt & Ruben, 1993). The concept of a common pattern of consumption indicates that an audience is not the entirety of the public, and getting all of the public to react a certain way is not necessarily the communication objective, although trying to attract as large of an audience as possible is a goal. Hunt and Ruben (1993) broke down the audience into those who have access (individuals to whom the information products and services were available) and those who are exposed (individuals who actually saw, heard, or read particular information about products and services). They stated, "Specific measures of exposure are critical from a marketing and advertising perspective for the purpose of targeting advertising and public messages for particular audiences" (p. 62).

In terms of audience behavior dictating future content, Shaw and Martin (1992) commented that audiences respond to the content they are provided and "perhaps even influence it as the news media try to match audience interests" (p. 906). Dennis (1994) argued, "News organizations that are a part of big business are governed by market forces, and market research is said to determine what America (and the rest of the world) reads, hears, and watches" (p. 32). In studying a large daily newspaper, Sumpter (2000) found that editors often selected stories based on trying to "forecast the reactions of various audiences to stories, the audience appeal to a collection of stories, and a story's ability to compete with other non-print sources" (p. 343).

Branham commented that even the media routine is very much dictated by the expectations of the readers (personal communication, March 28, 2003). She cited that when working as the senior vice president and executive editor of the *Tallahassee Democrat*, hometown newspaper of Florida State University, she could expect calls from readers if scores and stories about Florida State University football were not in the next day's newspaper. She also pointed out that newspapers look to market research to learn what readers want, and they allocate resources on those types of stories. Branham indicated that this type of research could serve as an indication to audiences that are perhaps being neglected, and if more stories were geared toward that audience it could lead to an increase in readership and a group of advertisers trying to reach that demographic. For example, there could be an emphasis to do more stories about a certain demographic to try to attract that group as readers.

The aspect of the argument that the audience is the driving force behind content decision making that becomes somewhat faulty is that the choice that any audience member can make in his or her media usage is only made from the content options provided. Success is determined by the audience, but trying to predict what the audience will like and continue to participate in is difficult (e.g., Buchman, 2000). This could lead to a system where mass media organizations produce content that is safe, has worked in the past, and will not offend a large portion of the audience. This certainly speaks to the concerns of diversity and large corporate conglomeration ownership.

McQuail (2000) commented that "media organizations tend to reproduce selectively according to criteria that suit their own goals and interests. These may sometimes be professional and craft criteria, but more weight is usually given to what sells most or gets higher ratings" (p. 295). Although some would find McQuail's statement problematic in terms of weight being given to what sells and implying that mass media organizations should be held to a different standard from other industries, the fact that mass media organizations are after all a business and should have the right to earn a profit and continue to provide products that inform and entertain people should not be construed as a negative. Concerns about a lack of diversity and producing only safe content might be exaggerated. With the number of cable television channels available, the Internet, and the more traditional media forms of print and broadcast, it is hard to find a large aggregate of people without some content aimed at them and an advertiser looking to expose its brand to that niche group.

It was not easy to predict the success of 24-hour all-news channel, 24-hour all-sports television, political talk radio, a newspaper focused only on business, magazines that present more of a conservative or liberal perspective, or any of the various Internet sites before some entrepreneur took a chance and financed the industry. Now all of these are vital parts the culture's mass media experience and components essential to the public discourse of the nation. With predictability of audience use being difficult to determine, other than what has worked in the past, content tends to repeat itself with similar stories, movies, television shows, and actors and actresses. Sandy Grushow, chairmen of Fox Entertainment Group, simply stated, "The audience is never wrong" (cited in Carter, 2003a, p. A20).

SUGGESTED READINGS

Buchman, J. G. (2000). Television newscast promotion and marketing. In S. T. Eastman (Ed.), *Research in media promotion* (pp. 265–296). Mahwah, NJ: Lawrence Erlbaum Associates.

Hunt, T., & Ruben, B. D. (1993). *Mass communication: Producers and consumers*. New York: HarperCollins.

Webster, J. G., & Lin, S. F. (2002). The Internet audience: Web use as mass behavior. *Journal of Broadcasting & Electronic Media, 46*(1), 1–12.

Webster, J. G., Phalen, P. F., & Lichty, L. W. (2000). *Ratings analysis: The theory and practice of audience research*. Mahwah, NJ: Lawrence Erlbaum Associates.

Conclusion

The multiple complex practices and detailed standard operating procedures of any industry are difficult to chronicle, yet easy to criticize. Such is the case with the mass media industry. Not only are the practices within the mass media organization complex, but so many constituency groups that have agendas, desires, and a stake in what messages are exposed and how those messages are presented to the audience complicate the process. The importance of learning about this process is that the audience constantly uses the mass media to satisfy a variety of needs. There is also the potential impact that these messages can have on the audience.

This book began with a few premises—the first being that although the responsibility of the mass media is to produce content, the mass media organization is simply not the sole entity involved in the content decision-making process. Media employees do not make decisions unilaterally, as several different people and constituency groups constantly and simultaneously try to influence the mass media organizations and their decisions regarding the content they select to make available to the audience. In addition to mere exposure and getting stories selected, these constituency groups are equally focused on how that content is framed, the facts and perspectives that will be highlighted in the story.

The interactions between the mass media organization and the various constituency groups are complex relationships that always have the potential to influence the content decision-making process. The constituency groups of content providers, advertisers, and the audience all use the mass media organization as the vehicle to expose their message or brand name to the audience. These constituency groups, in essence, depend on the mass media organization to be the exposure vehicle necessary to get noticed by the audience. These groups try to influence the content decision-making process because they know the audience depends and uses the mass media to satisfy many needs such as information, entertainment, and social desires.

Another major premise of this book is that the business of the media is to produce content that will attract an audience. The audience of this content is then offered to advertisers, giving the mass media organization its opportunity for economic profit. The business objective of the decision-making process of a mass media organization is to produce content that will attract audience participation, which in turn will attract advertiser support and eventual profit to the mass media organization. A relationship of interdependency emerges between the mass media organization and content providers through the recognition that the mass media organizations also depend on many of these content providers to obtain the quality content needed to attract an audience and subsequent advertisers.

Complicating the mass media organization decision-making process is that selection and framing of content are a necessary condition of the process because of time and space restrictions. The agenda-setting theoretical model indicates that not all of the stories can be selected and that even the stories that are covered cannot be done so with the same standard. This selection and framing can signify the importance of the topic. Although behavioral effects based on mass media messages can be debated, the ability to select and frame messages is a power that the mass media organization always possesses.

It is these necessary conditions of decisions of selection and framing that begin to set up a logical conclusion: The mass media system is not, and can never be perfect. All of the stories cannot be covered, and once there is selection and framing inevitably there will be complaints: Why was this story covered? Why wasn't that story covered? Why was the story covered from this angle? Why wasn't more time spent on this story? It becomes virtually impossible to please everyone from both the distribution and retrieval perspectives.

How "should" the mass media operate and how "do" the mass media operate thus become two entirely different questions. How should they operate invites as many opinions and answers as there are people. When questions of how the mass media should operate are posed, issues of ideology and bias are raised. Because selection and framing are necessary conditions, inevitably there are many stories not covered and therefore there is ample opportunity for people to complain about what is and is not covered. This critique, however, is rarely, if ever, objective and is often, if not always, examined through the ideological prism of the receiver. Republicans complain that stories are being shaded to favor Democrats, and vice versa. Interest groups complain that their organization or cause is not getting enough coverage. Complaints come from the people trying to influence content and from the audience receiving the content. Even national sports announcers get criticized for being biased against a favorite team if the announcer makes an analysis with which the viewer does not agree.

Add the fact that mass media organization employees are human beings making critical content decisions while dealing with human problems of family and trying to maintain or improve their job status, and the system gets even more complicated (or in some ways simplified if taking the position that the individual employee is only acting on his or her own behalf). For all of these reasons the mass media become an easy target for criticism. Therefore, the system of mass media content decision making can best be categorized as human and imperfect. The characteristics of constant audience media use and dependence make it an imperfect system with potentially large consequences.

BASIC GENERALIZATIONS OF THE MASS MEDIA CONTENT DECISION-MAKING PROCESS

In trying to explain the mass media content decision-making process there are some general conclusions that can be drawn. The process demonstrates that several successful interdependent relationships occur at the same time. Constituency groups compete simultaneously for exposure, and the people of the mass media organization have to sort them out. The sorting-out process also has to be done quickly, and decisions regarding content might not receive the deliberation the various constituency groups might hope or even the personnel of the mass media organization desire.

These relationships are successful because all of the entities understand what the other groups need and try to make the relationships work in a way that is beneficial to all entities. Advertisers know what mass media organizations need, and mass media organizations know how to be accommodating to fulfill advertisers' needs. Mass media organizations know what content providers desire and content providers know what mass media organizations desire. All of these organizations hope to know what the audience desires by providing content that produces a positive behavior response.

The audience emerges as a powerful entity factored into every stage of the process. Even at the earliest stages of establishing media routines, not all of the content that is possible is considered when making decisions. The philosophical establishing of media routines and developing the mass media organization as a brand help journalists simplify the complex process and begin to organize decision making. The routines also create a set of expectations on the part of the audience, and these expectations can help predict future audience behavior. The mass media routine does not account for every decision, and decisions need to be made within the routine.

Therefore, the strategic communication of what each mass media organization and each constituency group is doing is made with the expectations of the audience in mind. The content decision-making process is dictated by the expectations, desires, dependencies, and ultimately the behavior of the audience. The arguments of many theorists that the mass media organizations are only trying to please advertisers and stockholders are a little misleading in that advertisers most want an audience, particularly a desired target audience, that might buy their product. Advertisers pay the mass media organizations and invest in commercials and other communication strategies only if that content delivers an audience. If the mass media organization only does stories to please stockholders and advertisers and if these groups are only satisfied if a profit is being made, the item advertisers most desire is not control of content but instead stories or content that deliver a large audience. A large audience generates advertising revenue and profit for the mass media organization. If the mass media organizations are all about profits, they have to attract an audience—no audience, no advertisers, no profits.

How the process works is very much a function of whom the process is intended for—the audience. Sanders pointed out that at *Time* magazine there is certainly a sense of duty to the readers in providing them with stories that the staff at *Time* deem important, but there is also a realization that the magazine has to appeal to the audience and has to sell. One situation that Sanders explained is that when he was covering the Supreme Court he was not to write using extensive legal jargon but was to write the story so that it is more understandable. According to Sanders, the reporter should "always write for the masses" (personal communication, August 8, 2003).

In his article about being a Nielsen family, Susswein (2003) explained that he found himself watching more television, but claimed, "I watched for the same reasons I've always watched: to connect to the world, to escape and to have some familiar background noise in my life" (p. E8). He concluded, "In the television-viewing world, there are two groups that decide the fate of programs. One is the network executives. The other consists of ordinary viewers" (p. E8).

There are a couple of caveats to the idea that the audience drives the process that need to be addressed. The first is that audiences can only select from the content that is provided to them. Mass media organizations make an initial choice as to what content to show, although even that is often based on what has been successful with the audience in the past. After that initial choice, it does not take long for the organizations to receive the feedback of the audience's behavior and make decisions whether to continue with that content. Mass media organizations as profit entities can either give the people what they want and follow the behavior of the audience or convince the audience that what is being shown is important and should be watched. By doing the latter, the chances of gaining an audience that is in essence being lectured to by media elites is problematic. Therefore, the trend in media is always to provide a form of content and, if the audience responds well, continue to provide more of the same.

On the idea of giving people what they will watch or read or providing them with stories they should know about, Webber, senior vice president and publisher of usatoday.com, pointed out that news judgments have to be made, and it is important to reflect the fullness of the readers' life. He stated, "Our mission is to provide information on a variety of topics" (personal communication, May 25, 2004).

Westin, president of ABC News, commented that you want to lead the audience but not by too much so that you are speaking past them. However, if you simply follow the audience you do not add anything for them. He stated that you try to "find information that is interesting, important, and get the audience to understand why it is important" (personal communication, May 28, 2004). Westin explained that the mission of ABC News is to "do the best broadcast journalism for the most people and the challenge is to do both" (personal communication, May 28, 2004). He contended that it is easy to accomplish one of these mission objectives, as you could do a great journalistic story that people are not interested in and conversely do a shallow story that many people might watch but does not have any journalistic value. Westin added, "We try to help the American people live their lives and provide information on all of the things that are important for the over 200 million people that experience ABC News content in some capacity in a given week" (personal communication, May 28, 2004).

The second important caveat for the importance of the audience in the content decision-making process is there does not have to be participation by the majority of the audience, just enough to sustain the business and maintain its place in the market. The system places a tremendous amount of trust in the audience. The notion that the audience most dictates the decision-making process is not a bad thing. It is not a perfect system; it is a market similar to every other industry. The mass media are essentially operating under the primary business model governed by the laws of supply and demand where the market decides which content (products) stays and which goes.

Having the laws of supply and demand govern the mass media industry is problematic for some. McManus (1994) devalued the role of the audience, claiming they do not understand how to evaluate news quality. He said, "It is difficult for consumers to gain the knowledge necessary to critically evaluate news coverage outside of news departments' self-promotion and advertising campaigns" (p. 64). Zelizer (1993) contended, "Journalistic power burgeons largely due to the public's general acquiescence and its reluctance to question journalism's parameters and fundamental legitimacy" (p. 80). Critical theorists see the mass media as the essential agent for the continuance of the capitalist system. The story they are most complaining about not being told is their perceived shortcomings of the capitalist system. In their view it is the market system that has led to media conglomeration, a lack of diversity, and ultimately a hindering of democracy. They would also call for more state control of the media industry, but it seems the state would have even more control over messages and the flow of information if the media were state run. At least the current system has some form of independence and an allowance for the audience to make some determinations about the success or failure of media content.

Is having a market system for an industry as far reaching in its impact as the mass media the best system, with mass media organizations giving the people only what they want? Perhaps not. Are there some stories or issues that people should know and learn of, but are not being covered because they will not deliver a larger audience? Possibly. The criticism about the media system as currently constructed is: What stories are we not learning about?

PROCESS SUGGESTIONS

In an imperfect system, concerns are often raised, but viable alternatives to the current system might not be practical. This does not make any of these concerns any less justifiable, but asking the mass media organization to operate in a different economic system from other industries is not realistic. It costs money to produce quality news. Even if the economic variables were removed and the mass media had unlimited resources of money and personnel and did not care about ratings or circulations and attracting advertisers, the responsibility to select and frame remains, and there would be just as much criticism of their content decision making from the people and the constituency groups with a vested interest in the content. Once the necessary selection and framing had been done, complaints would emerge and an imperfect system would be exposed.

It is too simplistic to say that the media should be more democratic as a final solution, as articulated by some (e.g., Mazzocco, 1994). That ideal sounds terrific in theory, but how does this work in practice? Even if the "ideal" network was created, how do you guarantee people will watch? You cannot force people to participate in messages they do not want to waste their time watching or listening to. Certain brands in each product category are better, and these businesses that risked the investment are rewarded through consumer behavior. News and information industries are no different.

The system has strengths and flaws and perhaps the best that can be done is to provide suggestions of how to cope with a flawed system. Suggestions have been made to improve the mass media organization itself. In terms of news coverage, Dennis (1994) saw a need for a commitment from news organizations to engage in quality news. Again, quality is a very ambiguous, subjective term and often in the eye of the beholder in terms of the perspectives that are emphasized. He offered a plausible solution, requesting editors and broadcast executives to indicate how their news organization guides itself; what resources it devotes to news gathering; how the public should access and evaluate news organizations; how individuals might provide feedback to news organizations; and what the goals, purposes, and measures of quality are. This book tried to point out some of these objectives as put forth by Dennis.

Gomery (2000), too, provided suggestions for the mass media organization by offering six media performance norms that could serve as a guide for how mass media organizations should operate: (a) not to waste resources and be efficient; (b) facilitate free speech and political discourse; (c) facilitate public order; (d) to protect and maintain cultural quality, offering some role of media diversity; (e) bring to the marketplace new technologies as quickly as possible; and (f) be equitable and not shut out members of society as media employees and managers (p. 523).

Although all are laudable goals, can they all be achieved simultaneously? The answer to the question of being able to serve democracy and be a profit-oriented company is also subjective. Critics point to a mass media company earning a profit and argue that they should be doing more for democracy. Berkowitz (1993) offered a realistic description of the situation in that there are "tradeoffs between journalistic judgment and the imperatives from the business side of a media organization" (p. 67).

With all of the criticisms of the mass media system, Miller (1986) still contended that "they [the media] are designed to fulfill consensually agreed upon societal functions and they generally accomplish this goal admirably" (p. 138). Baron (2003) argued that "the news media's diversity, ubiquity, and competitive instincts have, for the most part, served America exceedingly well, and not only America, because CNN and other major news outlets have become world brands, delivering news and information around the clock to audiences around the globe" (p. 67). Gardner (1990) offered an overall perspective on the performance of the mass media, arguing that "it is easy to indict the media. But for anyone who has observed the devastating consequences of a controlled press, the bottom line is clear. Throughout our history our free press has made an overwhelmingly positive contribution" (p. 87).

Westin pointed out that the evaluation of the news media tends to overlook the people and that a news division is only as smart and creative as its people. He contended that "many in journalism are deeply committed to bring information to people and more than business reasons or political reasons content decisions are made by people who really believed they thought it was important to put that information on the air" (personal communication, May 28, 2004).

Price (2003) offered another important group where suggestions to improve the system can occur, the audience. She stated that "people may have to watch more than one news program to get the objectivity that they desire or the definition of news itself may need to be changed" (p. 187). The idea of an informed democracy does not place all of the responsibility on the mass media organization or content providers, but also on the audience who has to become engaged in the issues and learn the variety of perspectives that are available. Part of the responsibility of an informed citizenry is on the citizenry to become actively informed.

The current mass media system through communication technologies is at unprecedented "mass" for delivering a diversity of ideas. This communication environment creates challenges and opportunities for both the mass media organizations and their constituency groups, including the audience. Westin (2004) wrote in an editorial:

> The challenge we face is how to take this new world of media and make it a new world for great journalism. We're being given an opportunity. There are no assurances of success. The splintering of the media has not, in the past, always led to stronger journalism. With intelligence, daring and a bit of luck, maybe we can earn the audience's attention through the strength of our reporting and presentation, even when there are virtually unlimited choices. (p. 15)

As far as the audience is concerned, with all of the different mass media organizations distributing important content in many convenient forms and mediums, there is little excuse for people not to be aware of the happenings of the world or where candidates stand on certain issues so long as they put in a little time and effort to learn of the issues. So people might have to watch the *CBS Evening News*, but also *Special Report with Brit Hume* on the Fox News Channel. People might have to read columns by George Will, Charles Krauthammer, Thomas Friedman, and David Broder or visit a few different Internet sites to collect various opinions and make an informed decision about an issue.

In the descriptions of how the process operates hopefully what becomes inevitable is that the audience is the major constituency group driving the process, and the feeling here is that having the market decide, despite some flaws, is the best possible scenario. The audience has the power through its behavior to change the process and not accept mediocrity from mass media organizations.

If the audience is one of the major constituency groups that can influence the content decision-making process, it is incumbent on the audience to learn about the process and all of its intricacies. The audience should be aware that the comment they are seeing is by the public relations person for that organization and his or her comments are being made in the best interests of that client. The audience should be aware that advertisers are always trying to persuade them to purchase their product and their message is only from the perspective of the advertiser. By learning about the content decision-making process, people can better understand the mass media industry and learn about how and why certain decisions are made and certain content appears on their television sets, in their newspapers, or on the Internet. The audience is then in a better position to evaluate these messages and provide meaningful feedback to content providers, advertisers, and mass media organizations, thus raising the quality and efficiency of the content decision-making process at every stage.

References

Aaker, D. A. (1991). *Managing brand equity*. New York: Free Press.
Aaker, D. A., & Joachimsthaler, E. (2000). *Brand leadership*. New York: Free Press.
Aaker, J. L. (1997). Dimensions of brand personality. *Journal of Marketing Research, 34*(3), 347–356.
Adamic, L. A., & Huberman, B. A. (1999). *The nature of markets in the World Wide Web*. Palo Alto, CA: Xerox Palo Alto Research Center.
Akhavan-Majid, R., & Boudreau, T. (1995). Chain ownership, organizational size, and editorial role perceptions. *Journalism and Mass Communication Quarterly, 72*, 863–873.
Albarran, A. (1996). *Media economics: Understanding markets, industries and concepts*. Ames: Iowa State University Press.
Alger, D. (1998). *Megamedia: How giant corporations dominate mass media, distort competition, and endanger democracy*. New York: Rowman & Littlefield.
Alter, J. (1995, August 14). A call for Chinese walls. *Newsweek,* p. 31.
Altschull, J. H. (1995). *Agents of power* (2nd ed.). White Plains, NY: Longman.
Anderson, C. A. (1997). Effects of violent movies and trait hostility on hostile feelings and aggressive thoughts. *Aggressive Behavior, 23*, 161–178.
Anderson, D. (2002, December 8). Woods is not obliged to boycott. *The New York Times*, Section 8, pp. 1, 15.
Ang, I. (1990). Culture & communication. *European Journal of Communication, 5*, 239–261.
Anschuetz, N. (1997a). Point of view: Building brand popularity: The myth of segmenting to brand success. *Journal of Advertising Research, 37*, 63–66.
Anschuetz, N. (1997b). Profiting from the "80–20 rule of thumb." *Journal of Advertising Research, 37*, 51–56.
Arant, M. D., & Anderson, J. Q. (2001). Newspaper online editors support traditional standards. *Newspaper Research Journal, 22*, 57–69.
Ashley, L., & Olson, B. (1998). Constructing reality: Print media's framing of the women's movement, 1966 to 1986. *Journalism & Mass Communication Quarterly, 75*, 63–277.

Atkin, D. J., & Jeffres, L. W. (1998). Understanding Internet adoption as telecommunications behavior. *Journal of Broadcasting & Electronic Media, 42*(4), 475–490.

Atkin, D., & Litman, B. (1986). Network TV programming: Economics, audiences, and the ratings game, 1971–1986. *Journal of Communication, 36*(3), 32–50.

Austin, E. W., & Pinkleton, B. E. (1999). The relation between media content evaluations and political disaffection. *Mass Communication & Society, 2*, 105–122.

Bae, H. (2000). Product differentiation in national TV newscasts: A comparison of the cable all-news networks and the broadcast networks. *Journal of Broadcasting & Electronic Media, 44*, 62–77.

Bagdikian, B. H. (2000). *The media monopoly* (6th ed.). Boston: Beacon.

Baker, C. E. (1992). Advertising and a democratic press. *University of Pennsylvania Law Review, 140*, 2097–2243.

Ball-Rokeach, S. J. (1985). The origins of individual media-system dependency: A sociological framework. *Communication Research, 12*, 485–510.

Ball-Rokeach, S. J., & Cantor, M. G. (Eds.). (1986). *Media, audience, and social structure*. Newbury Park, CA: Sage.

Ball-Rokeach, S. J., & DeFleur, M. L. (1976). A dependency model of mass-media effects. *Communication Research, 3*, 3–21.

Ball-Rokeach, S. J., & DeFleur, M. L. (1986). The interdependence of the media and other social systems. In G. Gumpert & R. Cathcart (Eds.), *Inter/media: Interpersonal communication in a media world* (3rd ed., pp. 81–96). New York: Oxford University Press.

Ball-Rokeach, S. J., Hale, M., Schaffer, A., Porras, L., Harris, P., & Drayton, M. (1999). Changing the media production process: From aggressive to injury-sensitive traffic crash stories. In D. Demers & K. Viswanath (Eds.), *Mass media, social control, and social change: A macrosocial perspective* (pp. 229–262). Ames: Iowa State University Press.

Ball-Rokeach, S. J., Rokeach, M., & Grube, J. W. (1986). Changing and stabilizing political behavior and beliefs. In S. J. Ball-Rokeach & M. G. Cantor (Eds.), *Media, audience, and social structure* (pp. 280–290). Newbury Park, CA: Sage.

Baron, G. R. (2003). *Now is too late: Survival in an era of instant news*. Upper Saddle River, NJ: Prentice Hall.

Becker, L. B., & Kosicki, G. M. (1995). Understanding the message-producer/message receiver transaction. *Research in Political Sociology, 7*, 33–62.

Bednarski, P. J., & Higgins, J. M. (2003, March 24). Heyward: Objectivity a function of fairness. *Broadcasting & Cable*, p. 55.

Behr, R. L., & Iyengar, S. (1985). Television news, real-world cues, and changes in the public agenda. *Public Opinion Quarterly, 49*, 38–57.

Bellamy, R. V., Jr., & Traudt, P. J. (2000). Television branding as promotion. In S. T. Eastman (Ed.), *Research in media promotion* (pp. 127–159). Mahwah, NJ: Lawrence Erlbaum Associates.

Bennett, W. L. (2000). Introduction: Communication and civic engagement in comparative perspective. *Political Communication, 17*, 307–312.

Berger, B. K., & Park, D. J. (2003). Public relation(ship)s or private controls? Practitioner perspectives on the uses and benefits of new technologies. *New Jersey Journal of Communication, 11*, 76–99.

Berkowitz, D. (1991). Assessing forces in the selection of local television news. *Journal of Broadcasting & Electronic Media, 35*, 245–251.

Berkowitz, D. (1993). Work roles and news selection in local TV: Examining the business-journalism dialectic. *Journal of Broadcasting and Electronic Media, 37*, 67–81.

Berkowitz, D. (1997). *Social meaning of news: A text-reader.* Thousand Oaks, CA: Sage.

Bernays, E. L. (1955). *The engineering of consent.* Norman: University of Oklahoma Press.

Berry, S. T., & Biel, A. L. (1992). How brand image drives brand equity. *Journal of Advertising Research, 32*(6), RC6–RC12.

Binder, A. (1993). Media depictions of harm in heavy metal and rap music. *American Sociological Review, 58,* 753–767.

Black, J., Steele, B., & Barney, R. (1993). *Doing ethics in journalism: A handbook with case studies.* Greencastle, IN: The Sigma Delta Chi Foundation and the Society of Professional Journalists.

Blackston, M. (2000). Observations: Building brand equity by managing the brand's relationships. *Journal of Advertising Research, 40*(6), 101–105.

Blumler, J. G. (1979). The role of theory in uses and gratifications studies. *Communication Research, 6,* 9–36.

Blumler, J. G., Gurevitch, M., & Katz, E. (1985). Reaching out: A future of gratifications research. In K. E. Rosengren, L. A. Wenner, & P. Palmgreen (Eds.), *Media gratifications research: Current perspectives* (pp. 255–273). Beverly Hills, CA: Sage.

Blumler, J. G., & Katz, E. (Eds). (1974). *The uses of mass communication: Current perspectives on gratifications research.* Newbury Park, CA: Sage.

Blyskal, J., & Blyskal, M. (1985). *PR: How the public relations industry writes the news.* New York: Morrow.

Breed, W. (1955). Social control in the newsroom: A functional analysis. *Social Forces, 33,* 326–355.

Brill, A. M. (2001). Online journalists embrace new marketing function. *Newspaper Research Journal, 22,* 28–40.

Bryant, J., & Zillmann, D. (Eds.). (2002). *Media effects: Advances in theory & research* (2nd ed.). Mahwah, NJ: Lawrence Erlbaum Associates.

Buchman, J. G. (2000). Television newscast promotion and marketing. In S. T. Eastman (Ed.), *Research in media promotion* (pp. 265–296). Mahwah, NJ: Lawrence Erlbaum Associates.

Budd, M., Entman, R. M., & Steinman, C. (1990). The affirmative character of U.S. cultural studies. *Critical Studies in Mass Communication, 7,* 169–184.

Burns, J. E. (1998). Information subsidies and agenda building: A study of local radio news. *New Jersey Journal of Communication, 6,* 90–100.

Burson, H. (1997). Beyond "PR": Redefining the role of public relations. In G. R. Carter (Ed.), *Perspectives: Public relations* (pp. 16–22). St. Paul, MN: Coursewise.

Callison, C. (2002). Media relations and the Internet: How Fortune 500 company Web sites assist journalists in news gathering. *Public Relations Review, 29,* 13–28.

Cameron, G. T., Sallot, L., & Curtin, P. A. (1997). Public relations and the production of news: A critical review and a theoretical framework. In B. Burleson (Ed.), *Communication yearbook 20* (pp. 111–115). Thousand Oaks, CA: Sage.

Carey, J. W., & Kreiling, A. L. (1974). Popular culture and uses and gratifications: Notes toward an accommodation. In J. G. Blumler & E. Katz (Eds.), *The uses of mass communications: Current perspectives on gratifications research* (Vol. 3, pp. 225–248). Beverly Hills, CA: Sage.

Carragee, K., Rosenblatt, M., & Michaud, G. (1987). Agenda-setting research: A critique and theoretical alternative. In S. Thomas (Ed.), *Studies in communication* (Vol. 3, pp. 35–49). Norwood, NJ: Ablex.

Carrick, P. M. (1959). Why continued advertising is necessary. *Journal of Marketing, 23*, 386–98.

Carroll, C. E., & McCombs, M. E. (2003). Agenda-setting effects of business news on the publics images and opinions about major corporations. *Corporate Reputation Review, 16*, 1–24.

Carter, B. (2003a, January 25). Viewer shift will write new reality for TV, executives say. *Austin American-Statesman*, pp. A1, A20.

Carter, B. (2003b, February 28). CBS and White House quarrel over Saddam. *The International Herald Tribune*, p. 3.

Centerwall, B. (1989). Exposure to television as a risk factor for violence. *American Journal of Epidemiology, 129*, 643–652.

Chaffee, S. H. (1986). Mass media and interpersonal channels: Competitive, convergent, or complementary? In G. Gumpert & R. Cathcart (Eds.), *Inter/media: Interpersonal communication in a media world* (3rd ed., pp. 62–80). New York: Oxford University Press.

Chan-Olmsted, S. M., & Kim, Y. (2001). Perceptions of branding among television station managers: An exploratory analysis. *Journal of Broadcasting & Electronic Media, 45*, 75–91.

Chan-Olmsted, S. M., & Kim, Y. (2002). The PBS brand versus cable brands: Assessing the brand image of public television in a multichannel environment. *Journal of Broadcasting & Electronic Media, 46*, 300–320.

Chang, T. K., & Lee, J. W. (1992). Factors affecting gatekeepers' selection of foreign news: A national survey of newspaper editors. *Journalism Quarterly, 69*, 554–561.

Cohen, B. C. (1963). *The press and foreign policy*. Princeton, NJ: Princeton University Press.

Cohen, E. C. (2002). Online journalism as market-driven journalism. *Journal of Broadcasting & Electronic Media, 46*, 532–548.

Cohen, R. M. (1997). The corporate takeover of news: Blunting the sword. In E. Barnouw, P. Auderhide, R. M. Cohen, T. Frank, T. Gitlin, D. Lieberman, M. C. Miller, G. Roberts, & T. Schatz (Eds.), *Conglomerates and the media* (pp. 31–60). New York: New Press.

Cohen, S., & Young, J. (Eds.). (1973). *The manufacture of news: A reader*. Beverly Hills, CA: Sage.

Colford, P. D. (2002a, December 4). *Times* editors kill 2 columns in Augusta rift. *New York Daily News*, p. 50.

Colford, P. D. (2002b, December 6). Anderson says he'll still cover The Masters for *New York Times*. *New York Daily News*, p. x.

Compaine, B. M. (2000). Distinguishing between concentration and competition. In B. M. Compaine & D. Gomery (Eds.), *Who owns the media? Competition and concentration in the mass media industry* (3rd ed., pp. 537–581). Mahwah, NJ: Lawrence Erlbaum Associates.

Compaine, B. M., & Gomery, D. (Eds.). (2000). *Who owns the media? Competition and concentration in the mass media industry* (3rd ed.). Mahwah, NJ: Lawrence Erlbaum Associates.

Cooper, S. (1996). Military control over war news: The implications of the Persian Gulf. *New Jersey Journal of Communication, 4*, 3–20.

Cornwell, T. B., & Maignan, I. (1998). An international review of sponsorship research. *Journal of Advertising, 27*(1), 1–21.

Coulson, D. C. (1994). Impact of ownership on newspaper quality. *ournalism Quarterly, 71*, 403–410.

Coulson, D. C., & Hansen, A. (1995). The *Louisville Courier-Journal*'s news content after purchase by Gannett. *Journalism and Mass Communication Quarterly, 72*, 205–215.

Croteau, D., & Hoynes, W. (2001). *The business of media: Corporate media and the public interest*. Thousand Oaks, CA: Pine Forge Press.

Curran, J., Gurevitch, M., & Woollacott, J. (1982). The study of the media: Theoretical approaches. In M. Gurevitch, T. Bennett, J. Curran, & J. Woollacott (Eds.), *Culture, society and the media* (pp. 11–29). London: Methuen.

Cutlip, S. M., Center, A. H., & Broom, G. M. (1994). *Effective public relations* (7th ed.). Englewood Cliffs, NJ: Prentice Hall.

Danielian, L. H., & Reese, S. D. (1989). A closer look at intermedia influences on agenda-setting: The cocaine issue of 1986. In P. J. Shoemaker (Ed.), *Communication campaigns about drugs: Government, media and the public* (pp. 47–66). Hillsdale, NJ: Lawrence Erlbaum Associates.

Davis, S. M. (2002). *Brand asset management: Driving profitable growth through your brands*. San Francisco: Jossey-Bass.

Dean, D. H. (2002). Associating the corporation with a charitable event through sponsorship: Measuring the effects on corporate community relations. *Journal of Advertising, 31*(4), 77–88.

Demers, D. (1996). Corporate newspaper structure, profits and organizational goals. *Journal of Media Economics, 9*(2), 1–23.

Demers, D. (1998). Revisiting corporate newspaper structure and profit making. *Journal of Media Economics, 11*(2), 19–45.

Demers, D., & Merskin, D. (2000). Corporate news structure and the managerial revolution. *Journal of Media Economics, 13*(2), 103–121.

Dennis, E. E. (1994) News ethics and split-personality journalism. *Television Quarterly, 27*, 29–35.

De Vany, A. S., & Walls, W. D. (1999). Uncertainty in the movie industry: Does star power reduce the terror of the box office? *Journal of Cultural Economics, 23*, 285–318.

Dreier, P. (1978). Newsroom democracy and media monopoly: The dilemmas of workplace reform among professional journalists. *The Insurgent Sociologist, 8*(2/3), 70–86.

Eastman, S. T. (2000). Orientation to promotion and research. In S. T. Eastman (Ed.), *Research in media promotion* (pp. 3–18). Mahwah, NJ: Lawrence Erlbaum Associates.

Ehrlich, M. C. (1995). The ethical dilemma of television news sweeps. *Journal of Mass Media Ethics, 10*, 37–47.

Elber, L. (2003, August 25). TV gets aggressive in going after viewers. *Austin American-Statesman*, p. E7.

Engelhardt, T. (1994). The Gulf War as total television. In S. Jeffords & L. Rabinowitz (Eds.), *Seeing through the media* (pp. 81–95). New Brunswick, NJ: Rutgers University Press.

Entman, R. (1993). Framing: Toward clarification of a fractured paradigm. *Journal of Communication, 43*(4), 51–58.

Ettema, J. S., Whitney, D. C., & Wackman, D. B. (1987). Professional mass communicators. In C. H. Berger & S. H. Chaffee (Eds.), *Handbook of communication science* (pp. 747–780). Beverly Hills, CA: Sage.

Evans, W. A. (1990). The interpretive turn in media research: Innovation, iterations, or illusion. *Critical Studies in Mass Communication, 7*, 147–168.

Fahey, P. M. (1991). Advocacy group boycotting of network television advertisers and its effects on programming content. *University of Pennsylvania Law Review, 140*, 647–709.

Fallows, J. M. (1996). *Breaking the news: How the media undermine American democracy*. New York: Pantheon.

Farrelly, F. J., Quester, P. C., & Burton, R. (1997). Integrating sports sponsorship into the corporate marketing function: An international comparative study. *International Marketing Review, 14*, 170–182.

Ferguson, D. A. (1992). Channel repertoire in the presence of remote control devices, VCR's and cable television. *Journal of Broadcasting & Electronic Media, 38*, 83–91.

Ferguson, D. A., Eastman, S. T., & Klein, R. A. (1999). Marketing the media: Scope and goals. In S. T. Eastman, D. A. Ferguson, & R. A. Klein (Eds.), *Promotion and marketing for broadcasting and cable* (3rd ed., pp. 1–28). Boston: Focal Press.

First, A. (1997). Television and the construction of social reality: An Israeli case study. In M. E. McCombs, D. L. Shaw, & D. Weaver (Eds.), *Communication and democracy: Exploring the intellectual frontiers in agenda-setting theory* (pp. 41–50). Mahwah, NJ: Lawrence Erlbaum Associates.

Fishman, M. (1980). *Manufacturing the news*. Austin: University of Texas Press.

Fishman, M. (1997). News and nonevents: Making the visible invisible. In D. Berkowitz (Ed.), *Social meaning of news: A text-reader* (pp. 210–229). Thousand Oaks, CA: Sage.

Fortunato, J. A. (2000). Public relations strategies for creating mass media content: A case study of the National Basketball Association. *Public Relations Review, 26*, 481–497.

Fortunato, J. A. (2001). *The ultimate assist: The relationship and broadcast strategies of the NBA and television networks*. Cresskill, NJ: Hampton.

Fortunato, J. A., & Dunnam, A. E. (2004). The negotiation philosophy for corporate sponsorship of sports properties. In B. G. Pitts (Ed.), *Sharing best practices in sports marketing: The Sports Marketing Association's inaugural book of papers* (pp. 73–86). Morgantown, WV: Fitness Information Technology.

Franklin, M. (1987). *Mass media law: Cases and materials* (3rd ed.). New York: The Foundation Press.

Futterman, M. (2003, December 21). Cable games: Soaring sports-programming costs drive monthly television bills higher. *Newark Star-Ledger*, Section 3, pp. 1, 2.

Gamson, W. A. (2001). Foreword. In S. D. Reese, O. H. Gandy, & A. E. Grant (Eds.), *Framing public life: Perspectives on media and our understanding of the social world* (pp. ix–xi). Mahwah, NJ: Lawrence Erlbaum Associates.

Gamson, W. A., & Modigliani, A. (1987). The changing culture of affirmative action. In R. G. Braungart & M. M. Braungart (Eds.), *Research in political sociology* (3rd ed., pp. 137–177). Greenwich, CT: JAI.

Gamson, W. A., & Modigliani, A. (1989). Media discourse and public opinion on nuclear power: A constructionist approach. *American Journal of Sociology, 95*, 1–37.

Gandy, O. H. (1982). *Beyond agenda-setting: Information subsidies and public policy*. Norwood, NJ: Ablex.

Gandy, O. H. (1991). Beyond agenda-setting. In D. L. Protess & M. E. McCombs (Eds.), *Agenda-setting: Readings on media, public opinion, and policymaking* (pp. 263–275). Hillsdale, NJ: Lawrence Erlbaum Associates.

Gandy, O. H. (2001). Epilogue—Framing at the horizon: A retrospective assessment. In S. D. Reese, O. H. Gandy, & A. E. Grant (Eds.), *Framing public life: Perspectives on media and our understanding of the social world* (pp. 355–378). Mahwah, NJ: Lawrence Erlbaum Associates.

Gans, H. J. (1979). *Deciding what's news: A study of CBS Evening News, NBC Nightly News, Newsweek, and Time*. New York: Pantheon.

Gantz, W., & Zohoori, A. R. (1982). The impact of television schedule changes on audience behavior. *Journalism Quarterly, 59*, 265–272.

Garcia, M., & Stark, P. (1991). *Eyes on the news*. St. Petersburg, FL: Poynter Institute.

Gardner, J. W. (1990). *On Leadership*. New York: Free Press.

Garnham, N. (1990). *Capitalism and communication: Global culture and the economics of information*. London: Sage.

Gay, J. (2003, May 19). At CBS, Les is more. *New York Observer*, p. 1.

Gerbner, G. (1972). Violence in television drama: Trends in symbolic functions. In G. A. Comstock & E. A. Rubinstein (Eds.), *Television and social behavior: Vol. 1. Media content and control* (pp. 28–187).

Gerbner, G. (1998). Cultivation analysis: An overview. *Mass Communication & Society, 1*, 175–194.

Gerbner, G., Gross, L., Morgan, M., Signorielli, N., & Shanahan, J. (2002). Growing up with television: Cultivation processes. In J. Bryant & D. Zillmann (Eds.), Media effects: Advances in theory and research (2nd ed., pp. 43–67). Mahwah, NJ: Lawrence Erlbaum Associates.

Ghanem, S. (1997). Filling in the tapestry: The second level of agenda-setting. In M. E. McCombs, D. L. Shaw, & D. Weaver (Eds.), *Communication and democracy: Exploring the intellectual frontiers in agenda-setting theory* (pp. 3–14). Mahwah, NJ: Lawrence Erlbaum Associates.

Gieber, W. (1964). News is what newspapermen make it. In L. A. Dexter & D. M. White (Eds.), *People, society and mass communication* (pp. 173–182). New York: Free Press.

Gitlin, T. (1972). Sixteen notes on television and the movement. In G. White & C. Neuman (Eds.), *Literature in revolution* (pp. 335–366). New York: Holt, Rinehart & Winston.

Gitlin, T. (1980). *The whole world is watching: Mass media in the making and unmaking of the new left*. Berkeley: University of California Press.

Gitlin, T. (1982). Prime time ideology: The hegemonic process in television entertainment. In H. Newcomb (Ed.), *Television: The critical view* (3rd ed., pp. 426–454). New York: Oxford University Press.

Gitlin, T. (1983). *Inside prime time*. New York: Pantheon.

Goffman, E. (1974). *Frame analysis: An essay on the organization of the experience*. Boston: Northeastern University Press.

Gomery, D. (1989). Media economics: Terms of analysis. *Critical Studies in Mass Communication, 6*, 43–60.

Gomery, D. (2000). Interpreting media ownership. In B. M. Compaine & D. Gomery (Eds.), *Who Owns the Media? Competition and concentration in the mass media industry* (3rd ed., pp. 507–535). Mahwah, NJ: Lawrence Erlbaum Associates.

Goodwin, M. (1999). Who's a journalist?: Welcome the new journalists on the Internet. *Media Studies Journal, 13*(2), 38–42.

Gordon, A. D., & Kittross, J. M. (1999). *Controversies in media ethics* (2nd ed.). New York: Longman.

Graber, D. A. (1984). *Media power in politics.* Washington, DC: Congressional Quarterly Press.

Graber, D. A. (1997). *Mass media and American politics.* Washington, DC: Congressional Quarterly Press.

Grant, A. E., Guthrie, K. K., & Ball-Rokeach, S. J. (1991). Television shopping: A media system dependency perspective. *Communication Research, 18,* 773–798.

Grunig, J. E. (1990). Theory and practice of interactive media relations. *Public Relations Quarterly, 35*(3), 18–23.

Gwinner, K. P. (1997). A model of image creation and image transfer in event sponsorship. *International Marketing Review, 14*(3), 145–158.

Gwinner, K. P., & Eaton, J. (1999). Building brand image through event sponsorship: The role of image transfer. *Journal of Advertising, 28*(4), 47–58.

Hallberg, G. (1995). *All consumers are not created equal.* New York: Wiley.

Halpern, P. (1994). Media dependency and political perceptions in an authoritarian political system. *Journal of Communication, 44*(4), 39–52.

Harvey, B. (2001). Measuring the effects of sponsorship. *Journal of Advertising Research, 41*(1), 59–65.

Henninger, W. (2001, December 17–23). Reporters haven't grown attached to e-mail attachments and links. *Street & Smith's Sports Business Journal,* p. 12.

Hills, J. (1986). *Deregulating telecoms: Competition and control in the United States, Japan, and Britain.* London: Pinter.

Hills, J., & Papathanassopoulos, S. (1991). *The democracy gap: The politics of information and communication technologies in the United States and Europe.* New York: Greenwood.

Hollifield, C. A., Kosicki, G. M., & Becker, L. B. (2001). Organizational vs. professional culture in the newsroom: Television news directors' and newspaper editors' hiring decisions. *Journal of Broadcasting & Electronic Media, 45*(1), 92–117.

Huesmann, L. R., & Eron, L. D. (Eds.). (1986). *Television and the aggressive child: A cross-national comparison.* Hillsdale, NJ: Lawrence Erlbaum Associates.

Hunt, T., & Ruben, B. D. (1993). *Mass communication: Producers and consumers.* New York: HarperCollins.

Husselbee, L. P. (1994). Respecting privacy in an information society: A journalist's dilemma. *Journal of Mass Media Ethics, 9*(3), 145–156.

Jacobs, M. T. (1992). Assessing the constitutionality of press restrictions in the Persian Gulf War. *Stanford Law Review, 44,* 675–726.

Jamieson, K. H., & Campbell, K. K. (2001). *The interplay of influence: News, advertising, politics, and the mass media* (5th ed.). Belmont, CA: Wadsworth.

Jamieson, K. H., & Waldman, P. (2003). *The press effect: Politicians, journalists, and the stories that shape the political world.* New York: Oxford University Press.

Jason, L. A., Kennedy, H. L., & Brackshaw, E. (1999). Television violence and children: Problems and solutions. In T. P. Gullota & S. J. McElhaney (Eds.), *Violence in homes and communities: Prevention, intervention, and treatment: Vol. 11. Issues in children's and families' lives* (pp. 133–156). Thousand Oaks, CA: Sage.

Jhally, S. (1990). *The codes of advertising: fetishism and the political economy of meaning in the consumer society.* New York: Routledge.

Johnson, T. J., & Kaye, B. K. (2000). Democracy's rebirth or demise? The influence of the Internet on political attitude. In D. Schultz (Ed.), *It's show time! Media, politics, and popular culture* (pp. 209–228). New York: Lang.

Johnson, T. J., & Kelly, J. D. (2003). Have new media editors abandoned the old media ideals? The journalistic values of online newspaper editors. *New Jersey Journal of Communication, 11*(2), 115–134.

Johnstone, J. W. C., Slawski, E. J., & Bowman, W. W. (1976). *The news people: A sociological portrait of American journalists and their world.* Urbana: University of Illinois Press.

Kanervo, E. W., & Kanervo, D. W. (1989). How town administrator's view relates to agenda building in community press. *Journalism Quarterly, 66,* 308–315.

Kaneva, N., & Lenert, E. (2003). Who wants to be a millionaire? How the press framed the role of the public in the dispute between Time Warner Cable and Disney's ABC Network in May 2000.*New Jersey Journal of Communication, 11*(2), 149–163.

Kapferer, J. N. (1992). *Strategic brand management and new approaches to creating and evaluating brand equity.* New York: Free Press.

Katz, E. (1959). Mass communication research and the study of popular culture: An editorial note on the possible future for this journal. *Studies in Public Communication, 2,* 1–6.

Katz, E., Blumler, J. G., & Gurevitch, M. (1974). Utilization of mass communication by the individual. In J. Blumler & E. Katz (Eds.), *The uses of mass communication* (pp. 19–32). Beverly, CA: Hills: Sage.

Kaye, B. K., & Johnson, T. J. (2002). Online and in the know: Uses and gratifications of the Web for political information. *Journal of Broadcasting & Electronic Media, 46,* 54–71.

Keller, K. L. (1993). Conceptualizing, measuring, and managing customer-based brand equity. *Journal of Marketing, 57*(1), 1–22.

Keller, K. L. (1998). *Strategic brand management: Building, measuring, and managing brand equity.* Upper Saddle River, NJ: Prentice Hall.

Kellner, D. (1990). *Television and the Crisis of Democracy.* Boulder, CO: Westview.

Kim, H. S. (2002). Gatekeeping international news: An attitudinal profile of U.S. television journalists. *Journal of Broadcasting & Electronic Media, 46,* 431–452.

Klapper, J. T. (1960). *The effects of mass communication.* New York: Free Press.

Kline, F. G., Miller, P. V., & Morrison, A. J. (1974). Adolescents and family planning information: An exploration of audience needs and media effects. In J. Blumler & E. Katz (Eds.), *The uses of mass communication* (pp. 113–136). Beverly Hills, CA: Sage.

Kosicki, G. M. (1993). Problems and opportunities in agenda-setting research. *Journal of Communication, 43*(2), 100–127.

Kubey, R., & Csikszentmihalyi, M. (1990). *Television and the quality of life: How viewing shape everyday experiences.* Hillsdale, NJ: Lawrence Erlbaum Associates.

Kubey, R., & Larson, R. (1990). The use and experience of the new video media among children and young adolescents. *Communication Research, 17,* 107–130.

Kurtz, H. (1998). *Spin cycle: Inside the Clinton propaganda machine.* New York: Free Press.

Kurtz, H. (2002, December 5). N.Y. Times's golf handicap; columns on Augusta killed for being out of line with paper's. *The Washington Post,* p. C1.

Lacy, S., & Niebauer, W. E., Jr. (1995). Developing and using theory for media economics. *Journal of Media Economics, 8*(2), 3–13.

Lacy, S., & Vermeer, J. P. (1995). Theoretical and practical considerations in operationalizing newspaper and television competition. *Journal of Media Economics, 8*(1), 49–61.

Lasorsa, D. L. (1997). Media agenda-setting and press performance: A social system approach for building theory. In M. E. McCombs, D. L. Shaw, & D. Weaver (Eds.), *Communication and democracy: Exploring the intellectual frontiers in agenda-setting theory* (pp. 155–167). Mahwah, NJ: Lawrence Erlbaum Associates.

Lauzen, M. M., & Dozier, D. M. (2002). Equal time in prime time? Scheduling favoritism and gender on the broadcast networks. *Journal of Broadcasting & Electronic Media, 46*(1), 137–153.

Lee, I. L. (1997). Publicity and propaganda. In G. R. Carter (Ed.), *Perspectives: Public relations* (pp. 3–7). St. Paul, MN: Coursewise.

Lee, M., & Solomon, N. (1990). *Unreliable sources*. New York: Carol.

Levy, M. R., & Windahl, S. (1985). The concept of audience. In K. E. Rosengren, L. A. Wenner, & P. Palmgreen (Eds.), *Media gratifications research: Current perspectives* (pp. 109–122). Beverly Hills, CA: Sage.

Lewin, K. (1947). Frontiers in group dynamics: II. Channels of group life; social planning and action research. *Human Relations, 1,* 143–153.

Lichter, S. R., & Noyes, R. E. (1996). *Good intentions make bad news: Why Americans hate campaign journalism*. Lanham, MD: Rowman & Littlefield.

Lin, C. A. (1993). Modeling the gratification-seeking process of television viewing. *Human Communication Research, 20,* 224–244.

Lin, C. A., & Jeffres, L. (1998). Predicting adoption of multimedia cable service. *Journalism Quarterly, 75,* 251–275.

Lippmann, W. (1922). *Public opinion*. New York: Macmillan.

Livingstone, S. M. (1990). *Making sense of TV: The psychology of audience interpretation*. Oxford, England: Pergamon.

Livingstone, S. M. (1993). The rise and fall of audience research: An old story with a new ending. *Journal of Communication, 43*(4), 5–12.

Loevinger, L. (1968). The ambiguous mirror: The reflective-projective theory of broadcasting and mass communication. *Journal of Broadcasting, 12*(2), 97–116.

Loges, W. E. (1994). Canaries in the coal mine: Perceptions of threat and media system dependency relations. *Communication Research, 21*(1), 5–23.

Luna, A. (1995). An economic philosophy for mass media ethics. *Journal of Mass Media Ethics, 10*(3), 154–166.

Madrigal, R. (2000). The influence of social alliances with sports teams on intentions to purchase corporate sponsors' products. *Journal of Advertising, 29*(4), 13–24.

Maher, T. M. (2001). Framing: An emerging paradigm or a phase of agenda setting. In S. D. Reese, O. H. Gandy, & A. E. Grant (Eds.), *Framing public life: Perspectives on media and our understanding of the social world* (pp. 83–94). Mahwah, NJ: Lawrence Erlbaum Associates.

Mazzocco, D. W. (1994). *Networks of power: Corporate TV's threat to democracy*. Boston: South End Press.

McAllister, M. P. (1996). *The commercialization of American culture: New advertising, control and democracy*. Thousand Oaks, CA: Sage.

McAllister, M. P. (1998). College bowl sponsorship and the increased commercialization of amateur sports. *Critical Studies in Mass Communication, 15*, 357–381.

McAllister, M. P. (2002). Television news plugola and the last episode of *Seinfeld. Journal of Communication, 52*(2), 383–401.

McChesney, R. (1997). *Corporate media and the threat to democracy.* New York: Seven Stories Press.

McCombs, M. E. (1976). Agenda-setting research: A bibliographic essay. *Political Communication Review, 1,* 1–7.

McCombs, M. E. (1997, August). *New frontiers in agenda-setting: Agendas of attributes and frames.* Paper presented at the annual convention of the Association for Education in Journalism and Mass Communication, Chicago.

McCombs, M. E., & Ghanem, S. I. (2001). The convergence of agenda-setting and framing. In S. D. Reese, O. H. Gandy, & A. E. Grant (Eds.), *Framing public life: Perspectives on media and our understanding of the social world* (pp. 67–81). Mahwah, NJ: Lawrence Erlbaum Associates.

McCombs, M. E., & Mauro, J. (1977). Predicting newspaper readership from content characteristics. *Journalism Quarterly, 54,* 3–7, 49.

McCombs, M. E., & Reynolds, A. (2002). News influence on our pictures of the world. In J. Bryant & D. Zillmann (Eds.), *Media effects: Advances in theory and research* (2nd ed., pp. 1–18). Mahwah, NJ: Lawrence Erlbaum Associates.

McCombs, M. E., & Shaw, D. L. (1972). The agenda-setting function of the mass media. *Public Opinion Quarterly, 36,* 176–187.

McCombs, M. E., & Shaw, D. L. (1993). The evolution of agenda-setting research: Twenty-five years in the marketplace of ideas. *Journal of Communication, 43*(2), 58–67.

McCombs, M. E., Shaw, D. L., & Weaver, D. (Eds.). (1997). *Communication and democracy: Exploring the intellectual frontiers in agenda-setting theory.* Mahwah, NJ: Lawrence Erlbaum Associates.

McCombs, M. E., & Weaver, D. H. (1985). Toward a merger of gratifications and agenda-setting research. In K. E. Rosengren, L. A. Wenner, & P. Palmgreen (Eds.), *Media gratifications research: Current perspectives* (pp. 95–108). Beverly Hills, CA: Sage.

McLeod, D. M., Kosicki, G. M., & McLeod, J. M. (2002). Resurveying the boundaries of political communication effects. In J. Bryant & D. Zillmann (Eds.), *Media effects: Advances in theory and research* (2nd ed., pp. 215–267). Mahwah, NJ: Lawrence Erlbaum Associates.

McLeod, J. M., & Becker, L. B. (1974). Testing the validity of gratification measures through political effects analysis. In J. G. Blumler & E. Katz (Eds.), *The uses of mass communications: Current perspectives on gratifications research* (Vol. 3, pp. 137–164). Beverly Hills, CA: Sage.

McLeod, J. M., & Becker, L. B. (1981). The uses and gratifications approach. In D. D. Nimmo & K. R. Sanders (Eds.), *Handbook of political communication* (pp. 67–99). Beverly Hills, CA: Sage.

McLuhan, M. (1964). *Understanding media.* New York: McGraw-Hill.

McManus, J. H. (1994). *Market-driven journalism: Let the citizen beware?* Thousand Oaks, CA: Sage.

McManus, J. (1995). A market-based model of news production. *Communication Theory, 5,* 301–338.

McQuail, D. (2000). *Mass communication theory* (4th ed.). London: Sage.

Meehan, E. R. (1993). Commodity audience, actual audience: The blindspot debate. In J. Wasko, V. Mosko, & M. Pendakur (Eds.), *Illuminating the blindspots: Essays honoring Dallas W. Smythe* (pp. 378–397). Norwood, NJ: Ablex.

Meenaghan, T. (1991). The role of sponsorship in the marketing communications mix. *International Journal of Advertising, 10*(1), 35–47.

Megwa, E. R., & Brenner, D. J. (1988). Toward a paradigm of media agenda-setting effect: Agenda-setting as a process. *Howard Journal of Communication, 1*(1), 39–55.

Mendelson, A., & Thorson, E. (2003). The impact of role-congruency and photo presence on the processing of news stories about Hillary Clinton. *The New Jersey Journal of Communication, 11,* 135–148.

Meyer, P. (1987). *Ethical journalism*. New York: Longman.

Mill, J. S. (1956). *On liberty*. Baltimore: Penguin. (Original work published 1859)

Miller, G. A. (1956). The magical number seven, plus or minus two: Some limits on our capacity for processing information. *Psychological Review, 63,* 81–97.

Miller, G. R. (1986). A neglected connection. Mass media exposure and interpersonal communicative competency. In G. Gumpert & R. Cathcart (Eds.), *Inter/media: Interpersonal communication in a media world* (3rd ed., pp. 132–139). New York: Oxford University Press.

Miller, M. M., & Riechert, B. P. (2001). The spiral of opportunity and frame resonance: Mapping the issue cycle in news and public discourse. In S. D. Reese, O. H. Gandy, & A. E. Grant (Eds.), *Framing public life: Perspectives on media and our understanding of the social world* (pp. 107–121). Mahwah, NJ: Lawrence Erlbaum Associates.

Miyazaki, A. D., & Morgan, A. G. (2001). Assessing market value of event sponsoring: Corporate Olympic sponsorship. *Journal of Advertising Research, 41*(1), 9–15.

Molotch, H., & Lester, M. (1974). News as purposive behavior: On the strategic use of routine events, accidents, and scandals. *American Sociologist Review, 39*(1), 101–112.

Moore, R. L. (1999). *Mass communication law and ethics* (3rd ed.). Mahwah, NJ: Lawrence Erlbaum Associates.

Morton, L. P. (1992/1993). Producing publishable press releases. A research perspective. *Public Relations Quarterly, 37*(4), 9–11.

Mosco, V. (1996). *The political economy of communication*. Thousand Oaks, CA: Sage.

Mulgan, G. (1991). *Communication and control: Networks and the new economics of communication*. New York: Guilford Press.

MWW Group. mwwpr.com

Nelson, T. E., Clawson, R. A., & Oxley, Z. M. (1997). Media framing of a civil liberties conflict and its effect on tolerance. *American Political Science Review, 91,* 567–583.

Office of Global Communications. http://www.whitehouse.gov/ogc/aboutogc.html

Papacharissi, Z., & Rubin, A. M. (2000). Predictors of Internet use. *Journal of Broadcasting & Electronic Media, 44,* 175–196.

Park, C. S., & Srinivasan, V. (1994). A survey-based method for measuring and understanding brand equity and its extendibility. *Journal of Marketing Research, 31,* 271–288.

Park, C. W., Jun, S. Y., & Shocker, A. D. (1996). Composite branding alliances: An investigation of extension and feedback effects. *Journal of Marketing Research, 32,* 453–466.

Parker, K. (2003, April 28). Corporate media aren't necessarily a conspiracy. *Austin Amercian-Statesman*, p. A9.

Parmar, A. (2002). Sponsorship. *Marketing News, 37*(1), 13.

Perse, E. M. (2000). Applying theory to the practice of promotion. In S. T. Eastman (Ed.), *Research in media promotion* (pp. 19–53). Mahwah, NJ: Lawrence Erlbaum Associates.

Perse, E. M. (2001). *Media effects and society*. Mahwah, NJ: Lawrence Erlbaum Associates.

Perse, E. M., & Dunn, D. G. (1998). The utility of home computers and media use. Implications of multimedia and connectivity. *Journal of Broadcasting & Electronic Media, 42*, 435–456.

Phillips, E. B. (1977). Approaches to objectivity: Journalistic vs. social science perspectives. In P. M. Hirsch, P. V. Miller, & F. G. Kline (Eds.), *Strategies for communication research* (pp. 63–77). Beverly Hills, CA: Sage.

Pinkleton, B. E., & Austin, E. W. (2002). Exploring relationships among media use frequency, perceived media importance, and media satisfaction in political disaffection and efficacy. *Mass Communication & Society, 5,* 141–163.

Pinkleton, B. E., Reagan, J., Aaronson, D., & Chen, C. (1997). The role of individual motivations in information source use and knowledge concerning divergent topics. *Communication Research Reports, 14,* 291–301.

Porter, M. E. (1980). *Competitive strategy: Techniques for analyzing industries and competitors*. New York: Free Press.

Price, C. J. (2003). Interfering owners or meddling advertisers: How network television news correspondents feel about ownership and advertiser influence on news stories. *Journal of Media Economics, 16*(3), 175–188.

Protess, D. L., & McCombs, M. E. (1991). The public agenda. In D. L. Protess & M. E. McCombs (Eds.), *Agenda setting: Readings on media, public opinion, and policymaking* (pp. 1–4). Hillsdale, NJ: Lawrence Erlbaum Associates.

Rachlin, A. (1988). *News as hegemonic reality: American political culture and the framing of news accounts*. New York: Praeger.

Reagan, J. (1995). The "repertoire" of information sources. *Journal of Broadcasting and Electronic Media, 42,* 34–49.

Redmond, J., & Trager, R. (1998). *Balancing the wire: The art of managing media organizations*. Boulder, CO: Coursewise.

Reese, S. D. (2001). Prologue—Framing public life: A bridging model for media research. In S. D. Reese, O. H. Gandy, & A. E. Grant (Eds.), *Framing public life: Perspectives on media and our understanding of the social world* (pp. 7–31). Mahwah, NJ: Lawrence Erlbaum Associates.

Reese, S. D., Gandy, O. H., & Grant, A. E. (Eds.). (2001). *Framing public life: Perspectives on media and our understanding of the social world*. Mahwah, NJ: Lawrence Erlbaum Associates.

Reilly, M., & Futterman, M. (2003, August 5). Benching Kobe: Lakers star has lost one endorsement. Will others follow? *The Newark Star-Ledger*, pp. 39, 42.

Richards, J. I., & Murphy, J. H. (1996). Economic censorship and free speech: The circle of communication between advertisers, media, and consumers. *Journal of Current Issues and Research in Advertising, 18*(1), 21–34.

Rideout, C. R. (1993). News coverage and talks shows in the 1992 presidential campaign. *PS: Political Science & Politics, 26,* 712–716.

Ridgway, J. (1998, April 20). Name of the game is branding. *Electronic Media, 16,* 37.

Ries, A., & Trout, J. (1997). *Marketing warfare.* New York: McGraw-Hill.

Roberts, M. (1997). Political advertising's influence on news, the public and their behavior. In M. E. McCombs, D. L. Shaw, & D. Weaver (Eds.), *Communication and democracy: Exploring the intellectual frontiers in agenda-setting theory* (pp. 85–96). Mahwah, NJ: Lawrence Erlbaum Associates.

Rogers, E. M., Dearing, J. W., & Bregman, D. (1993). The anatomy of agenda-setting research. *Journal of Communication, 43*(2), 68–84.

Rosengren, K. E., Wenner, L. A., & Palmgreen, P. (Eds.). (1985). *Media gratifications research: Current perspectives.* Beverly Hills, CA: Sage.

Roshco, B. (1975). *Newsmaking.* Chicago: University of Chicago Press.

Roy, D. P., & Cornwell, T. B. (1999). Managers' use of sponsorship in building brands: Service and product firms contrasted. *International Journal of Sports Marketing and Sponsorship, 1*(6), 345–360.

Rubin, A. M. (1983). Television uses and gratifications: The interactions of viewing patterns and motivations. *Journal of Broadcasting & Electronic Media, 27,* 37–51.

Rubin, A. M. (1984). Ritualized and instrumental television viewing. *Journal of Communication, 34*(3), 67–77.

Rubin, A. M. (1993). Audience activity and media use. *Communication Monographs, 8,* 141–165.

Rubin, A. M. (2002). The uses-and-gratifications perspective of media effects. In J. Bryant & D. Zillmann (Eds.), *Media effects: Advances in theory and research* (2nd ed., pp. 525–548). Mahwah, NJ: Lawrence Erlbaum Associates.

Rubin, A. M., & Perse, E. M. (1987). Audience activity and television news gratifications. *Communication Research, 14*(1), 58–84.

Rubin, A. M., & Rubin, R. B. (1985). Interface of personal and mediated communication: A research agenda. *Critical Studies in Mass Communication, 2*(1), 36–53.

Ryan, C., Carragee, K. M., & Meinhofer, W. (2001). Framing, the news media, and collective action. *Journal of Broadcasting & Electronic Media, 45*(1), 175–182.

Salwen, M. B. (1988). Effect of accumulation of coverage on issue salience in agenda setting. *Journalism Quarterly, 65,* 100–106.

Samuelson, R. J. (2003, August 7). The myth of the almighty big media. *The Newark Star-Ledger,* p. 17.

Sandman, P. M., Rubin, D. M., & Sachsman, D. B. (Eds.). (1976). *Media: An introductory analysis of American mass communications* (2nd ed.). Englewood Cliffs, NJ: Prentice Hall.

Scheufele, D. A. (1999). Framing as a theory of media effects. *Journal of Communication, 49*(1), 103–122.

Scheufele, D. A. (2000). Agenda-setting, priming, and framing revisited: Another look at cognitive effects of political communication. *Mass Communication & Society, 3,* 297–316.

Schiller, H. I. (1989). *Culture, Inc.: The corporate takeover of public expression.* New York: Oxford University Press.

Schoenbach, K., & Semetko, H. A. (1992). Agenda-setting, agenda-reinforcing or agenda-deflating? A study of the 1990 German national election. *Journalism Quarterly, 69,* 837–846.

Schramm, W. (1949). The nature of news. In W. Schramm (Ed.), *Mass communications.* Urbana: University of Illinois Press.

Schramm, W., Lyle, J., & Parker, E. (1961). *Television in the lives of our children.* Stanford, CA: Stanford University Press.

Schudson, M. (1978). *Discovering the news.* New York: Basic Books.

Schudson, M. (1995). *The power of news.* Cambridge, MA: Harvard University Press.

Schudson, M. (1997). The sociology of news production. In D. Berkowitz (Ed.), *Social meaning of news: A text-reader* (pp. 7–22). Thousand Oaks, CA: Sage.

Schultz, M., Mouritsen, J., & Gabrielsen, G. (2001). Sticky reputation: Analyzing a reputation system. *Corporate Reputation Review, 4*(1), 24–41.

Seitel, F. P. (1998). *The practice of public relations* (7th ed.). Englewood Cliffs, NJ: Prentice Hall.

Semetko, H. A., & Mandelli, A. (1997). Setting the agenda for cross-national research: Bringing values into the concept. In M. E. McCombs, D. L. Shaw, & D. Weaver (Eds.), *Communication and democracy: Exploring the intellectual frontiers in agenda-setting theory* (pp. 195–207). Mahwah, NJ: Lawrence Erlbaum Associates.

Semetko, H. A., & Valkenburg, P. M. (2000). Framing European politics: A content analysis of press and television news. *Journal of Communication, 50*(2), 93–107.

Shaw, D. L., & Martin, S. E. (1992). The function of mass media agenda setting. *Journalism Quarterly, 69,* 902–920.

Shaw, D. L., & McCombs, M. E. (Eds.). (1977). *The emergence of American political issues: The agenda setting function of the press.* St. Paul, MN: West.

Shocker, A. D., Srivastava, R. K., & Ruekert, R. W. (1994). Challenges and opportunities facing brand management: An introduction to the special issue. *Journal of Marketing Research, 31*(2), 149–158.

Shoemaker, P. J. (1991). *Gatekeeping.* Newbury Park, CA: Sage.

Shoemaker, P. J. (1999). Media gatekeeping. In M. B. Salwen & D. W. Stacks (Eds.), *An integrated approach to communication theory and research* (pp. 79–91). Mahwah, NJ: Lawrence Erlbaum Associates.

Shoemaker, P. J., & Reese, S. D. (1996). *Mediating the message: Theories of influences on mass media content.* New York: Longman.

Siebert, F., Peterson, T., & Schramm, W. (1974). *Four theories of the press.* Urbana: University of Illinois Press.

Sigal, L. (1973). *Reporters and officials: The organization and politics of newsmaking.* Lexington, MA: Heath.

Singhania, L. (2002, December 4). Times cites editorial standards in refusal to run two sports columns. *Associated Press.*

Slattery, K., Doremus, M., & Marcus, L. (2001). Shifts in public affairs reporting on the network evening news: A move toward the sensational. *Journal of Broadcasting & Electronic Media, 45,* 290–302.

Smyth, D. W. (1977). Communications: Blindspot of western Marxism. *Canadian Journal of Political and Social Theory, 1*(3), 1–27.

Soley, L. C., & Craig, R. L. (1992). Advertising pressures on newspapers: A survey. *Journal of Advertising, 21*(4), 1–10.

Soloski, J. (1997). News reporting and professionalism: Some constraints on the reporting of the news. In D. Berkowitz (Ed.), *Social meaning of news: A text-reader* (pp. 138–154). Thousand Oaks, CA: Sage.

Sparks, G. G., & Sparks, C. W. (2002). Effects of media violence. In J. Bryant & D. Zillmann (Eds.), *Media effects: Advances in theory and research* (2nd ed., pp. 269–285). Mahwah, NJ: Lawrence Erlbaum Associates.

Stewart, D. W., Pavlou, P., & Ward, S. (2002). Media influences on marketing communications. In J. Bryant & D. Zillmann (Eds.), *Media effects: Advances in theory and research* (2nd ed., pp. 353–396). Mahwah, NJ: Lawrence Erlbaum Associates.

Stipp, H., & Schiavone, N. P. (1996). Modeling the impact of Olympic sponsorship on corporate image. *Journal of Advertising Research, 36*(4), 22–28.

Sumpter, R. S. (2000). Daily newspaper editors' audience construction routines: A case study. *Critical Studies in Media Communication, 17,* 334–346.

Susswein, G. (2003, February 24). Confessions of a Nielsen family. *Austin American-Statesman*, pp. E1, E8.

Sutherland, M., & Galloway, J. (1981). Role of advertising: Persuasion or agenda-setting? *Journal of Advertising Research, 21*(5), 25–29.

Swanson, D. L. (1987). Gratification seeking, media exposure, and audience interpretations: Some directions for research. *Journal of Broadcasting & Electronic Media, 31*(3), 237–254.

Tan, A. S. (1980). Mass media use, issue knowledge, and political involvement. *Public Opinion Quarterly, 44,* 241–248.

Thayer, L. (1986). On the mass media and mass communication: Notes toward a theory. In G. Gumpert & R. Cathcart (Eds.), *Inter/media: Interpersonal communication in a media world* (3rd ed., pp. 41–61). New York: Oxford University Press.

Till, B. D., & Shimp, T. A. (1998). Endorsers in advertising: The case of negative celebrity information. *Journal of Advertising, 27*(1), 67–82.

Time Magazine Online. www.timemediakit.com

Trusdell, B. (1997). Life in the fast lane. *Sales & Marketing Management, 149*(2), 66–71.

Tuchman, G. (1978). *Making news: A study in the construction of reality*. New York: Free Press.

Underwood, D. (1993). *When MBA's rule the newsroom*. New York: Columbia University Press.

Wanta, W. (1988). The effects of dominant photographs: An agenda-setting experiment. *Journalism Quarterly, 65,* 107–111.

Wanta, W., & Wu, Y. (1992). Interpersonal communication and the agenda-setting process. *Journalism Quarterly, 69,* 847–855.

Weaver, D. H., & Elliott, S. N. (1986). Who sets the agenda for the media? A study of local agenda building. *Journalism Quarterly, 62,* 87–94.

Weaver, D. H., Graber, D. A., McCombs, M. E., & Eyal, C. H. (1981). *Media agenda-setting in a presidential election: Issues, images, and interest*. New York: Praeger.

Weaver, D. H., & Wilhoit, G. C. (1996). *The American journalist: A portrait of U.S. news people and their work*. Bloomington: Indiana University Press.

Webster, J. G., & Lichty, L. W. (1991). *Ratings analysis: Theory and practice*. Hillsdale, NJ: Lawrence Erlbaum Associates.

Webster, J. G., & Lin, S. F. (2002). The Internet audience: Web use as mass behavior. *Journal of Broadcasting & Electronic Media, 46*(1), 1–12.

Webster, J. G., Phalen, P. F., & Lichty, L. W. (2000). *Ratings analysis: The theory and practice of audience research*. Mahwah, NJ: Lawrence Erlbaum Associates.

Welch, J., & Byrne, J. A. (2001). *Jack: Straight from the gut*. New York: Warner Business.

Wenner, L. A. (1989). *Media, sports, and society*. Newbury Park, CA: Sage.

Westin, D. (2004, August 2). So many media, so many decisions. *The Newark Star-Ledger*, p. 15.

White, D. M. (1950). The gate-keeper: A case study in the selection of news. *Journalism Quarterly, 27*, 383–390.

White House News Releases. http://www.whitehouse.gov/news/releases/2003/01/20030121-3.html

Williams, D. (2002). Synergy bias: Conglomerates and promotion in the news. *Journal of Broadcasting & Electronic Media, 46*, 453–472.

Willnat, L. (1997). Agenda-setting and priming: Conceptual links and differences. In M. E. McCombs, D. L. Shaw, & D. Weaver (Eds.), *Communication and democracy: Exploring the intellectual frontiers in agenda-setting theory* (pp. 51–66). Mahwah, NJ: Lawrence Erlbaum Associates.

Wright, C. R. (1986). *Mass communication: A sociological perspective* (3rd ed.). New York: Random House.

Yioutas, J., & Segvic, I. (2003). Revisiting the Clinton/Lewinsky scandal: The convergence of agenda setting and framing. *Journalism & Mass Communication Quarterly, 80*, 567–582.

Zelizer, B. (1993). Has communication explained journalism? *Journal of Communication, 43*(4), 80–88.

Zillmann, D., Bryant, J., & Huston, A. (Eds.). (1994). *Media, children, and the family: Social scientific, psycho-dynamic, and clinical perspectives*. Hillsdale, NJ: Lawrence Erlbaum Associates.

Zillmann, D., Gibson, R., & Sargent, S. (1999). Effects of photographs in news-magazine reports on issue perception. *Media Psychology, 1*, 207–228.

Author Index

Subject Index

SEP 0 1 2005 **DATE DUE**

DEC 1 8 2005			
REC'D SEP 0 3 2005			
AUG 0 6 2010			
AUG 1 8 REC'D			